NEPAL
From Monarchy to Democratic Constitution

NEPAL: FROM MONARCHY TO DEMOCRATIC CONSTITUTION

S.K. Singh

PRASHANT PUBLISHING HOUSE
DELHI-110094

Published by :
Prashant Publishing House
C-34, 28 Foota Road, Gali-3,
West Karwal Nagar, Delhi-110094
Phone : 011-22963970, Mob. : 9810396373
e-mail.: prashantpublishinghouse@gmail.com

Nepal: From Monarchy to Democratic Constitution

First Published 2016

ISBN 978-93-80565-65-1

PRINTED IN INDIA
Published by Mr. R.K. Jha M/s Prashant Publishing House and Published at H.S. Offset House Press, Delhi.

Contents

Preface

Nepal finally has a formal constitution after nearly a decade of political paralysis.

The landlocked Himalayan nation's parliament passed the constitution on Wednesday with 507 out of 601 members of its Constituent Assembly voting in favor, Agence France-Presse reported.

The new charter replaces an interim constitution that has governed the country since 2007, when a decadelong civil war culminated in the end of its Hindu monarchy. Since then, rival political parties have been at loggerheads over the document's details, a disagreement that dragged on for years until this year's devastating earthquake that claimed nearly 9,000 lives prompted a hasty reconciliation. The constitutional logjam was widely blamed for the delay in mobilizing rescue efforts, prompting the country's three leading political stakeholders — the formerly antigovernment Maoists, the main communist party UML and the Nepali Congress — to begin the drafting process in June.

The constitution has not been without controversy, however, with the decision to divide the country into seven distinct provinces sparking protests that claimed at least 40 lives in recent weeks. Critics of the bill say the divisions will further marginalize Nepal's ethnic minorities like the Tharu and Madhesi communities. A clause that increases barriers to Nepali children automatically acquiring their mothers' citizenship has also been criticized as backward.

A constitutional monarchy, limited monarchy or parliamentary monarchy (in its most limited form, a crowned republic) is a form of government in which governing powers of the monarch are restricted by a constitution. Constitutional monarchy differs from absolute monarchy, in which a monarch in an absolute monarchy holds absolute power.

A constitutional monarchy may refer to a system in which the monarch acts as a non-party political head of state under the constitution, whether written or unwritten. While most monarchs may hold formal reserve powers and the government may officially take place in the monarch's name, they do not set public policy or choose political leaders. Political scientistVernon Bogdanor, paraphrasing Thomas Macaulay, has defined a constitutional monarch as "a sovereign who reigns but does not rule". In addition to acting as a visible symbol of national unity, a constitutional monarch may hold formal powers such as dissolving parliament or givingRoyal Assent to legislation.

The promulgation of the new constitution was immediately followed by virtual blockade of all checkpoints at Nepal-India border. Some ethnic groups in lowland Nepal have accused of being gender discriminatory especially in regards to citizenship provisions. They allege new constitution makes it difficult for woman to pass on citizenship to their children as compared to men. Similarly, Madhesi and indigenous population view that the new constitution fails to address demands of marginalized communities and support status-quo of the ruling groups. They are protesting mainly over the federal delineation of new states as proposed in the constitution fearing existing demarcation could affect their political representation. With the protest ongoing since August 15, 2015 or earlier, at least 45 people, including 8 security personals and one Indian National, have been killed. Human Rights Watch has criticized the Nepal Government as well as the protesters for violation of human rights during the protest.

As the book addresses this crucial issue quite deftly, it is hoped that it would prove to be a source of great information for the reader.

—*Editor*

1

Constitutional Monarchy

A constitutional monarchy, limited monarchy or parliamentary monarchy (in its most limited form, a crowned republic) is a form of government in which governing powers of the monarch are restricted by a constitution. Constitutional monarchy differs from absolute monarchy, in which a monarch in an absolute monarchy holds absolute power.

A constitutional monarchy may refer to a system in which the monarch acts as a non-party political head of state under the constitution, whether written or unwritten. While most monarchs may hold formal reserve powers and the government may officially take place in the monarch's name, they do not set public policy or choose political leaders. Political scientistVernon Bogdanor, paraphrasing Thomas Macaulay, has defined a constitutional monarch as "a sovereign who reigns but does not rule". In addition to acting as a visible symbol of national unity, a constitutional monarch may hold formal powers such as dissolving parliament or givingRoyal Assent to legislation.

However, the exercise of such powers is generally a formality rather than an opportunity for the sovereign to enact personal political preference.

In *The English Constitution*, British political theorist Walter Bagehot identified three main political rights which a constitutional monarch could freely exercise: the right to be consulted, the right to advise, and the right to warn. Some constitutional monarchs, however, still retain significant power and influence and play an important political role.

The United Kingdom and fifteen of its former colonies are constitutional monarchies with aWestminster system of government. Three states – Malaysia, Cambodia and the Holy See – employ true elective monarchies, where the ruler is periodically selected by a small,aristocratic electoral college.

History

The oldest constitutional monarchy dating back to ancient times were the Hittites. They were an ancient Anatolian peoples that lived during the Bronze age whose king had to share his orher authority with an assembly, called Panku, equivalent to a modern-day deliberative assembly of a legislature. These were scattered noble families that worked as representatives of their subjects in an adjutant or subaltern federal-type landscape.

The most recent country to transition from an absolute monarchy to a constitutional monarchy was Bhutan, in 2007–08.

CONSTITUTIONAL AND ABSOLUTE MONARCHY

In the Kingdom of England, the Glorious Revolution of 1688 led to a constitutional monarchy restricted by laws such as the Bill of Rights 1689 and the Act of Settlement 1701, although limits on the power of the monarch ('a limited monarchy') are much older than that (seeMagna Carta). At the same time, in Scotland the Convention of Estates enacted the Claim of Right Act 1689, which placed similar limits on the Scottish monarchy. From the Hanoverian accession to the throne of Great Britain, monarchs saw their powers pass further to their ministers, and Royal neutrality in politics became cemented early in the reign of Queen Victoria (although she had her personal favorites) following enlargements to the franchise. Today, the role of the British monarch is by convention effectively ceremonial. Instead, the British Parliament and the Government - chiefly in the office of Prime Minister - exercise their powers under 'Royal (or Crown) Prerogative': on behalf of the monarch and through powers still formally possessed by the Monarch. No person may accept significant public office without swearing an oath of allegiance to the Queen. With few exceptions, the monarch is bound by convention to act on the advice of the Government.

Constitutional monarchy occurred first in continental Europe, briefly in the early years of the French Revolution, but much more widely afterwards. Napoleon Bonaparte is considered the first monarch proclaiming *himself* as an embodiment of the nation, rather than as a divinely-appointed ruler; this interpretation of monarchy is germane to continental constitutional monarchies. G.W.F. Hegel, in his *Elements of the Philosophy of Right* (1820), gave it a philosophical justification that concurred with evolving contemporary political theory and the Protestant Christian view of natural law. Hegel's forecast of a constitutional monarch with very limited powers whose function is to embody the national character and provide constitutional continuity in times of emergency was reflected in the development of constitutional monarchies in Europe and Japan. His forecast of the form of government suitable to the modern world may be seen as prophetic: the largely ceremonial offices of president in some modern parliamentary republics in Europe and Israel can be perceived as elected or appointed versions of Hegel's constitutional monarch; the Russian and French presidents, with their stronger powers, may also be regarded in Hegelian terms as wielding powers suitable to the embodiment of the national will.

Executive Monarchy versus Ceremonial Monarchy

There exist at least two different types of constitutional monarchies in the modern world — executive and ceremonial. In executive monarchies, the monarch wields significant (though not absolute) power. The monarchy under this system of government is a powerful political (and social) institution. By contrast, in ceremonial monarchies, the monarch holds little actual power or direct political influence.

Executive constitutional monarchies: Bhutan, Bahrain, Jordan, Kuwait, Liechtenstein, Monaco, Morocco, and Tonga.

Ceremonial constitutional monarchies: Andorra, Antigua and Barbuda, Australia, The Bahamas, Barbados, Belgium, Belize, Cambodia,Canada, Denmark, Grenada, Jamaica Japan, Lesotho, Luxembourg, Malaysia, the Netherlands, New Zealand, Norway, Papua New Guinea, Saint Kitts and Nevis, Saint Lucia, Saint Vincent and the Grenadines, Solomon Islands, Spain, Sweden, Thailand,

Tuvalu and theUnited Kingdom. Ceremonial and executive monarchy, should not be confused with democratic and non-democratic monarchical systems. For example, in Liechtenstein and Monaco, the ruling monarchs wield significant executive power. However, they are *not* absolute monarchs, and these countries are generally reckoned as democracies.

MODERN CONSTITUTIONAL MONARCHY

As originally conceived, a constitutional monarch was head of the executive branch and quite a powerful figure, even though his or her power was limited by the constitution and the elected parliament. Some of the framers of the US Constitution may have envisaged the president as an elected constitutional monarch, as the term was then understood, following Montesquieu's account of the separation of powers.

The present-day concept of a constitutional monarchy developed in the United Kingdom, where the democratically elected parliaments, and their leader, the prime minister, exercise power, with the monarchs having ceded power and remaining as a titular position. In many cases the monarchs, while still at the very top of the political and social hierarchy, were given the status of "servants of the people" to reflect the new, egalitarian position. In the course of France's July Monarchy, Louis-Philippe I was styled "King of the French" rather than "King of France".

Following the Unification of Germany, Otto von Bismarck rejected the British model. In the constitutional monarchy established under theConstitution of the German Empire which Bismarck inspired, the Kaiser retained considerable actual executive power, while the Imperial Chancellor needed no parliamentary vote of confidence and ruled solely by the imperial mandate. However this model of constitutional monarchy was discredited and abolished following Germany's defeat in the First World War. Later, Fascist Italy could also be considered as a constitutional monarchy, in that there was a king as the titular head of state while actual power was held by Benito Mussolini under a constitution. This eventually discredited the Italian monarchy and led to its abolition in 1946. After the Second World War, surviving European monarchies almost invariably adopted some variant of the constitutional monarchy model originally developed in Britain.

Nowadays a parliamentary democracy that is a constitutional monarchy is considered to differ from one that is a republic only in detail rather than in substance. In both cases, the titular head of state—monarch or president—serves the traditional role of embodying and representing the nation, while the government is carried on by a cabinet composed predominantly of elected Members of Parliament.

However, three important factors distinguish monarchies such as the United Kingdom from systems where greater power might otherwise rest with Parliament. These are: the Royal Prerogative under which the monarch may exercise power under certain very limited circumstances; Sovereign Immunity under which the monarch may *do no wrong* under the law because the responsible government is instead deemed accountable; and the monarch may not be subject to the same taxation or property use restrictions as most citizens. Other privileges may be nominal or ceremonial (e.g., where the executive, judiciary, police or armed forces act on the authority of or oweallegiance to the Crown).

Today slightly more than a quarter of constitutional monarchies are Western European countries, including the United Kingdom, theNetherlands, Belgium, Norway, Denmark, Spain, Luxembourg, Monaco, Liechtenstein, and Sweden. However, the two most populous constitutional monarchies in the world are in Asia: Japan and Thailand. In these countries the prime minister holds the day-to-day powers of governance, while the King or Queen (or other monarch, such as a Grand Duke, in the case of Luxembourg, or Prince in the case of Monaco and Liechtenstein) retains residual (but not always insignificant) powers. The powers of the monarch differ between countries. In Denmark and in Belgium, for example, the Monarch formally appoints a representative to preside over the creation of a coalition governmentfollowing a parliamentary election, while in Norway the King chairs special meetings of the cabinet.

In nearly all cases, the monarch is still the nominal chief executive, but is bound by convention to act on the advice of the

Cabinet. Only a few monarchies (most notably Japan and Sweden) have amended their constitutions so that the monarch is no longer even the nominal chief executive.

There are sixteen constitutional monarchies under Queen Elizabeth II, which are known as Commonwealth realms. Unlike some of their continental European counterparts, the Monarch and her Governors-General in the Commonwealth realms hold significant "reserve" or "prerogative" powers, to be wielded in times of extreme emergency or constitutional crises, usually to uphold parliamentary government. An instance of a Governor-General exercising such power occurred during the 1975 Australian constitutional crisis, when the Australian Prime Minister, Gough Whitlam, was dismissed by the Governor-General. The Australian senate had threatened to block the Government's budgetby refusing to pass the necessary appropriation bills. On 11 November 1975, Whitlam intended to call a half-Senate election in an attempt to break the deadlock. When he sought the Governor-General's approval of the election, the Governor-General instead dismissed him as Prime Minister, and shortly thereafter installed leader of the opposition Malcolm Fraser in his place. Acting quickly before all parliamentarians became aware of the change of government, Fraser and his allies secured passage of the appropriation bills, and the Governor-General dissolved Parliament for a double dissolution election. Fraser and his government were returned with a massive majority. This led to much speculation among Whitlam's supporters as to whether this use of the Governor-General's reserve powers was appropriate, and whether Australia should become a republic. Among supporters of constitutional monarchy, however, the experience confirmed the value of the monarchy as a source of checks and balances against elected politicians who might seek powers in excess of those conferred by the constitution, and ultimately as a safeguard against dictatorship.

In Thailand's constitutional monarchy, the monarch is recognized as the Head of State, Head of the Armed Forces, Upholder of the Buddhist Religion, and Defender of the Faith. The current King, Bhumibol Adulyadej, is the longest reigning current monarch in the world and in all of Thailand's history. Bhumibol has reigned through several political changes in the Thai government. He has played an influential role in each incident, often acting as mediator between disputing political opponents. Among the powers retained by the monarch under the constitution, lèse majesté protects the image of the monarch and enables him to play a role in politics. It carries strict criminal penalties for violators. Generally, the Thai people are reverent of Bhumibol. Much of his social influence arises from this reverence and from the socio-economic improvement efforts undertaken by the royal family.

In both the United Kingdom and elsewhere, a frequent debate centers on when it is appropriate for a monarch to use his or her political powers. When a monarch does act, political controversy can often ensue, partially because the neutrality of the crown is seen to be compromised in favour of a partisan goal, while some political scientists champion the idea of an "interventionist monarch" as a check against possible illegal action by politicians. For instance, the monarch of the United Kingdom can theoretically exercise an absolute veto over legislation by withholding Royal Assent. However, no monarch has done so since 1708, and it is widely believed that this and many of the monarch's other political powers are lapsed powers.

There are currently 44 monarchies, and most of them are constitutional monarchies.

Former constitutional monarchies

- The Anglo-Corsican Kingdom was a brief period in the history of Corsica (1794–1796) when the island broke with Revolutionary Franceand sought military protection from Great Britain. Corsica became an independent kingdom under George III of the United Kingdom, but with its own elected parliament and a written constitution guaranteeing local autonomy and democratic rights.
- Brazil from 1815 (United Kingdom of Portugal, Brazil and Algarves) until 1822, with the proclamation of independence and rise of theEmpire of Brazil by Pedro I

of Brazil. The empire ended in 1889, when Pedro II was deposed by a military coup.

- Kingdom of Bulgaria until 1946 when Tsar Simeon was deposed by the communist assembly.
- Many Commonwealth republics were constitutional monarchies for some period after their independence.
- The Grand Principality of Finland was a constitutional monarchy though its ruler, Alexander I, was simultaneously an autocrat andabsolute ruler in Russia.
- France, several times during the 19th century. Napoléon Bonaparte proclaimed himself Emperor of the French in what was ostensibly a constitutional monarchy, though modern historians often coin his reign as an absolute monarchy. The Bourbon Restoration (under Louis XVIII and Charles X), the July Monarchy (under Louis-Philippe), and the Second Empire (under Napoleon III) were also constitutional monarchies, although the power of the monarch varied considerably between them.
- The German Empire from 1871 to 1918, (as well as earlier confederations, and the monarchies it consisted of) was also a constitutional monarchy—see Constitution of the German Empire.
- Greece until 1973 when Constantine II was deposed by the military government. The decision was formalized by a plebiscite December 8, 1974.
- Hawaii, which was an absolute monarchy from its founding in 1810, transitioned to a constitutional monarchy in 1840 when King Kamehameha III promulgated the kingdom's first constitution. This constitutional form of government continued until the monarchy was overthrown in 1893 in American conspiracy.
- The Kingdom of Hungary. In 1848–1849 and 1867–1918 as part of Austria-Hungary. In the interwar period (1920–1944) Hungaryremained a constitutional monarchy without a reigning monarch.
- Iceland. The Act of Union, a December 1, 1918 agreement with Denmark, established Iceland as a sovereign kingdom

united with Denmark under a common king. Iceland abolished the monarchy and became a republic on June 17, 1944 after the Icelandic constitutional referendum, May 24, 1944.

- Iran under Mohammad Reza Shah Pahlavi was a constitutional monarchy, which had been originally established during the Persian Constitutional Revolution in 1906.
- Italy until June 2, 1946, when a referendum proclaimed the end of the Kingdom and the beginning of the Republic.
- Korean Empire proclaimed in October 1897 to the Annexation of Korea by Japan on August 20, 1910. It succeeded the Joseon Dynasty.
- The Kingdom of Laos was a constitutional monarchy until 1975, when Sisavang Vatthana was forced to abdicate by the communistPathet Lao.
- Mexico was twice an Empire. The First Mexican Empire was from July 21, 1822, to March 19, 1823, with Agustín de Iturbide serving as emperor. Then, with the help of the Austrian and Spanish crowns, Napoleon III of France installed Maximilian of Habsburg as Emperor of Mexico. This attempt to create a European-style monarchy lasted three years, from 1864 to 1867.
- Montenegro until 1918 when it merged with Serbia and other areas to form Yugoslavia.
- Kingdom of Mysore
- Nepal until May 28, 2008, when King Gyanendra was deposed, and the Federal Democratic Republic of Nepal was declared.
- Ottoman Empire from 1876 till 1878 and again from 1908 until the dissolution of the empire in 1922.
- The Polish–Lithuanian Commonwealth, formed after the Union of Lublin in 1569 and lasting until the final partition of the state in 1795, operated much like many modern European constitutional monarchies (into which it was officially changed by the establishment of theConstitution

of May 3, 1791, which historian Norman Davies calls "the first constitution of its kind in Europe"). The legislators of the unified state truly did not see it as a monarchy at all, but as *a republic under the presidency of the King*. Poland–Lithuania also followed the principle of "Rex regnat et non gubernat", had a bicameral parliament, and a collection of entrenched legal documents amounting to a constitution along the lines of the modern United Kingdom. The King was elected, and had the duty of maintaining the people's rights.

- Portugal was a monarchy since 1139 and a constitutional monarchy from 1822 to 1828 and again from 1834 until 1910, when Manuel IIwas overthrown by a military coup.
- Kingdom of Romania From its establishment in 1881 until 1947 when Michael I was forced to abdicate at gunpoint by the communists.
- Kingdom of Serbia until 1918, when it merged with the State of Slovenes, Croats and Serbs into the unitary Yugoslav Kingdom, that was led by the Serbian Karadjordjevic dynasty.
- The West African Songhai Empire was considered a powerful constitutional monarchy before annexation by Morocco and later France, when it became a colony and presently, a secular Sufist republic.
- Yugoslavia from 1918 (as Kingdom of Serbs, Croats and Slovenes) until 1929 and from then (as Kingdom of Yugoslavia) until 1944 when under pressure from the Allies Peter II recognized the communist government.

Unique constitutional monarchies

- Andorra is the only monarchy where the head of state is vested jointly in two individuals ("Co-Princes"): the Bishop of Urgell and thePresident of France.
- Andorra, Monaco and Liechtenstein are the only countries with a reigning Prince.
- Japan is the only country with an Emperor.
- Luxembourg is the only country with a Grand Duke.

THE FIRST DEMOCRATIC CONSTITUTION IN THE HISTORY OF NEPAL APPROVED

Nepal is at a turning point. "We have endorsed a federal democratic republic. This is no ordinary event; it is an historic event," said Pushpa Kamal Dahal, leader of the Unified Communist Party of Nepal (Maoist), the country's third largest party, as he greeted the final approval of the country's new constitution after many years of discussion and delays.

With 507 votes in favour and 25 against, the Constituent Assembly approved the draft proposal, the first by elected representatives. Nepal's long and tortuous journey towards a new constitution began in 2006 when a Comprehensive Peace Agreement was signed under the auspices of the United Nations ending a decade-long civil war between the regular army and Maoist guerrillas.

The first constituent assembly was elected in 2007 after 240 years of absolute Hindu monarchy but ended in 2012 in a stalemate. A second Assembly came into being in November 2013 but it too failed to come up with a constitution by the January 2015 deadline.

The tragic earthquake on 25 April (which killed more than 9,000 people) speeded up the reform process, which is set to end this Saturday, 20 September, with the promulgation of the constitution by the president of Nepal, Ram Baran Yadav. This will be followed by two days (Sunday and Monday) of celebrations across the country.

The new constitution is divided in 37 parts, 302 articles and 9 annexes. Its key aspects are a republican form of government, federalism, secularism, inclusiveness and proportional representation of disadvantaged minorities, as well as policies of social justice.

For Prime Minister Sushil Koirala, head of the Nepali Congress, this was a "moment of pride," the happiest day of his political career. "We have made our dream come true," he said. The demands of those who are dissatisfied "will be met through dialogue" and amendments.

Parties representing the Madhese and Tharu minorities boycotted yesterday's vote, whilst the Hindu-centred Rastriya

Prajatantra Party-Nepal opposed it, calling instead for the restoration of the monarchy and the Hindu kingdom.

The adoption of the constitution comes after weeks of discussion, centred on the content of the draft approved in late June. When the draft was first made public,Madhese and Tharu leaders complained immediately that it ignored their communities.

This led to clashes with the army and eventually casualties. So far, about 40 people have died, including a child, trampled to death by a crowd.

More recently, the growing climate of insecurity led Nepali authorities to ask the Holy See to cancel a visit by one of its officials, Card Fernando Filoni. The latter was scheduled to meet with survivors of the earthquake of 25 April.

The escalation reached a crescendo Tuesday night when bombs exploded in front of three Protestant churches in the Terai region, killing three police officers.

"Our demands were not heard," said Bijaya Kumar Gachchhadar, a leader of the Madhese minority who boycotted the vote. "The new constitution will not improve as long as it does not incorporates the voices of minority groups."

Conversely, the speaker of the Constituent Assembly Subas Nembang stressed the importance of the event. Although the country has had six constitution since the 1950s, this "is the first one that was democratically approved."

2

Constitution of Nepal

Nepal is governed according to the Constitution of Nepal, which came into effect on September 20, 2015, replacing the Interim Constitution of 2007. The Constitution was drafted by the Second Constituent Assembly following the failure of the First Constituent Assembly to produce a constitution in its mandated period. The constitution was endorsed by over 84% of the total lawmakers. Out of 598 CA members, 507 voted in favor of the constitution while 25 voted against and 66 others did not take part in the election process.

Nepal Constituent Assembly

The Interim Constitution provides for a Constituent Assembly, which was charged with writing Nepal's permanent constitution. Under the terms of the Interim Constitution, the new constitution was to be promulgated by May 28, 2010, but the Constituent Assembly postponed the promulgation by a year because of disagreements. On May 25, 2011, the Supreme Court of Nepal ruled that the 2010 extension of the Interim Constitution was not right. Since May 29, 2011 the Constituent Assembly repeatedly extended the Interim Constitution.

On May 28, 2012, the Constituent Assembly was dissolved after it failed to finish the constitution after the latest extension, ending four years of constitution drafting and leaving the country in a legal vacuum. New elections were held on November 19, 2013 to the Second Nepalese Constituent Assembly and political leaders pledged to draft a new constitution within a year.. The new assembly expressly committed that the new constitution would be promulgated on January 22, 2015. However, due to continued differences on key issues including system of governance, judicial system and federation issues like number, name and areas of the states to be carved, the constitution could not be finalized and promulgated in time.

Controversy over Constitution

The promulgation of the new constitution was immediately followed by virtual blockade of all checkpoints at Nepal-India border. Some ethnic groups in lowland Nepal have accused of being gender discriminatory especially in regards to citizenship provisions. They allege new constitution makes it difficult for woman to pass on citizenship to their children as compared to men. Similarly, Madhesi and indigenous population view that the new constitution fails to address demands of marginalized communities and support status-quo of the ruling groups. They are protesting mainly over the federal delineation of new states as proposed in the constitution fearing existing demarcation could affect their political representation. With the protest ongoing since August 15, 2015 or earlier, at least 45 people, including 8 security personals and one Indian National, have been killed. Human Rights Watch has criticized the Nepal Government as well as the protesters for violation of human rights during the protest.

Comparison with Constitution of India

Experts state that Nepal's constitution is one of the best in South Asia. Some of the important aspects of the constitution include the following:

- Same sex marriage is protected by the Constitution. In contrast, same-sex relationship is a crime in India under Section 377 of the Penal Code, which awards punishment of "imprisonment for life or with imprisonment of either description for a term which may extend to ten years and shall also be liable to fine." The Supreme Court in 2013 upheld Section 377 but left it to the wisdom of the parliament to decide whether to retain or repeal the draconian law.

- Recognizing the rights of women, the constitution of Nepal explicitly states that "women shall have equal ancestral right without any gender-based discrimination." India has yet to introduce a similar right for women from all faiths. Moreover, ancestral property rights for women are not a fundamental right in India.
- Nepal also has become the second country after Bhutan in South Asia to abolish the death penalty. The Supreme Court of India in the past has accepted the fact that on various occasions innocent people have been executed.
- Under the new constitution, victims of environmental pollution or degradation in Nepal now have the fundamental right to receive compensation from the polluter. In India the "right to a clean environment" is not explicitly mentioned in the constitution, but the Supreme Court has interpreted it be included under the right to life. However, unlike Nepal, the victims of environmental pollution or degradation in India are not entitled to any compensation as a fundamental right. The state may impose a penalty on polluters but this does not necessarily mean that the affected will be compensated.

Previous Constitutions

Previous constitutions of Nepal were enacted in 1948, 1951, 1959, 1962, 1990 and 2007.

In 1948, the Government of Nepal Act was enacted. Since the mid-nineteenth century, the country had been a monarchy where the prime ministers, from the Rana dynasty, had sweeping control over the affairs of the state. The 1948 document introduced limited democratic elements, but the experiment was not successful due to the misgivings of the Rana rulers to give away power.

The Interim Government of Nepal Act 1951 was promulgated after the Revolution of 1951 that the end of the Rana period. This text strengthened the authority of the king, and introduced relevant reforms such as the creation of the Supreme Court and the inclusion of fundamental rights and socio-economic goals to be pursued by the state.

The CONSTITUTION OF THE KINGDOM OF NEPAL, 1959 followed the previously mentioned interim text. Interestingly, despite the establishment of a bicameral parliament, the king continued to hold important powers such as the prerogative to appoint half of the members of the Senate and the suspension of parliament under certain circumstances.

The democratic experiment was short-lived, as in 1962 a new constitution came in to eliminate political parties, and to introduce the so-called *panchayat* system. In this model, *panchayats* were councils organized at the local level, presumably to ensure the representation of citizens. However, the king exercised much stronger authority than in the 1959 regime. and could modify the constitution or suspend it in case of emergency.

In 1990, the first *Jana Andolan*, Popular Revolt, brought multi-party democracy back to Nepal. The CONSTITUTION. OF THE KINGDOM OF NEPAL(1990) lifted the ban on political parties, described a democratic representative system where the authority of the king was curtailed, and enshrined fundamental rights. Although the 1990 constitution substantially increased the democratic character of the state in comparison with the Panchayat Regime, critiques have argued that this text did not adequately represent all sectors of society, even though Nepal is a multi-cultural country where diverse social groups coexist

Again following the 2006 democracy movement in Nepal, Interim Constitution was promulgated in 2007.

NEPAL CONSTITUTION: A HISTORIC STEP

The adoption of a federal, democratic and secular Constitution in Nepal is a historic occasion. The protracted struggle of the Nepalese people against feudal authoritarianism and for democracy has culminated in the establishment of a federal, democratic and secular State. Eight years after the interim Constitution, after a tortuous political process, the Constituent Assembly voted overwhelmingly (507 out of 601) to approve the Constitution. We congratulate the people of Nepal, the three major political parties – the Nepali Congress, the CPN(UML) and the UCPN(M) – and all democratic forces for this significant achievement.

India should have been the first to welcome the adoption of the Constitution. Instead, the Modi government has adopted a negative attitude and an unwarranted interventionist stance. Two days after the adoption of the Constitution in the Constituent assembly, the Modi government sent Foreign Secretary Jaishankar to Kathmandu to meet the president and the prime minister and leaders of major political parties in an attempt to stall the formal proclamation of the Constitution which took place on September 20. The plea made for this blatant interference in Nepal's sovereign matters is that that Constitution was not inclusive enough and there was serious unrest among the Madhesi people. After the formal promulgation of the Constitution, the Indian foreign ministry issued a statement expressing concern at the protests and violence and just "noted" the adoption of the Constitution. This was followed by two statements on successive days expressing concern about the situation in the Terai region and calling upon the Nepalese government to take the Madhesi people's concern on board as far as the Constitution is concerned. The Indian Ambassador was also recalled for consultations.

There has often been a big brother attitude to Nepal on the part of the Indian ruling establishment. This has however been taken to new heights now with the callous disregard shown to Nepal's sovereign right to formulate the country's Constitution as per their own democratic process.

The Constitution has enunciated fundamental rights of citizens which are more wide-ranging than those provided in the Indian Constitution. The electoral system has provision for proportional representation for 45 percent of the seats in the House of Representatives. Quotas are provided for women, dalits, Madeshis and janjatis in various constitutional bodies. There are seven provinces and three levels of government – the federal, provincial and local. There are many features of the Constitution which represent an advance over existing democratic Constitutions in South Asia, though there may be some shortcomings too.

One of the clauses in the draft constitution which was opposed vehemently by some sections in Nepal was the definition of Nepal State as secular. The pro-monarchy Rashtriya Prajatantra Party and various other Hindutva outfits organised protests throughout the country demanding that Nepal be declared a Hindu State. The Constituent Assembly rejected this demand overwhelmingly. The RSS and all the Hindutva forces in India campaigned, supported and propped up the forces within Nepal who wanted a Hindu Rashtra. BJP MP Avaidyanath had written to the president of Nepal and the chairman of the Constituent Assembly calling for Nepal to be declared a Hindu Rashtra. Earlier, Rajnath Singh, the union home minister, as a BJP leader had visited Nepal to attend the funeral of then Prime Minister GP Koirala in March 2010. On that occasion he had said "We used to feel proud that Nepal was the only Hindu kingdom in the world. I will be happy when Nepal is a Hindu state again." (IANS, March 22, 2010). The Hindutva organisations from India sent their sadhus and leaders to participate in the campaign for a Hindu Rashtra in Nepal.

The rejection of the demand for a Hindu State and the assertion that Nepal will be a secular republic has outraged the Hindutva forces in India. The BJP shares this anger, though it cannot display it openly. This has probably contributed to the negative stance taken by the Modi government.

The Madhesi people who constitute 50 percent of the population of Nepal may have legitimate grievances. But the Modi government's open stance advocating their cause cannot but be construed as an interference in the internal affairs of a neighbouring country. The Modi government's stance of tacit support to the Madhesi agitation is also motivated by the Bihar assembly elections where a large number of people in the border districts are linked to the Madhesi people across the border. Such narrow political considerations are also at play in harming relations with Nepal. The government and the political leadership in Nepal will have to consider how to accommodate the aspirations of the Madhesi people. Constitutions are not rigid static documents and changes can be made through the democratic process.

The Modi government's arrogant intervention has only vitiated the good neighbourly relations between the two countries. It will also send a cautionary message to all other countries in South Asia to be wary of India's big brotherly attitude.

NEITHER PEACE NOR CONSTITUTION IN NEPAL

The ongoing Nepalese Peace Process (PP) has been virtually postponed and the deadline for writing the constitution has somehow ended without even the coarse draft of the new constitution being submitted. The Constituent Assembly (CA) and its Government have totally failed to achieve its principle tasks. They are neither able to complete the constitution writing process nor to enforce properly the comprehensive peace accord.

Mainly, the Peace Process was simply destroyed due to the consensual confrontation between the Maoists and the Nepal Government for the integration issues of vieux jeu-Maoist combatants into Nepalese security force. It is comic to mention that both parties agreed to integrate the former Maoist guerrillas into the Nepalese security system but have always been undecided about the number of guerrillas that should integrate and why?

The United Nations Mission in Nepal (UNMIN) is supposed to provide technical support in the peace process, however the role of UNMIN has not been very useful. It has become a burden on the Nepalese Peace Process, and the UN too, because its role pushed the entire process into political polarization and left the parties in the position of confrontation and mayhem due to faulty peace diplomacy.

Surprisingly, the Internal and external stakeholders in the Nepalese Peace Process have remained silent on these issues, as they say they consider it an internal matter for the nation. For this reason, the bilateral confrontation on integration affairs has become one of the major hurdles to achieving peace through a comprehensive peace accord.

Unfortunately, the Peace Process is not a true priority on the agenda of the Nepalese political parties, which we can easily see by observing the progress in implementation of the comprehensive peace accord. The Government and the Maoists have failed and wavered from their commitment and duties to carry out the comprehensive peace accord in a systematic manner. There is no political culture of self-examination on their own lapses in performing roles and responsibilities towards the peace process and constitution writing. They deliberately failed to rule and operate the CA, Cabinet and Peace Process through political consensus in a constitutional manner as agreed. Most of the political parties are on a mission to capture the cabinet and seek to extend their powers in multifarious ways as much as possible.

Sadly, the CA has become a huge national burden and just a salary provider for its members. In other words, the CA members are temporary jobholders and it was just strategically created to provide employment for political workers. So we should not have expected any great and historical things like a new constitution for New Nepal and sustainable peace from such people who have not even delivered even the minimum characters, role and performance of CA member. Many People have started to comment that CA is a just crowed of ineligible political citizens who are unaware of the interest of our nation and people. This crowd only care about their individual interests, ignoring the people's mandate and national priority.

CA members must be accountable and should start to refund immediately all received incentives, salary, privileges and facilities to the state. Nepal has no ability to afford such huge administrative and financial expenses against the uncertainty of constitution writing and peace process. They should stop playing with the future and emotions of the people and the nation. The CA members and government have worked against the peace process, mandate of CA election and second peoples' movement.

Woefully, the routine jobs of the Nepalese political parties are to demonstrate and organize strike against the ruling parties and people. The Nepalese politicians and political parties abuse their own proclamations, commitments and public promise and mandates. They feel proud to declare general strikes, transportation halts, gheraos, bandhs, stoning, and other unconstitutional and illegal activities.

Shamefully, they claim that the baleful activities are done on behalf of the people to achieve public and national interests, but ignoring their political future and ethics, they never think about their constructive role and contribution. They just act to oppose everything just because they are in opposition. The mentality and poor attitude of political parties is a major cause of the postponing the Peace Process and barring the nation from a new constitution. The complete comprehensive peace accord in new dimension and new approach through multi-partner-partnership approach since the exiting peace accord and its proper implementation have been proved faulty at many ways i.e. cantonment management, guerrilla integration, political harmonization, disarmament, transitional justice etc., and constitution of various commissions for New Nepal as agreed in CPA and mentioned in the Interim constitution of Nepal.

The existing comprehensive peace accord and the Interim Constitution of Nepal have failed to drive the nation in accordance with the mandate and spirit of CA election and mandate of Janaandolan-2. UNMIN and other national and international stakeholders were in favour of the peace process, so the United Nations, Government of Nepal and the Maoist Party itself must rethink before further extending UNMIN in Nepal.

It is highly risky to continue the expired and defective Comprehensive Peace Accord of Nepal. So, the stakeholders must concentrate on the technical parts of the peace accord especially in the areas that are obstacles in execution of the Peace Accord, while restructuring the accord. Empirical assessment of the activities of the exiting CA assembly has already concluded that the CA model of constitution building is a failure here. The Janaandolan-2 and election efforts of CA were wasted; there are no exemplary products of the existing CA. People do not see any countable respect towards the motto of janaandoalan-2 and institutionalization of its achievement.

It is a pity to see that everything is in transition except the selfishness of the political parties and leaders. The nation is in a state of confrontation, and civil war and riots could start anytime, if the political scenario does not change properly. The impunity, crime, corruption, violence appears to be beyond control. Life, liberty, property, public freedoms and the rights of people are in serious danger. Governance and judicial systems are in disorder. All people should wake up urgently against the corrupt political parties and leaders to force them to dissolve the CA and work in favour of a fresh start for the nation.

Nepalese need a fresh start to begin constitution building process that could be managed by amending provision of the Interim Constitution of Nepal. We cannot be held any longer under the captivity of constitutional uncertainty and transitional state. The people of the nation have no more patience, they cannot wait to get and practice defective pieces and provisions of constitutional and governance products.

The existing CA cannot fulfil their minimum roles and assigned responsibilities, they are just disqualified political workers. Every Nepalese wants to save the nation from political, economical, administrative, judicial and diplomatic failure, otherwise the existing political parties and leaders will collapse the nation for fulfilment of their own political and individual vested interests.

It is a huge challenge for all honest citizens to address the trivialities and contemporary transitional scenario of Nepal, which has arisen due to inefficiency and incapability of the existing CA and Government. In plain language, most of the existing political parties and leaders are great cheaters, who have committed crimes against the nation and the people of Nepal by ignoring the Peace Process and delaying the constitution. Indeed, the CA has victimized the currents generations and will cause problems for future generations too. Our nation is about to collapse politically and financially. It is being listed as failed nation.

Therefore, we must think at least about protection and prevention of our future generations from political deadlocks, they will not excuse us for our deeds if we do not play a constructive and fair role. So, every individual and institutional actor must start to raise productive voices against the criminalized political scenario in Nepal. Let's try to minimize the results of the ongoing political crimes and dilemmas; otherwise we will achieve neither peace nor constitution.

CONSTITUTIONAL DEVELOPMENT

The Rana System

Beginning in 1856, the centre of power in Nepal rested with the Rana prime ministers, who retained sovereign power until the revolution of 1950-51. Many of the nobles who participated in the consultative court called the Assembly of Lords, or Bharadari Sabha, had been slaughtered at the Kot Massacre in 1846. Following his official visit to Britain and Europe in 1851, Jang Bahadur Kunwar (later called Jang Bahadur Rana) began to use the Bharadari Sabha as deliberative body for state affairs. For almost 100 years, this council served as a rubber stamp for the Rana autocracy. The next major effort at institutional development was initiated in 1947 by Padma Shamsher Rana, a liberal prime minister, who appointed a Constitutional Reform Committee to draft the first constitution. Known as the Government of Nepal Constitution Act, 1948, this constitution, written with the help of Indian advisers, superficially changed the Rana system. It established a bicameral legislative body. The entire membership of one house and a majority of the other was selected by the prime minister, who could reject any measure that the legislature might pass. There was a cabinet of at least five members, of whom at least two were chosen from among the few elected members of the legislature.

The act also specified that a *panchayat* system of local self-government would be inaugurated in the villages, towns, and districts. It enumerated certain fundamental rights and duties, which included freedoms of speech, the press, assembly, and worship; equality before the law; free elementary education for all; and equal and universal suffrage. Despite the appearance of reform, the alterations made in the Rana system by the constitution were slight. The more conservative Ranas perceived the constitution as a dangerous precedent, forced Padma Shamsher to resign, and suspended promulgation of the constitution. The constitution became effective in September 1950 but remained in force only until February 1951, when the Rana monopoly was broken and the creation of a new constitutional system began.

The Interim Constitution, 1951

The revolution of 1950-51 resulted in the overthrow of the Rana system. In 1951 King Tribhuvan Bir Bikram Shah announced by royal proclamation an interim government and an interim constitution until a new Constituent Assembly could be elected. The interim constitution, based on principles in India's constitution and entitled the Interim Government of Nepal Act, 1951, ratified the end of the authority of the prime minister and the system surrounding that office. It also reasserted the king's supreme executive, legislative, and judicial powers. The king exercised his executive authority through, and was aided and advised by, a Council of Ministers, which he appointed and which served at his pleasure.

The king also appointed an Advising Assembly to sit until the Constituent Assembly was elected. The king retained sovereign and plenary legislative powers. The Advising Assembly was, with certain exceptions, authorized only to discuss matters and to recommend measures to the king for enactment into law. The final authority to approve any legislative measure lay with the king. The constitution also established a Supreme Court, made the king supreme commander of the armed forces, reiterated and enlarged upon the fundamental rights included in the Rana constitution, and proclaimed numerous social and economic objectives of the government. These objectives were to promote the welfare of the people by securing a social order in which social, economic, and political justice pervaded all the institutions of national life. King Mahendra (reigned 1955-72) vigorously sought to broaden the monarch's political base, but the Nepali National Congress succeeded in gaining some democratic reforms. Although the constitution was expected to be temporary pending the election of a Constituent Assembly and the preparation of a permanent organic law, King Mahendra was unable to resist the increasingly well-orchestrated political demands by the Nepali National Congress for a more democratic and representative government, and was forced to promulgate a new constitution.

The Royal Constitution of 1959

The most significant aspect of the constitution of 1959 was that it was granted by the king rather than drawn up by elected representatives of the people as had been specified in the 1951 constitution. Although the constitution formally brought into being a democratically elected parliamentary system under a constitutional monarchy, the king retained ultimate sovereignty, even though the document itself did not explicitly grant this power.

The 1959 constitution, modelled on British and Indian constitutional custom, vested executive power in the king, who was advised and assisted by a Council of State (Raj Sabha) and a Council of Ministers (cabinet). The Council of State, which consisted of officers of Parliament, ministers ex officio, former ministers, and royal appointees, advised the monarch on legislation and handled the details of regency and succession in the event of his death or disability. The general direction and control of the government were entrusted to the Council of Ministers, headed by a prime minister required to command a majority in the lower house of Parliament, to which the council was collectively responsible.

The king was an integral part of the legislative arm of the government. Parliament was defined as consisting of the king; the House of Representatives, composed of 109 popularly elected members; and the Senate, composed of 36 members of whom half were elected by the house and half were nominated by the king. All bills approved by the two houses required the assent of the king to become law. The constitution granted the king wide latitude to nullify the parliamentary system. The king could suspend the operation of the cabinet and perform its functions himself if he determined that no person could command a majority in the house as prime minister. In the event of a breakdown of the parliamentary system or of any one of a number of emergency conditions, the king could suspend either or both houses of Parliament, assume their powers, and suspend the constitution in whole or part. In December 1960, King Mahendra invoked these emergency powers to dissolve the Nepali Congress Party government. The constitutional system that had prevailed before 1959 was then returned to operation.

The Panchayat Constitution, 1962

By royal proclamation on December 16, 1962, King Mahendra announced a new constitution that radically reformed the 1959 constitution but also adopted many features of the Rana system. Known as the Panchayat Constitution, it was the fourth constitution in fifteen years.

The *panchayat* system was an institution of great antiquity. Historically, each caste group system of Nepal formed its own *panchayat*, or council of elders, a sociopolitical organization operational on a village level that could expand to include neighbouring districts, or even function on a zonal basis. Although it could be argued that the *panchayat* system was adopted from India, King Mahendra had argued for its incorporation at the national level as an exponent of Nepalese culture—a worthy and historically correct representation of cultural expression.

The 1962 constitution was based on some elements from other "guided democracy" constitutional experiments—notably "Basic Democracy" in Pakistan, "Guided Democracy" in Indonesia, and the "Dominant Party System" in Egypt. The Panchayat constitution not only codified the irrelevance of political parties, but also declared them illegal.

The 1962 constitution contained a stronger and more explicit statement of royal authority than did previous constitutions. Real power remained with the king, who was the sole source of authority and had the power not only to amend the constitution but also to suspend it by royal proclamation during emergencies. The Council of Ministers, selected from the members of the legislative (Rashtriya Panchayat, or National Panchayat), served as an advisory body to the king. Members of the Rashtriya Panchayat were elected indirectly by the members of local *panchayat* as well as by the members of professional and class organizations such as the Nepal Workers' Organization, the Nepal Ex-servicemen's Organization, and the Nepal Youth Organization. The constitution abolished all political parties.

Constitutional Amendments

The Panchayat Constitution was amended several times, primarily to increase the power and prerogatives of the monarchy against the increasing popular demand for liberalization of the political institutions and processes. In view of the mounting criticism against the Panchayat Constitution, King Birendra, who had succeeded his father in 1972, pursuant to recommendations of a specially created Constitutional Reform Commission, announced in 1975 that the constitution would be amended to include provisions governing the amending procedure itself. Previously the king could not amend the constitution unless two-thirds of the Rashtriya Panchayat ratified the proposed amendment. Under the proposed amendment, the king would have to consult a special committee of the Rastriya Panchayat before amending the constitution. In addition, the term of a delegate to the Rashtriya Panchayat was reduced from six years to four years.

The Referendum of 1980

In May 1979, concerned by the unabated political demonstrations and considerable general unrest, King Birendra called for a nationwide referendum to determine the future form of government. The referendum offered two choices: a continuation of the partyless *panchayat* system, with prospects for further reform; or a multiparty system. Although no clear definition of a multiparty system was provided, the implication was that it stood for a parliamentary system of government run on a party basis. The referendum, the first nationwide vote in twenty-two years, was held on May 2, 1980, and 67 percent of the eligible voters participated. The *panchayat* system was chosen with a majority of 54.7 percent of the votes. On May 21, 1980, the king appointed an eleven-member Constitution Reforms Commission to be chaired by the acting chief justice of the Supreme Court. On December 15, the king promulgated three constitutional amendments: direct elections to the Rashtriya Panchayat would be held every five years for 112 seats, with 28 additional seats filled by the king's personal nomination; the prime minister would be elected by the Rashtriya Panchayat; the cabinet would be appointed by the king on the recommendation of the prime minister and would be accountable to the Rashtriya Panchayat; and Nepal would commit to the Nonaligned Movement as a zone of peace. These provisions, with a few minor modifications, remained in operation until early 1990, when the prodemocracy movement successfully agitated for a multiparty democratic system.

The Constitution of 1990

Widespread prodemocracy protests toppled the *panchayat* system in April 1990. The king appointed an independent

Constitution Recommendation Commission to represent the main opposition factions and to prepare a new constitution to accommodate their demands for political reform. On September 10, 1990, the commission presented King Birendra with the draft of a new constitution, which would preserve the king's status as chief of state under a constitutional monarchy but establish a multiparty democracy with separation of powers and human rights. As agreed upon earlier, the king turned the draft constitution over to Prime Minister K.P. Bhattarai and his cabinet for review and recommendations. The draft was discussed extensively and approved by the interim cabinet. A major obstacle to approval was avoided when the commission removed a disputed provision under which both the constitutional monarchy and multiparty system could have been eliminated by a three-quarters majority vote of Parliament.

On November 9, 1990, King Birendra promulgated the new constitution and abrogated the constitution of 1962. The 1990 constitution ended almost thirty years of absolute monarchy in which the palace had dominated every aspect of political life and political parties were banned. The constitution, broadly based on British practice, is the fundamental law of Nepal. It vests sovereignty in the people and declares Nepal a multiethnic, multilingual, democratic, independent, indivisible, sovereign, and constitutional monarchical kingdom. The national and official language of Nepal is Nepali in the Devanagari script. All other languages spoken as the mother tongue in the various parts of Nepal are recognized as languages of the nation. Although Nepal still is officially regarded as a Hindu kingdom, the constitution also gives religious and cultural freedom to other religious groups, such as Buddhists, Muslims, and Christians. The preamble of the constitution recognizes the desire of the Nepalese people to bring about constitutional changes with the objective of obtaining social, political, and economic justice. It envisages the guarantee of basic human rights to every citizen, a parliamentary system of government, and a multiparty democracy. It also aims to establish an independent and competent system of justice with a view to transforming the concept of the rule of law into reality.

Other safeguards include the right to property; the right to conserve and promote one's language, script, and culture; the right to education in the student's mother tongue; freedom of religion; and the right to manage and protect religious places and trusts. Traffic in human slavery, serfdom, forced labour, or child labour in any form is prohibited. The right to receive information about matters of public importance and the right to secrecy and inviolability of one's person, residence, property, documents, letters, and other information also are guaranteed.

Part three of the constitution provides for the fundamental rights of citizens. Although some elements of fundamental rights guaranteed in the 1962 constitution are reflected in the 1990 constitution, the latter provides new safeguards in unequivocal language and does not encumber the fundamental rights with duties or restrictions purported to uphold public good. All citizens are equal before the law, and no discrimination can be made on the basis of religion, race, sex, caste, tribe, or ideology. No person shall, on the basis of caste, be discriminated against as an untouchable, be denied access to any public place, or be deprived from the use of public utilities. No discrimination will be allowed in regard to remuneration for men and women for the same work. No citizen can be exiled or be deprived of liberty except in accordance with the law; and capital punishment is disallowed.

In addition, sections on fundamental rights provide for freedom of thought and expression; freedom to assemble peacefully and without arms; freedom to form unions and associations; freedom to move and reside in any part of Nepal; and freedom to carry out any profession, occupation, trade, or industry. Similarly, prior censorship of publications is prohibited, and free press and printing are guaranteed. Unfettered cultural and educational rights also are guaranteed. Articles twenty-three and eighty-eight provide for a citizen's right to constitutional remedy. Any citizen can petition the Supreme Court to declare any law or part thereof as void if it infringes on the fundamental rights conferred by the constitution.

Rights regarding criminal justice include the guarantee that no person will be punished for an act unpunishable by law or subjected to a punishment greater than that prescribed by the laws in existence at the time of commission of the offense; no person will be prosecuted more than once in any offense; and no one will be compelled to bear witness against himself or herself. Inflicting cruelty on a person in detention is prohibited, as is detaining a person without giving information about the grounds for such detention. Further, the person in detention must be produced within twenty-four hours of such arrest before the judicial authorities. Any person wrongly detained will be compensated.

The constitution lays down various directives in matters of political, economic, and social development, and foreign policy. These lofty policies are guidelines to promote conditions of welfare on the basis of the principles of an open society. One objective is to transform the national economy into an independent and self-reliant system by making arrangements for the equitable distribution of the economic gains on the basis of social justice. The constitution stresses the creation of conditions for the enjoyment of the fruits of democracy through the maximum participation of the people in governance of the country. Other aims include the pursuit of a policy in international relations that will enhance the dignity of the nation and ensure sovereignty, integrity, and national independence and the protection of the environment from further ecological damage

OTHER FEATURES OF THE CONSTITUTION

The constitution guarantees the citizens' unfettered rights to political pluralism and a multiparty democracy. All legitimate political organizations or parties that register with the Election Commission are allowed to publicize and broadcast for the purpose of securing support and cooperation of the general public toward their objectives and programs. Any law, arrangement, or decision that restricts any of these activities is inconsistent with the constitution and void. Any law, arrangement, or decision to impose a one-party system is also inconsistent with the constitution and void. Under the section on political organization, any political party is not eligible for registration if it discriminates, if at least 5 percent of its candidates are not women, or if it fails to obtain at least 3 percent of the total votes cast in the previous election to the House of Representatives. The constitution may be amended or repealed by a majority of two-thirds in each house of Parliament. However, such amendment or repeals may not be designed to frustrate the spirit of the preamble of the constitution, which recognizes the Nepalese people as the source of sovereign authority. After passing in both houses, any bill to repeal or amend the constitution must receive royal assent.

The Executive

Executive powers are vested in the king and the Council of Ministers—a prime minister, deputy prime minister, and other ministers as required. The direction, supervision, and conduct of the general administration of the country are the responsibility of the Council of Ministers. All transactions made in the name of the king, except those within his exclusive domain, are authenticated by the Council of Ministers. The king appoints the leader of the political party commanding a majority in the House of Representatives as prime minister. If a single party does not have a majority in the house, the member commanding a majority on the basis of two or more parties is asked to form the government. When this alternative also is not possible, the king may ask the leader of a party holding the largest number of seats in the house to form the government. In this case, the leader forming the government must obtain a vote of confidence in the house within thirty days. If a vote of no confidence is obtained, the king will dissolve the house and order new elections within six months. Other ministers are appointed by the king from members of Parliament on the recommendation of the prime minister.

The constitution declares the king the symbol of the nation and the unity of its people. Expenditures and privileges of the king and royal family are determined by law. The king is obliged to obey and protect the constitution. Although, as in previous constitutions the monarch remains the supreme commander of the Royal Nepal Army, a three-member National Defence Council, headed by the prime minister, commands the military.

Nonetheless, the king retains his power over the army because if there were a threat to sovereignty, indivisibility, or security because of war, foreign aggression, armed revolt, or extreme economic depression, he could declare a state of emergency. During the period of emergency—which would have to be approved by the House of Representatives within three months and which would remain in effect for six months from the date of its announcement, renewable for six months—fundamental rights, with the exception of the right of habeas corpus, could be suspended.

Additional prerogatives of the king include the power to grant pardons; suspend, commute, or remit any sentence passed by any court; confer titles, honours, or decorations of the kingdom; appoint all ambassadors and emissaries for the kingdom; and remove any barriers to enforcing the constitution. The king also nominates the members of the Raj Parishad (King's Council), the body that determines the accession to the throne of the heir apparent.

The Legislature

The constitution provides for a bicameral legislature, the Parliament. This body consists of the king and two houses, the House of Representatives (Pratinidhi Sabha) and the National Council (Rashtriya Sabha). The House of Representatives has 205 directly elected members.

The term for the House of Representatives is five years unless it dissolves earlier, pursuant to the provisions of the constitution. On the recommendation of the prime minister, the king may dissolve the house, but new elections must be held within six months.

Administrative districts are the election districts; and each district's allocation of seats is proportional to its population. All persons eighteen years or older are enfranchised.

The National Council has sixty members consisting of ten nominees of the king; thirty-five members, including at least three women, to be elected by the House of Representatives by means of a single transferable vote, pursuant to the system of proportional representation; and fifteen members to be elected by the electoral college comprising the voters, including the chair and deputy chair of the village and town and district committees of various development regions. The National Council is a permanent body; onethird of its members must retire every two years. Council members serve six-year terms.

With the exception of finance bills, introduced only in the House of Representatives, bills may be introduced in either house. All bills, however, must be passed by both houses before receiving royal assent. When a bill is rejected by the National Council, the House of Representatives has the overriding authority. If the joint session of Parliament receives and passes a bill that the king returned for reconsideration, it receives royal assent within thirty days. The king may, when both the Houses of Parliament are not in session, promulgate ordinances, which are not effective unless approved by both the houses when reconvened. Financial procedures are outlined in part ten of the constitution, which states that taxes cannot be levied or loans raised except in accordance with the law.

The Judiciary

An independent judiciary, unencumbered by the executive branch of the government and palace interference, was a stated goal of all political parties. Of the many changes which have taken place since the fall of the Ranas in 1951, among the most striking have been the growing autonomy of the courts and the gradual liberalization of many basic judicial principles. Despite major improvements, however, the judicial system has suffered from serious impediments in providing speedy, expeditious, and equal justice. The independence and integrity of the judiciary were repeatedly questioned in the press; intervention of political figures and government officials in the judicial process was a frequent occurrence; and caste and economic status were important determinants of the availability of justice.

The court system formerly was one of many instruments used by the prime minister to maintain the authoritarian rule of the Rana family, and the concepts of law it applied were arbitrary, punitive, and oppressive. After an initial attempt to keep the judiciary subordinate when the monarchy was restored, it was allowed to become a relatively independent branch of government. Reforms in the legal system rendered both substantive and procedural law progressively more systematic. Never clearly demarcated, the jurisdiction of the courts became further complicated with the introduction of the *panchayat* system, which at the local level exercised some quasijudicial functions. Therefore, the fundamental role of the judiciary and its position within the government became a subject of national focus during the prodemocracy movement. According to the constitution, the courts comprise three tiers: the Supreme Court, appellate courts, and district courts. In addition, courts or tribunals may be constituted for the purpose of hearing special types of cases.

The Supreme Court is the highest court. All other courts and institutions exercising judicial powers, except the military courts, are under its jurisdiction. The Supreme Court has the authority to inspect, supervise, and give directives to all subordinate courts and all other institutions that exercise judicial powers. The Supreme Court has both original and appellate jurisdiction and consists of a chief justice and fourteen other judges. The chief justice is appointed on the recommendation of the Constitutional Council. Other judges of the Supreme Court, appellate courts, and district courts are appointed on the recommendation of the Judicial Council.

All appointments are made by the king. The tenure of office of the chief justice is limited to seven years from the date of appointment. Supreme Court justices can be impeached in the House of Representatives for reasons of incapacity, misbehaviour, or malafide acts while in office. The Judicial Council, presided over by the chief justice of the Supreme Court, makes recommendations and advises on appointments, transfers, and disciplinary actions of the judges and other matters relating to judicial administration.

All appointments, promotions, transfers, and disciplinary actions of the judges of the appellate and district courts are under the jurisdiction of the Judicial Council. An independent Judicial Service Commission, appointed by the king, and with the chief justice of the Supreme Court serving as ex-officio chairman, appoints, transfers, promotes, and provides departmental punishment of the gazetted officers of the civil service.

An Abuse of Authority Investigating Commission is empowered to investigate the misuse of authority or corruption by public officials. Members of the commission have no specific party affiliation and are appointed by the king on the recommendation of the Constitutional Council.

The Supreme Court is the supreme judicial authority of the nation. All orders and decisions made by the court are binding. Any interpretation of a law or any legal principle laid down by the court is binding on all, including the king. As a guarantor of personal liberty and fundamental rights conferred by the constitution, the Supreme Court has the authority to declare a law as void ab initio if it finds that the impugned law contravenes the provisions of the constitution. The Supreme Court also has the power to issue appropriate orders and writs, including habeas corpus, mandamus, certiorari, prohibition, and quo warranto.

The Civil Service

The Nepal Civil Service Act, passed in 1956, classified all civil employees of the government into two categories—gazetted services and nongazetted services. Gazetted services included all services prescribed by the government by notification in the *Nepal Raj Patra*, the government gazette. In 1991 categories of the gazetted services were education, judicial, health, administrative, engineering, forest, agricultural, and miscellaneous services. The gazetted posts were further grouped into classes I, II, and III. Nongazetted posts also had several class echelons. As of 1990, there were approximately 80,000 civil service employees in all ranks.

According to the 1990 constitution, all members of the civil service are recruited through an open competitive examination conducted by the Public Service Commission. Police and military officers are excluded from the jurisdiction of the commission. The chairman and other members of the commission are appointed by the king on the recommendation of the Constitutional Council. The commission must be consulted in all matters concerning laws relating to the civil service—such as appointment, promotion, transfer, or departmental punishment. Tenure, benefits, and postings were regulated by the Nepal Civil Service Act of 1956.

The Administrative System

The *panchayat* system represented "democracy at the grassroots," and until April 1990 it included four integrated levels: local or village, district, zonal, and national—the Rashtriya Panchayat. Only the village *panchayat* was directly elected by the people. Championing *panchayat* rule as a political system, king Mahendra was able to tap into nascent Nepalese nationalism and also to outmaneuver the evolving political parties which had posed a challenge to the monarchy's vested power.

The country was divided into fourteen zones and seventy-five districts in support of the complex hierarchy of the *panchayat* system. The lowest unit of government was the *gaun panchayat* (village committee or council), of which there were 3,524. A locality with a population of more than 10,000 persons was organized as a *nagar panchayat* (town committee or council). The number of *nagar panchayat* varied from zone to zone. Above the *gaun panchayat* and *nagar panchayat* was the district *panchayat*, of which there were seventyfive. At the apex of the *panchayat* system was the Rashtriya Panchayat, which served as the unicameral national legislature from 1962 until 1990.

The district *panchayat* had broad powers for supervising and coordinating the development programs of the village and carried out development projects through the district development boards and centers. Each of the seventy-five districts was headed by a chief district officer, who was an elected official, responsible for maintaining law and order, and for coordinating the work of the field agencies of the various ministries.

The zonal *panchayat* was responsible for implementing development plans forwarded by the central government, formulating and executing programs of its own, and planning, supervising, and coordinating district development programs within its jurisdiction. Zonal commissioners exercised full administrative and quasijudicial powers. Each zone was administered by a zonal commissioner and one or two assistant zonal commissioners, all directly appointed by the king. Zones and districts were further regrouped into five development zones in 1971-72, an administrative division that remained in effect in

1991. A drive for political liberalization, which had begun shortly after the 1959 constitution was abrogated and all political activities were banned in 1960, did not climax until the prodemocracy movement of 1990. At that point, ongoing debilitating interparty conflicts and halting demands for reforms of the political system ended, and national energy focused on a movement to achieve democratic rights. During the prodemocracy movement, some of the *pancha* (*panchayat* members) loyalists even were openly friendly with their former adversaries.

The interim government that was installed in April 1990 consisted of strange bedfellows, who, however, succeeded in steering the nation to its first free and fair elections in thirtytwo years. In April 1990, the *nagar panchayat* was renamed *nagar polika* (municipal development committee), and the *gaun panchayat* became *gaun bikas samiti*, or village development committee. The Ministry of Local Development posted an officer to each district to help with the various programs of the development committees. In mid-1991, a Nepali Congress Party government was in power, and a conglomerate of communist parties was playing the role of constitutional opposition. At that time, there were 4,015 village development committees and thirty-three municipal development committees. Elections for the heads of the development committees were scheduled for June 1992.

The Panchayat System

For centuries the government had been run by a number of interrelated aristocratic families. Despite the limitations of a royal ban on political parties and other impediments, political parties did exist and operated clandestinely. To escape harassment or imprisonment, many political leaders went to India, where they also received logistical and other support.

Under the *panchayat* system, there were six government-sponsored class and professional organizations for peasants, laborers, students, women, former military personnel, and college graduates. These organizations were substitutes for the prohibited political parties and provided alternate channels for the articulation of group or class—rather than national—interests. The professional and class organizations were warned repeatedly against engaging in political activity; nevertheless, they offered the only political forum open to many Nepalese, and even some Nepali Congress Party and communist partisans considered them worthy of infiltration.

The king also launched an independent national student association, the National Independent Student Council (Rashtriya Swatantra Vidyarthi Parishad), to control the political activities of the students. The association failed to gain support, and successful student agitation in 1979 forced the king not only to abolish it but also to initiate constitutional reforms leading to the national referendum of 1980. Also in 1980, a group of dissident *pancha* brought a no-confidence motion against Prime Minister Surya Bahadur Thapa on charges of bureaucratic corruption, food shortages, and lack of economic discipline. Surya Bahadur, however, was a perennial political survivor and was returned to office in 1981.

King Birendra devised the Back-to-the-Village National Campaign (BVNC) in 1975. The BVNC was intended to circumvent the possibility of opposition within the *panchayat* and to create a loyal core of elites to select and endorse candidates for political office, thereby neutralizing the influence of underground political party organizers in the rural areas. Although it was envisioned as a means to mobilize the people for the implementation of development plans and projects, the shortlived BVNC—it was suspended in 1979—was in reality an ideological campaign to reinforce the importance of the partyless system. The campaign stressed that the partyless system was appropriate to the ways of the Nepalese people; the party system was a divisive and culturally alien institution.

Each zonal committee had a BVNC structure, with a secretary nominated by the king. The BVNC network was extended to the district and village levels so as to reinforce a national communication system. However inasmuch as the government paid the BVNC central and zonal committee members and restricted chances for popular participation, the committees carried out the same activities as the *panchayat*. In actuality, the BVNC was created by the king to ensure a loyal organization and circumvent active party members from gaining seats in the *panchayat* elections. The BVNC became an organization of centrally controlled loyal *panchayat* elites and an insurance policy for palace initiatives.

The only significant opposition to the monarchy came from the Nepali Congress Party, which operated from exile in India. Other parties either accepted and operated within the *panchayat* system on a supposedly nonpartisan basis or merged with the exiled Nepali Congress Party, polarizing politics over the issue of monarchical rule. Even the Communist Party of Nepal, divided on the tactical question of whether to seek the direct and immediate overthrow of the monarchical system or to work within it, had split into factions—a radical wing operated in India and a moderate wing underground in Nepal. Some party members, to gain tactical advantage over the Nepali Congress Party, entered the *panchayat* system with the tacit approval of the palace.

Ethnic plurality, income disparity, linguistic diversity, pervading regional loyalties, underdeveloped communications, and a paucity of written and electronic media also hindered party organization. The dominant high-caste political leaders were more interested in sharing or gaining access to power than in developing lasting foundations for party politics.

Reportedly, before political organizations were banned, there were sixty-nine political parties, most of which were characteristically fluid in their membership and inconsistent in their loyalties. Personalities rather than ideologies brought individuals and groups under the nominal canopy of a party. Fragmentation, recombination, and alliances for convenience were the outstanding aspects of party behaviour.

In the polarized political climate, the monarchy looked at the *panchayat* system as its only dependable support base. The *panchayat* apparatus provided access for politically motivated individuals to form a new elite. Although the political leadership and following of the Nepali Congress Party initially stayed away from the *panchayat* system, over time, and in the absence of an outlet for political activities, some defections took place. Nevertheless, the lateral entry of some pro-Nepali Congress Party elements did not substantially change the character of the *panchayat* leadership, which was dominated by rural elites of the Hill Region rather than the urban Kathmandu and Tarai Region elites who had been in the forefront of political activities.

The system was designed so that the established parties would gradually shrink and lose their influence and control. Once the new *panchayat* leadership matured, however, some members became restive under the excessive control of the palace. This group of the *panchayat* elite opposed the system from within and overtly joined the prodemocracy movement.

In the last four decades, there was significant progress towards democracy in Nepal's traditionally authoritarian political system. The first national elections in Nepal took place in 1959— some eight years after the overthrow of the Rana system.

The Nepali Congress Party-dominated government, victorious in the 1959 parliamentary elections, was overthrown by King Mahendra within two years—resulting in the ban on political parties. The pattern that developed over the following decades was that of a monarchy reinforcing its power through the traditional institution of the *panchayat*.

The *panchayat* system, co-opted and easily manipulated by the monarchy to suit its political ends, nevertheless was slowly but steadily subjected to pressures to change.

Over time the monarchy was forced by necessity to expand the role of elections in response to the mounting discontent of a citizenry living in an age of heightened political awareness and rising expectations. This trend culminated in May 1991 with the first truly free elections in over thirty years, ushering in a new political era. The Nepali Congress Party obtained a workable majority within the framework of a constitutional monarchy and affirmed the rise of a nascent democratic force.

One of the ramifications of the prodemocracy movement was the beginning of a process of integration in national politics and decision making. With an elected Parliament and demands for an equitable allocation of resources to different regions, it was likely that all regions would compete for equality in national politics and that the monopoly of power by select families would erode, as would the excessive influence of the Kathmandu Valley Brahman,

Chhetri, and Newar elites. At the beginning of 1990, the *panchayat* system still dominated Nepal.

Although the institution itself was the object of derision from opponents of the *panchayat* system, it appeared unthreatened. Within a few months, however, its position eroded and then crumbled with bewildering speed. The surge of the successful prodemocracy movement sweeping Eastern Europe, parts of the Soviet Union, and several Asian countries profoundly inspired the Nepalese people.

Also contributing to the sudden transformation were the economic woes of Nepal, exacerbated by India's refusal to renew a trade and transit agreement; widespread bureaucratic inefficiency and corruption at all levels of government; the misgivings openly expressed by the international donors over the country's inefficient use of aid; and a deplorable record on human rights. In January 1990, the Nepali Congress Party held its first national convention in thirty years in Kathmandu.

It was well attended by party delegates from all districts and observers from all political parties. Also present was a multiparty delegation from India, headed by Janata Dal (People's Party) leader Chandra Shekhar, who subsequently became Indian's prime minister. The Nepali Congress Party cooperated with the United Left Front parties, a coalition of seven communist factions, in a joint program to replace the *panchayat* system with a multiparty political system and launched the Movement for the Restoration of Democracy, or prodemocracy movement.

Beginning on February 18, 1990—the thirty-ninth anniversary of King Tribhuvan's declaration of a multiparty democracy and the thirtieth anniversary of the antidemocratic usurpation of power by the palace—a series of spontaneous and sometimes turbulent mass demonstrations rocked major cities. People took to the streets to demand the restoration of a multiparty democracy, human rights, and fundamental freedoms.

The success of the Kathmandu *bandh* (general strike) by prodemocracy forces on March 2 was repeated in other parts of the country over the course of seven weeks. By the time the movement succeeded in totally uprooting the *panchayat* system, at least fifty people were dead, and thousands were injured as a result of the force used by the authorities in suppressing the agitation. The government also had incarcerated national and district-level leaders of both the Nepali Congress Party and the United Left Front.

Unable to contain the widespread public agitation against the *panchayat* system and the mounting casualties, and fearing for the survival of his own monarchical status, King Birendra lifted the ban on political parties on April 8.

The unrest persisted. In the midst of continued violence, a royal proclamation on April 16 dissolved the Rashtriya Panchayat and invalidated provisions of the 1962 constitution inconsistent with multiparty democracy.

The next day, the king named Nepali Congress Party President K.P. Bhattarai, a moderate who had spent fourteen years as a political prisoner, as prime minister and head of the interim government. The government also freed all political prisoners, lifted control of all domestic and foreign publications, and established a commission, known as the Mullick Commission, to investigate the recent loss of life and property.

The eleven-member Bhattarai cabinet, composed of four members of the Nepali Congress Party, three members of the United Left Front, two human rights activists, and two royal nominees, was immediately entrusted with the task of preparing a new constitution and holding a general election. Pending the adoption of a new constitution, the interim government agreed that Nepal should remain under the 1962 constitution. In the interest of continuity and orderly management of public business, the interim government resisted demands from the left for a mass purge of the bureaucracy and die-hard *panchayat* elements. Bhattarai's goal was national reconciliation in a multiparty democracy.

After nine months of politicking, the constitution was proclaimed on November 9, 1990. Elections to the House of Representatives were held on May 12, 1991. The new government faced the immediate problems of restoring law and order, providing economic relief to the populace, and establishing its claim to sound administration, a somewhat difficult task because the parties of the interim government had been in the opposition for a long period of time.

Furthermore, pro-*panchayat* thugs who had tried to foment chaos and law and order problems to discredit the new government had to be brought under control. The situation improved as many former *panchayat* leaders who had previously supported moves for a multiparty democracy openly supported the political changes and offered to cooperate with the new government-taking advantage of political opportunism.

3

Constitution of Nepal 2072: Under Fire

"It was the best of the times; it was the worst of the times. It was the age of wisdom, it was the age of foolishness... it was the session of light; it was the session of darkness. We had everything before us; we had nothing before us..."

These lines by Charles Dickens in A Tale of Two Cities aptly describe our political situation today, nobody knows where Nepal is headed amidst several ups and downs. Leaders of the three parties, Nepali Congress, CPN-UML, and UCPN-Maoist, who got united to promulgate the new constitution, are now looking differently in the context of power sharing.

When president Dr. Ram Baran Yadav promulgated the new constitution from Birendra International Convention Center (BICC), there was joy and happiness inside the hall, where the constitution received a thunderous welcome. The next hour all the students loyal to the three ruling parties celebrated the promulgation of constitution as an historic and life-time achievement.

Political leaders of the three big parties, civil society leaders affiliated with them and students and young political forces showed up in streets with flags and candles. Similarly, business communities welcomed it as an opportunity for an all-round economic development.

"This is a victory day of all Nepalese who fought almost 66 years to write the new constitution by the elected representatives of Constituent Assembly," said Prime Minister Sushil Koirala following the promulgation of the new constitution. "After the promulgation of the constitution, the republic, federalism and secularism have been institutionalized in the country and no one can grab these achievements any longer."

UCPN-Maoist leader Pushpa Kamal Dahal thundered that the day made him the happiest in his life as Nepalese people's long dream to write the constitution through an elected Constituent Assembly got translated into reality.

Leaders of big three parties and their supporters were distributing the sweet dream to their followers that the new constitution would open economic opportunities for them. Having listened for a long time to the false promise that the end of transition would bring economic prosperity in the country, many young people celebrated the occasion as the victory day.

However the situation is violent and dark in the bordering cities. An agitator was killed and three injured in police firing in Birjung, a southern border city where Madheshi parties have been launching the agitation for almost 42 days following the demarcation of provinces.

Despite the use of force and announcement of curfew and prohibitory orders in various district headquarters, the agitation continues to flare up and escalate deep inside Terai.

As Nepal is heading for a festive season next month, the general strike in Terai has created an uncertainty as the market is empty and there is already the scarcity of essential goods, including the petroleum products. With over 40 dead and more than hundred injured, the wound of Terai is deepening.

"September 20 was the darkest day in Madhesh as two young sons of Madhesh got the martyrdom from police firing," said Sadbhavana Party leader Rajendra Mahato. "Three Brahmin leaders of Kathmandu are killing Madheshis, who are demanding just rights and shares in their own country. "

As people in Kathmandu and other hill cities celebrated September 20 as the day of victory, the entire Madhesh observed it as a black day in its history. When youngsters in capital Kathmandu were lighting candles and praying for a unified country, the Madheshi youth were burning the copies of Constitution of

Nepal 2072 throughout Madhesh and threatening to declare the Madhesh plains as a separate country. Youth of the capital were escorted by security personnel granting security. However, youth in terai were fighting with police in the streets.

Blaming India

As the agitation flares up and Indian response to the promulgation of New Constitution chills, leaders of big three are blaming India for the unrest in areas bordering India.

Social media, online and print news sites are full of stories blaming India for the present problems. Even scholars regarded as soft on India are accusing the Indian establishment as a factor in the situation.

Although Prime Minister Sushil Koirala is quietly describing India's role, UCPN-Maoist leader Pushpa Kamal Dahal and CPN-UML leader K.P. Sharma Oli are openly chanting anti-India slogans in the public forums.

UCPN-Maoist leader Prachanda threatened India not to indulge in Nepal's internal politics. "Nepalese cannot bow down to anybody as they don't want to sacrifice their pride with India," said Prachanda.

Out of big three, UCPN-Maoist leader Prachanda is the most vocal, followed by CPN-UML leader and prime minister aspirant K.P. Sharma Oli. The situation is such that Nepal and India are witnessing their official relations at their lowest ebb since the impasse of 1988-1989.

As Nepal heavily depends on India for its economic development, the deteriorating relations with India will harm the common people. "We will talk with India on issues if there are certain misunderstandings between us," said K.P.Sharma Oli.

Political Move

As per the gentlemen's agreement, Nepali Congress, CPN-UML and UCPN-Maoist have already fixed the positions of power for new Nepal, with Nepali Congress likely to get the post of president, CPN-UML leader K.P. Sharma Oli prime minister and UCPN-Maoist leader Krishna Bahadur Mahara speaker of the Legislature Parliament.

Given the ongoing agitation, building pressure from agitators, the plan of the three parties is likely to change in case of early agreement. In case the leaders of the three parties agreed the proposal of the leader of Madheshi Janaadhikar Forum (Loktantrik), who proposed to incorporate the demands of disgruntled parties in bulk as political agenda, there will be new provisions in the constitution and the present power sharing model will be likely to change.

Prime Minister Sushil Koirala will be in New York for two weeks after leaving Nepal on 23 September and the parties in Kathmandu are likely to work on power sharing and accommodation of demands of Madheshis, Tharus and Janjatis through an amendment.

"Since the demands of Madheshis, Tharus and Janajatis are political in nature, one cannot find these addressed looking at the legal and constitutional means," said Gachchhadar.

Given the nature of the political leaders, it is unlikely that the current unity among the top brass of the three parties will remain intact forever when they will sit across the table to bargain for various constitutional and political positions.

Challenges

Nepal has promulgated seven constitutions in the past 68 years, this is the first constitution which faced the strong challenges from the hour of promulgation. Nepal has experimented with Nepal Constitutional Act, 1948, Interim Constitution of Nepal 1951, Constitution of Kingdom of Nepal 1959, Constitution of Nepal 1962, Constitution of Nepal 1990, Interim Constitution of Nepal 2007 and Constitution of Nepal 2015.

However, none of the constitutions has survived for an adequate time. All the previous constitutions died because of failure of Nepalese leaders to stick to institutions and rule of law. One after another, these constitutions were burnt whenever the opposition felt betrayed.

This time also, similar forces have appeared to threaten the longevity of the constitution. Instead of warm welcome or candle light, the constitution was put in fire on the same evening with blackout in half of the country. This has indicated that the new constitution is likely to face a number of challenges in its implementation.

The process of negotiations has already been initiated by prime minister Sushil Koirala, K.P.Sharma Oli and Pushpa Kamal Dahal Prachanda, who started the initiative by visiting the party offices of two leaders Mahant Thakur and Bijaya Kumar Gachchhadar. Even as 40 days of violent agitation and clashes have already taken the lives of over 40 people, no sign of immediate solution is near the horizon.

Along with Madhesis, Tharus and disgruntled Janajatis, Dalits and Hindu religious groups are opposing the constitution. And the opposition is gradually increasing expanding as the groups join hands with one another to press the rulers in Kathmandu.

History of Constituent Assembly

Although many Nepalis mistakenly consider that the Constituent Assembly is the agenda of Nepali people, it is wrong. Nepal's Constituent Assembly was first proposed in the Indian parliament by Indian Prime Minister Jawaharlal Nehru in December 21,1950.

In a process for trip rate agreement, India handed over an eight-point memorandum to Rana's representatives on 8 December 1950 which said that a Constituent Assembly, composed entirely of properly elected members, should be brought into being as soon as possible to draw up a constitution for Nepal.

Many political circumstances had changed during the period and political parties finally agreed to write the new constitution through the Constitutional Commission which drafted the Constitution of Kingdom of Nepal 1960 and replaced the Interim Constitution 1951.

After dismissal of 1960 Constitution, King Mahendra proclaimed Constitution of Nepal 1962. Then, Constitution of Kingdom of Nepal 1990 was promulgated and, before long, the Constituent Assembly demand rose again following the announcement of People's War in 1996 by Maoist Party. The present Constituent Assembly became possible only after the signing of the 12-point agreement in November 2005 between the seven-party alliance and Maoists in New Delhi through an Indian brokered peace agreement.

It was expected that promulgation of Federal, Democratic, Republic, Secular and Inclusive constitution creates a conducive and peaceful environment in Nepal.

The challenge for the constitution now is to accommodate the left out and disgruntled people, giving them space. Other challenges for the new constitution are to erase the divisions between hills and Terai on the constitution. With disrespect in the process and promulgation of constitution in Terai, there was celebration in capital Kathmandu and many hill cities.

"After years of political infighting, Nepal has adopted a constitution creating a federal state. But for it to become a success the nation must also tackle issues affecting women and minorities," said George Vaurgese.

Highlights of Constitution

Following years of political deadlock and violent protests, Nepal's parliament approved a new national constitution on September 20 that divides the country into seven federal states, each with three levels of government: federal, provincial and local. This is Nepal's first complete political framework since the monarchy was abolished in 2008.

The country's first constitution written by elected representatives ensures secularism, granting citizens the right to practice any religion. Some of the provisions feature a president with a ceremonial role who will be elected by parliament for a five-year term and a ministerial council elected by the people that will have executive duties.

The long-delayed charter was pushed through by the country's three major political parties. But smaller opposition parties as well as ethnic and religious groups - especially in Nepal's southern plain regions - have rejected the document amid concerns over how state borders should be defined.

They had even announced a nationwide general strike on the day the constitution was going to be promulgated, followed by protests where they would burn copies of the new charter, thus potentially setting the stage for a prolonged conflict.

With the promulgation of the new Constitution by president Dr. Ram Baran Yadav, the Constituent Assembly was dissolved and Nepal entered into a new phase of history. Following the promulgation, the eight-year political transition has come to an end.

As a constitution is a living document, the ruling party leaders must give up their arrogant behavior and show flexibility to incorporate the demands of Madheshis, Tharus and Janajatis so that everybody can have a sense of ownership on it. It is worthwhile noting what T.S.Eliot says in Murder in the Cathedral,

Kings rule or barons rule;
We have suffered various oppressions,
But mostly we are left alone to our own devices,
And we are content if we are left alone.

NEW NEPAL, OLD POLITICS

Republican Nepal finally adopted a constitution on September 20, nearly ten years after the initiation of the peace process. It had held two elections to the Constituent Assembly to produce a constitution based on 'consensus' as agreed in the comprehensive peace agreement of 2006, which was midwifed by New Delhi. But the constitution, rather than resolving the fundamental problem of political representation and mainstreaming minority communities and women who were historically at the bottom of both the social and political structure, has marginalised them further. The issue of 'consensus' that has been at the core of writing a constitution has been eroded through majoritarianism to secure the entrenchment in power of the hill political elites.

The argument that has been a driving force behind the new constitution is this: an elected Constituent Assembly (CA) representing the will of the people should write a new constitution taking into account the aspirations of the people based on transparency and consensus. This was the reason why the Maoists had rejected the Constitution of 1990 as a compromise document dictated by the Monarchy and agreed to by the leaders of political parties who were in a hurry to acquire power when the transition was made from the Panchayat regime to multiparty democracy and constitutional monarchy. It was at that time, the Masal and Mashal radical left groups came together and formed the Communist Party of Nepal (Unity Centre), which, as part of the United National Peoples Movement (UNPM), participated in the pro-democracy movement that engulfed Nepal in 1990.

One of their demands was an elected constituent assembly to write a constitution. Though the Unity Centre participated in the 1990 election, it suffered a split before the 1994 election because Prachanda's faction was not allowed to contest, which thereupon boycotted the election and declared armed struggle, a 'people's war', against a system that was a symbol of the Hindu religion, Nepali language and *khas* nationality. The Prachanda faction also carried forth the demand for a republic, secularism and a constitution written by the elected representatives of the people. This was reflected in the various agreements that the political parties signed after *Jan Andolan II*.

After the formation of an elected Constituent Assembly in 2008, all the political parties jostled to frame a constitution keeping in mind their particular electoral constituency. The victory of the Maoists and the end of constitutional monarchy gave hope to the marginalised groups, especially the Janajatis, that their political aspirations would find a place in the new constitution. Similarly, the Madhesis who have had historic grievances about the lack of proportional representation in jobs, in the army and in Parliament also aspired for accommodation. When their political concerns were not addressed in the 2007 interim constitution, the Madhesis even engaged in violent protest demanding 'ek Madhesh ek Pradesh'. The UCPN-M (United Communist Party of Nepal – Maoist) was reluctant to support the cause of Madhesis because of the fear that its own support base among the Paharis would get eroded. It was only belatedly, that too after Jay Krishna Goit and Jwala Singh broke away to form a separate party, the Janatantrik Terai Mukti Morcha (JTMM), that the UCPN-M extended support for the Madhesi cause. Subsequently, the Madhesis also received assurances from Prime Minister G. P. Koirala in the form of a 22-

point agreement with the Madhesi Janadhikar Forum, an umbrella group of Madhesi leaders from different political parties led by Upendra Yadav.

While Nepal managed to resolve most contentious issues, it could not resolve the issue of federalism. This remained a sticking point when Baburam Bhattarai dissolved the Constituent Assembly in 2012 and called for fresh elections. There was complete disagreement regarding the basis of creating federal units and their numbers. The problem persisted in the second Constituent Assembly. But since the Madhesis and Janajatis did not have adequate numbers of seats in the second CA, they depended on the UCPN-M's support to attain their demand.

Kathmandu was rife with rumours of a post-constitution making power sharing deal between the UCPN-M and Communist Party of Nepal-United Marxist-Leninist (CPN-UML). It was therefore not surprising that Prachanda decided to abandon the causes of Madhesis and other minorities as well as the principle of consensus that guided the peace-process. The split in the UCPN-M became apparent when Baburam Bhattarai, former Prime Minister, second in command in the UCPN-M, and chairman of the CA committee on dialogue and consensus building, was not present in the ceremony where the new constitution was promulgated. His subsequent resignation from the party as well as from Parliament indicates a certain degree of disagreement within the party on the constitution.

It is true that the absence of consensus on the constitution prevented a settlement given the stance adopted by Madhesi parties and the Janajati groups. But what cannot be ignored at the same time is the fact that the Kathmandu political elites were not sincere about initiating a dialogue process to address the grievances of Madhesis and Janajatis. Ironically, the Maoists who waged a People's war demanding an elected CA to draw up a constitution by taking into account people's aspirations, now supports a constitution that is approved only by the majority and in the process marginalising the marginalised classes that at one point in time formed the backbone of their movement. The boundaries of the new provinces have been drawn with a view to preserving the base of the political elite dominated by *bahuns* and *chetris*. It is true that the Madhesi parties have remained hopelessly fragmented. As a result, their strength declined precipitously between the first and second Constituent Assemblies; while they held 84 seats in the first CA, it declined to only 46 seats in the second CA election. This made them politically ineffective.

Three issues are of major concern in the Constitution that has been promulgated. First, many of the highest constitutional positions are reserved for those who are citizens by descent only; naturalized citizens are ineligible to hold these posts. The fact that many Madhesis have marriage and familial ties across the border make them ineligible for these posts. Second, children of a Nepali mother married to a foreigner will not get citizenship by descent, thus perpetuating a gender bias in the constitution.

Third is the issue of the boundaries of the newly created provinces, which affects the Tharus, Limbus and the Madhesis. In June, the four major political parties including the Madheshi Janadhikar Forum (Democratic) led by Bijay Gachchedar had agreed to the 16 point formula which promised that "The Federal Democratic Republic of Nepal will have eight provinces based on five criteria of identity and four criteria of capability." It was also decided that since the names of the provinces and demarcation of their boundaries was a contentious issue, these would be decided by a Commission. But this agreement was struck down by the single bench of the Supreme Court as contravening Articles 82 and 138 of the interim constitution, resulting in the present crisis. Thereafter, on August 10, top political leaders agreed to divide the country into six provinces in such a manner as to dilute the majority of the Madhesis and Tharus and reduce their political salience in terms of electoral politics.

While Nepal moved to a new era of democratic politics after adopting a constitution drafted by an elected CA which made Nepal a secular, federal republic, its failure to address the grievances of Madhesis and Janajatis and women's rights make the constitution non-inclusive. Adoption of this constitution and the manner in which the provincial boundaries have been drawn only ensure that the political and electoral base of the Kathmandu based hill elites gets further entrenched.

Indian Concerns

From the outset, India had supported a consensus constitution. Prime Minister Modi while addressing Nepal's Parliament last year had emphasised upon the need to build a consensus. Nepali political leaders assured New Delhi that they will keep in mind the interests of Janajatis, Madhesis, Dalits and women in the new constitution. Yet, these were completely ignored and the constitution was passed through a majority vote.

India's reaction has been curt especially since it had held a series of consultations with all Nepali leaders regarding the need to adopt an inclusive constitution. Yet, Nepal's political parties went back on the assurances that they had given to India. Even Foreign Secretary Jaishankar's last ditch effort did not help matters with Nepal adopting the constitution by majority voting on 17 September. India has consequently not hidden its displeasure as it is concerned about the increasing polarisation in Nepali politics.

The need for building a consensus is clearly reflected in the MEA statement: "India has been strongly supportive of constitution making in Nepal. We would like its completion to be an occasion for joy and satisfaction, not agitation and violence. We hope that Nepal's political leaders will display the necessary flexibility and maturity at this crucial time to ensure a durable and resilient Constitution that has broad-based acceptance."

Nepal has decided to send a Special Envoy to brief the Indian leadership about the constitution and the latest security situation. In the meanwhile, attempts are being made to initiate talks with Madhesi and Janajati leaders. Without a concrete road map and without disbanding the law and order approach to the Madhesi demand, the offer of talks is unlikely to yield result. The continuing violence by agitating parties in the Terai has created a situation where Indian trucks carrying goods and oil are reluctant to venture into Nepal.2 Economic hardship due to shortage of fuel and goods would have a long term impact on India-Nepal relations.

Given the fact that India shares an open border with Nepal, the consequences of violence and instability in the Terai would have consequences for India's security and may threaten the security of Indian businessmen and traders who are engaged in business in Nepal. Moreover, cross border ethnic linkages and familial ties makes India an interested party. While Nepali political leaders blame India and Indian 'interference' and try to arouse anti-Indianism, the same political leaders use New Delhi to further their political ambitions and do not hesitate to take New Delhi's help to entrench themselves in power. If Nepal does not want India's involvement, it needs to not only ensure that developments in the Terai do not have a spill over effect but also stop courting the Indian establishment to gain political power.

CRAFTING A CONSTITUTION FOR NEPAL

Nepal is trying to write a constitution for the second time, after the first Constituent Assembly (CA) of four years collapsed in May 2012. The entire polity and economy of the country have suffered a state of suspension since 2006, when the People's Movement and the end of the decade-long internal conflict promised peace and prosperity.

For a land richly endowed by nature, Nepal's lot has been poverty and marginalisation since the unification two-and-half centuries ago down to the present, through oligarchy, monarchy, and obstinately unstable democracy. The ongoing attempt is to erect the newborn republic on a strong foundation of pluralism and representative politics, and make Nepal an exemplary democracy of South Asia, which its size and sensibility allow.

But these are precarious days. There are hurdles to the constitution drafting that have to be resolved urgently if the radical leftists and the royalist (Hindutva) right are not to rear up and blow away hard-won freedoms. India has been a player on the complex Nepal chessboard, recently leaning towards micromanagement of internal affairs, and the best support it can provide is staying outside the *laxman rekha* of constitution writing.

Passionate discourse

There are three main pending issues before the second CA, more or less the same ones that brought down the earlier one — secularism, electoral process and definition of federalism. On secularism, there is a rising undercurrent to redefine Nepal as a

Hindu state, and a whole phalanx has taken energy from the Bharatiya Janata Party's electoral success in India. However, such a definition would be incompatible with the range and layers of Hindu belief and practice in Nepal, plus the fact that 20 per cent of the population is non-Hindu.

The term "secularism", on the other hand, is imported from the Indian Constitution (as amended) and, translated as "*dharma nirpekchhata*", carries an exclusionary denotation that rankles many. All else remaining the same, the framers can probably agree on declaring Nepal "*dharma bahool*" (with religious pluralism) or do away with mention of religion altogether, to respect all and injure none.

On the electoral scheme, the tussle is between those favouring the first-past-the post system for effective governance and others who maintain that only proportional representation can reflect Nepal's diversity of marginalised communities. The effort is on to find the acceptable proportional-to-direct elections ratio, and a compromise will probably be reached between half-half and 70:30.

It is the demarcation of federal provinces that has the hackles up on all sides, and it is here that communal passions could flare up, particularly on the hill-and-plain dimension. The resulting polarisation would set the country back by another decade, and impact variously the neighbouring States of India as well.

Demarcation debate

Nepal was officially declared a federal democratic republic in 2008, but the debate on federalism has yet to mature to the level of allowing demarcation. There is a bewildering web of positions and demands that the CA has failed to address; some have not even made it to the table.

"It is vital to satisfy the Madhesi and ethnic activists that the deferral of decision on federalism does not at all mean abandoning it."

At its core, the argument is between those who believe (as does this writer) that provincial division should follow the logic of economic geography, to bring prosperity to all communities in a country of mixed habitation, and especially those of the plains where there is a disproportionate volume and density of poverty. Others argue forcefully for demarcation by identity, to make up for historical wrongs committed by the Kathmandu-centric state. The heightened rancour of today has mainly to do with the parcelling of the Terai, with the Madhesi Morcha combine of parties seeking exclusive plains-only province or provinces.

In the CA, the Nepali Congress (NC) and the Communist Party of Nepal (Unified-Marxist-Leninist)-UML can come up with the two-thirds majority required for promulgation. However, they have not been able to generate momentum for constitution drafting, laid low by the lacklustre performance of their coalition government. More importantly, the two parties have not been able to effectively counter the position of the Maoist-Madhesi Morcha, which is that the November 2013 election results (*"mataadhesh"*) do not reflect the people's will (*"janaadhesh"*), an argument that is anti-political as much as it is anti-people.

Truth be told, the roadblock to constitution writing is not on the matter of principle, but the political careers of a dozen or so senior opposition leaders. In the case of both Maoist Chairman Pushpa Kamal Dahal ('Prachanda') and senior leader Baburam Bhattarai, their instigation of the 'people's war', the stonewalling on accountability for war crimes, as well as the economic devastation wrought by their party's actions make them fearful of the future.

Seeking collapse

Mr. Dahal is pursued by several personal demons — the possibility of investigation into alleged loot of the exchequer, international jurisdiction for conflict era crimes, and the collapse of his ambitions of emerging as directly elected president. Mr. Bhattarai, for his part, has remained deputy to Mr. Dahal for too long and is desperate to get the party chairmanship. He recently visited New Delhi in early March hoping to reinforce his known image of being "India-friendly" for political advantage back home.

Both leaders suffer under the knowledge that there is another two-and-half years remaining in the life of the second CA (also serving as Parliament). Meanwhile, the Supreme Court has just confirmed that grave human rights abuse of the conflict era must undergo criminal procedure, striking at the heart of the political aspirations of Mr. Dahal and Mr. Bhattarai. Under the circumstances, without a plan at hand, the Maoist leaders would like to foment political chaos hoping that something, somewhere will collapse to their advantage.

Others who lost badly in the 2013 elections were the stalwarts of the Madhesi Morcha, when the Terai (the plains) voters opted for the NC, the UML and the Hindutva-oriented Rastriya Prajatantra Party (Nepali) party of Kamal Thapa. And yet, the Madhesi Morcha's line against Kathmandu's "*pahadiya*" (hill-dweller) elites resonates among the restless Madhesi youth, giving it traction.

While the sense of alienation provides a level of unity against Kathmandu, however, the plains are not as homogeneous as the Morcha leaders (mostly from the east-central belt of the Terai) would like to suggest. Beyond the division by language (Awadhi, Maithili, Bhojpuri, etc), there are many permutations of identity among the citizens of plains origin, with cross-cutting layers including the Madhesi (incorporating the Dalits from the plains as the most marginalised nationally), Muslim, Tharu and other plains ethnicities, as well as a significant number of *pahadiyas*.

The demography of the plains is thus rather intricate, and it would be unwise to concede on any proposed federal arrangement out of sheer exasperation, whether identity-based or on economic geography. We need a way to hold off on a decision, to allow a more considered approach in which the protagonists do not talk past each other. Simultaneously, it is vital to satisfy the Madhesi and ethnic activists that the deferral of decision on federalism does not at all mean abandoning it.

The India hand

By some believable accounts, the plains-specific province(s) idea was thought up by Indian diplomats and intelligence operatives, with the Madhesi Morcha leaders made to carry the burden as a kind of ideology. If the plan is to create a geopolitical buffer for India astride the open border, that itself is objectionable for seeking to render the Terai plains and its Nepali citizens as some kind of bulwark for India.

With the arrival of the Narendra Modi-led government in New Delhi, there seems to be second thoughts, at least in some quarters, about the viability of the proposed plains-specific provinces. Some strategists in India are now wondering whether this prescription is not geopolitically fraught, with dangers of making Nepal a stomping ground for international adventurism.

From this writer's perspective, however, the most important concern is that nothing should be done to further impoverish the Terai population, the likely result of a plains-only province when the concentration of investment in the coming years is likely to be in the hills.

Last week, the Maoists and Madhesi Morcha, unlikely collaborators, announced agitations against the attempt by the NC-UML to take forward the proper procedure of constitution drafting, leading ultimately to a vote on provisions The upcoming protests could well lead to a collapse of the second CA, and the people's opportunity to write their own constitution wrested by the very leaders who claim to have birthed the idea of both the Constituent Assembly and federalism.

The best option for now is to promulgate a constitution that confirms a democratic, federal, non-denominational Republic of Nepal, while leaving the matter of federal arrangement to parliament or to a credible, high-level commission. If the country finds itself without a constitution after eight years of trying, the politicians and political parties of Kathmandu will be the first to be held accountable. But history will also ask New Delhi about its role in the debacle.

4

Nepal's New Constitution: An Analysis from the Madheshi Perspective

A new Constitution was promulgated in Nepal on 20 September 2015. It has failed to satisfy the Madheshis and Tharus who constitute 70 per cent of the Terai population, who regard the formation of seven federal provinces as per the Constitution as grossly unfair to them. Only eight districts in the Terai region, from Saptari in the East to Parsa in the West, have been given the status of a province (State 2, see Map below); the remaining 14 districts are to be joined with the hill districts, with the sole purpose of converting the local people into a minority. The Madheshis and Tharus were sidelined in the entire constitution making process due to prevailing distrust towards them among the mainstream political parties. Of course, the Bijay Kumar Gachhadar-led Madhesi Janaadhikar Forum–Democratic was initially involved in the constitution drafting process; but later on it also had no option but to quit the alliance as its point of view was not entertained.

Flaws

Consequently, none of the major Madhesh-based parties signed the Constitution, which has serious flaws. The new Constitution has a provision for a 165-member Parliament, but the constituencies have been demarcated in such a way that the people of the hill and mountain region would get 100 seats, despite the fact that their share in Nepal's total population is less than 50 per cent. On the other hand, the Terai region constituting over half of the country's population has been allocated only 65 seats.

Because of the insensitivity shown towards the demands of the Madheshi parties, a call was given by the Unified Democratic Madheshi Front and Tharuhat/Tharuwan Joint Struggle Committee for an indefinite strike in Terai beginning August 8. Security Forces personnel used excessive force to suppress the agitation. Even the army was mobilized for this purpose. But the situation deteriorated fast. During the last month and half of protests, over 46 people, including 10 security personnel, have been killed. Besides, hundreds of protesters have been injured. Almost all the Terai districts have turned into war-like zones.

Immediately after the promulgation of the Constitution, the ruling political parties including Nepali Congress and CPN-UML celebrated "Diwali", while the Madheshi political parties and Tharuhat Struggle Committee observed it as a black day. Both within and outside the country, the new Constitution was welcomed by one community, while it was burnt by others. Nepal is now widely polarised between those who support and those who oppose the Constitution. China, Pakistan and a few other countries have welcomed the new Constitution, but India has indirectly shown its displeasure over the development, which is worrisome.

Marginalisation

The changing demography of Terai deserves critical scrutiny in light of the developments taking place in the region today. Until 1954, the Madheshis and the Tharus formed 94 per cent of the total population in the Terai region. But since the 1970s, the state—during the years of monarchy— helped hundreds of thousands of hill migrants to settle in Terai mostly by clearing the thick forest land. For this, even resettlement companies were set up. Though landlessness among the Madheshis is common, none of them got any piece of land as part of the resettlement policy adopted by the state.

Those who suffered the most due to the state-sponsored migration and settlement of population in Terai were the tribal groups like the Tharus, the Rajbanshis and the Satars. Land belonging to many of these people was confiscated on one or other excuse for distribution among the migrants. A sizeable chunk of the local people were forced to migrate to India. But those who stayed at home in Terai were virtually made Kamaiyas (paupers) whose only means of survival was to work as domestic help in the houses of the hill migrants. As if this were not enough, in the early 1980s a Commission on Internal and International Migration was constituted under Hark Gurung. The Commission recommended that whatever remaining forest that was left along the East West Highway be cleared with a view to settle the hill migrants.

Both under the rules of the Kings and the Ranas, large tracts of land in Terai were gifted away to civil servants, army officers and family members of the ruling class through the infamous system of *Birta*. The Kings of Nepal advocated a policy of not employing the Madheshis in the civil services. This deficit of trust towards the Madheshis and the Tharus was one of the major reasons why their presence in the civil services, judiciary and security agencies have remained minimal. Even their presence in corporations, industries and private sector agencies have been far from satisfactory. Until the mid-1950s, the Madheshis had to receive permits from the government authorities to enter Kathmandu, the capital city! Even in matters concerning the grant of citizenship, they were discriminated against. The Madheshis comprise the bulk of such stateless citizens in Nepal even to this day. All the major political parties usually field hill-elites as their candidates in the Terai region during the elections. They would never allow any Madheshi as their candidate in the hill constituencies.

In order to get rid of discrimination, the Terai Congress in 1950 gave a call for a federal state for the area situated in the Terai belt. But the idea could not gain much traction as the party was defeated in the 1959 General Elections. After the restoration of multi-party democracy in 1990, Nepal Sadbhavana Party was formed to protect the interests of the Madheshis. This party also echoed its voice for a federal state. Later on, the idea of federalism was picked up by the Communist Party of Nepal (Maoist).

Subsequently, in 2007, there was a major Terai uprising, which was controlled only when the government made a formal agreement with the Madheshi leaders for the formation of a single autonomous Madhesh Pradesh with the right to self-determination.

From Disarray to Unity

Despite the overwhelming size of population of the Madheshis and Tharus in Terai, they could get only 10 per cent seats in the 601-member Constituent Assembly (CA)-2 in the December 2013 elections. Many of the Madheshi leaders were defeated in CA-2 elections because they failed to address the people's problems. Out of lust for money and power, they did not hesitate to fragment the parties. During the CA-1 elections in 2008, only three Madhesh-based parties had contested the elections and hence they had a substantial presence in CA-1. In contrast, during the CA-2 elections in 2013, there were 13 Madhesh-based parties. Though both during CA-1 and CA-2 elections, the overall voting percentage for the Madhesh based parties remained almost the same— about 12 per cent— Madhesh leaders lost the elections because their votes were divided, making it easier for non-Madheshi leaders to win.

Nevertheless, the Madhesh-based parties did not learn any lesson from the election debacle and they could not come together to form a united front to protect their interests. By the time they formed the Unified Democratic Madheshi Front this year, it was too late to exhibit their strength. The three major political parties, including the NC, CPN-UML and UCPN-Maoist, took advantage of this split. Because they had 90 per cent seats in the CA-2, they excluded the Madheshi parties in the constitution-making process. But this was a major blunder. It was forgotten that the Madheshis and the Tharus have always been humiliated ever since the central and eastern parts of Terai were gifted away by the British East India Company to Nepal partly after the Sugauli Treaty of 1816 and partly after the Sepoy Mutiny (1857) in 1860 The hill elites always doubted the loyalty of the Madheshis towards the nation. This distrust towards the Madheshis and the Tharus provided these groups with ample reason to unite and protest against the constitution when a call was given for an indefinite strike.

Impact of Strike

The impact of the ongoing Madheshi agitation in Nepal as a whole in general and in the Terai region in particular is quite severe. For more than one-and-a-half months now, life in the Terai region has been paralysed.

All the educational institutions, hospitals, government offices, industries, banks, shops, agricultural activities and transport services have been crippled. Most of the essential items including food grains, petrol and gas are in short supply.

Those who depend on daily wages for their livelihood are suffering the most. Movement of people is restricted because of continuous curfew in several places and also due to the deteriorating law and order situation. Amidst all this, unscrupulous elements hostile to India could pose a security risk by taking advantage of the open border between the two countries.

However, the government and the main political parties in Nepal are least sensitive to the needs of their own people, leave alone their concerns about security challenges such a protracted crisis could pose for Nepal and India.

Instead of taking any initiative to defuse the crisis, some of them have started blaming India for the troubles in Nepal. Rumours are rife that India has imposed a blockade as trucks loaded with goods are not coming from India to Nepal.

In a deliberate manner, wrong information is being fed to the people of Nepal by the media that the sealing of the border by India at certain locations has caused food scarcity in Nepal. The truth, however, is that the private trucks plying on the Indian side of the border cannot afford to cross the border and come to Nepal because of the fragile law and order situation, which is due to the mishandling of the situation by the Nepalese government.

Conclusion

If the government and the main political parties are really serious about defusing the present crisis, they should accept it as a political problem and take steps to ensure that Nepalese people of all ethnicities, including the Madheshis and the Tharus, develop a sense of ownership in the new Constitution. For this, it is urgently required to initiate a dialogue with the aggrieved Madeshi and Tharu political leaders and address some of the demands put out by them at the moment, as follows:

- Formation of two autonomous states in the Terai – one extending from Jhapa to Parasa to be called "Mithila state" with Janakpur as its capital, and the other from Chitwan to Kanchanpur to be called "Buddha State" with Lumbini as its capital.
- Provision of 83 parliamentary seats for Terai Region in the new parliament.
- Reservation of seats for the Madheshis and the Tharus in administrative, security, judiciary and diplomatic services on the basis of their population.
- Adequate representation of the Madheshis and the Tharus in decision-making process in all constitutional bodies, including in Public Service Commission at the central and state levels.
- Formation of an independent commission to investigate the excesses committed by the security forces and punish the culprits; and provision of adequate compensation for those killed during the agitation and also to those injured.

A forward looking Constitution must take adequate care to accommodate rather than leave out the genuine aspirations of a substantial cross-section of people.

If such aspirations remain unmet, as the persisting movement by the people of the Terai region would indicate, the ongoing crisis may deepen causing trouble for one and all in Nepal. In such a situation, there is always a temptation to find an external scapegoat. It would require exemplary courage on the part of the Nepalese leadership to own up their mistakes and put their house in order before it is too late.

NEPAL: A 7-YEAR STRUGGLE FOR A NEW CONSTITUTION

Nepal's struggle to establish a constitutional government has been long and tumultuous. Beginning in 1996, a ten-year conflict between the Government of Nepal and the Communist Party of Nepal (Maoist) left over 13,000 dead and approximately 1,300 forcibly disappeared. Hereditary chief ministers, known as Ranas, ruled the country for over a century before the monarchy took power in 1951. Nearly forty years later, a popular pro-democracy movement, the Jana Andolan (People's Movement), spawned a series of violent street protests.

But it took a civil war for the monarchy to finally agree to end its direct rule in 2006. Soon thereafter, the Maoists began peace talks with the parliamentary government, and in 2008 a nationwide election for a Constituent Assembly (CA) completely abolished the monarchy and declared Nepal a federal democratic republic.

Nearly a decade after the war's end, Nepal continues to struggle with the effects of this turbulent civil war. Disappeared persons still have not been accounted for and few efforts have been made to ensure accountability.

The Comprehensive Peace Accord (CPA) signed in 2006 included a number of promises, such as justice for the victims and their families, and an end to impunity. By some estimates both sides of the conflict may have committed up to 9,000 international human rights law or international humanitarian law violations, with enforced disappearances among the most serious.

Earlier this year the government established two separate commissions, the Truth and Reconciliation Commission and a Commission of Inquiry on the Disappearances, though little progress has been made.

A key point in the CPA called for the promulgation of a new democratic constitution that would ensure the protection of marginalized communities. Historically, Nepal's nearly 28 million inhabitants have been highly stratified into some 125 caste/ethnic groups, and many were hopeful for social progress and greater equality under a new founding document.

Efforts to draft a new constitution began in 2008, but the main political parties have yet to agree on a final version. A major stumbling block has been disagreement over the administrative division of Nepal. Having been centrally governed for more than two centuries, Nepalese politicians cannot agree on how to federalize the country along ethnic lines. A new president and prime minister cannot be elected until a constitution is adopted, further compounding the country's governance issues.

The devastating earthquakes earlier this year seemed to break the seven-year stalemate, however. In the aftermath, the leading political parties agreed to organize Nepal into eight federal provinces, only to see dozens of small parties reject the deal. Since then, violent protests have erupted in response to subsequent proposals on the number of provinces. Ethnic groups across Nepal are demanding that a new draft of the constitution address their concerns. The Madhesi and Tharu communities both object to plans for their regions to merge with districts that they claim belong to political elites. The Tharus, a group that numbers about 1.7 million, want a separate province. The Madhesis and other groups, fear the proposed division of the provinces will diminish their political power.

The government has responded with violence. The Nepali Police and the Armed Police Force have reportedly beaten and even used lethal force against protestors. In turn, people in the streets have vandalized buildings and attacked officers, including one who was doused with kerosene and set on fire last month. Despite continuing protests from ethnic minority groups, the CA began voting on a draft of the constitution on Sunday.

With approximately 40% of the population living in poverty and the April earthquakes causing widespread devastation, an end to almost a decade of negotiations over the constitution could provide a modicum of much needed political stability. The current draft is supported by the three major parties, but the smaller opposition parties (about 9 percent of the assembly) are refusing to vote. As protests continue throughout the country, Nepal's many challenges are likely to continue into the foreseeable future.

NEPAL ADOPTS FIRST DEMOCRATIC CONSTITUTION

Nepal adopted its first democratic Constitution, a historic step for a nation that has seen war, a palace massacre and devastating earthquakes since a campaign to create a modern state began more than 65 years ago.

President Ram Baran Yadav promulgated the charter intended to unite the country, but it has already exacerbated divisions in some places with 40 people killed in protests against it in recent weeks.

"Our country is multi-ethnic, multi-lingual, multi-religious and multi-cultural... this new document will safeguard the rights of all Nepali brothers and sisters," Yadav said, signing five copies of the Constitution into law as lawmakers thumped tables. Some of them cried.

There were no reports of major violence on Sunday though three people were wounded when police fired at people trying to break a curfew in Birgunj in the south. In the capital Kathmandu, a crowd of more than 2,000 people cheered and took pictures of the constituent assembly building decked out in red and blue Nepali flags.

Neighbouring powers India and China are keen to see stability and to limit each other's influence in the poor Himalayan country sandwiched between them.

The earthquakes that killed more than 9,000 people in Nepal this year galvanized politicians, who had squabbled for seven years to finish the charter.

It creates seven states in a secular, federal system, but is opposed by some groups who wanted to re-establish Nepal as a Hindu nation, and others who feel it is unfavourable to people in the plains, near India.

Demonstrations in the lowlands in recent weeks were met with a tough response from Kathmandu, which ordered in the army after protesters attacked and killed police. More than 40 protesters and police died.

The unrest troubles India, which on Sunday urged Nepal to resolve differences between groups through dialogue. China has welcomed the new Constitution saying that as a "friendly neighbour" it hoped for increased stability and growth. The government says an imperfect document is better than nothing, and the Constitution can be amended to reflect the aspirations of dissenting groups.

Nepal's 239-year old monarchy was abolished in 2008, seven years after an unhinged crown prince killed the king and eight members of his family at the height of a Maoist uprising. Disgruntled royalist politicians voted against the charter on Wednesday, while some parties from the southern lowlands abstained.

The Maoists laid down their arms in 2006 and joined democratic politics in an India-brokered peace deal that paved the way for the Constitution. Wrangling hampered progress on the draft and several governments have come and gone in the interim.

Prime Minister Sushil Koirala is expected to stand down to allow a new government under the charter. He may be replaced by KP Oli, from a moderate Communist party.

Clauses over citizenship in the country of 28 million people were some of the most contentious with critics saying they discriminate against women who marry foreigners, and that their children are denied equal access to citizenship.

Estimates of the number of stateless people in Nepal range from 800,000 to 4 million.

Suman Sapkota, 19, a student in Kathmandu, recalled the days when his father, mother and grandparents would take turns to go out on to the streets for protests against the monarchy. He hopes his country will now have a chance to prosper.

"The main thing I want, and what we all want, is for the country to be peaceful, and never return to the violence we saw in the war," Sapkota said.

"I got used to hearing the sounds of gunshots when I was very young, and it's something I don't want to hear any more."

NEPAL'S DEMOCRACY LANDMARK (A CONSTITUTION) LEADS TO INSTABILITY

To set the framework for its infant democracy, to recognize its rich pluralist character, and to enshrine its secular ideals Nepal had finally awarded itself a new constitution. Barely five months after earthquakes struck Kathmandu and neighboring districts an agreement that had eluded Nepal's constituent assembly for eight years was finalized. Perhaps its resolve came from pressure exerted by global humanitarian donors meeting to award earthquake relief; perhaps in the face of this national disaster Nepal's citizens realized how desperately they needed clear governance.

The constitution, signed into law September 20, provides the essential framework for country-wide elections, introduces a proportional electoral system at the federal and state levels, and spells out leadership powers. Many compromises had to be made but across the country most citizens felt a sense of relief and stopped work for two days to indulge in a self-congratulatory holiday.

The final document is far from perfect and there were disappointments over many provisions. Even before celebrations had ended serious discontent surfaced.

Notwithstanding hasty statements by some ministers that the constitution could be changed, opposition to the agreement in the south of the country turned violent. Eight police were killed; in the mayhem that followed another 45 people were dead. Within days, India advised Nepal that its hard won sacred document should be amended; a border blockade went into effect preventing essential imports, mainly fuel, from Indian suppliers..

This cutoff of fuel has disrupted life across the country and the resulting crisis is now in its second month. Although the embargo isn't a stated Indian government policy, no one in Nepal doubts that Delhi is not fully supporting it.

Some say today's emergency is as serious as the one which preceded the end of the monarchy in 2007. Except today there is no king to blame, or eject. This predicament is not new; it's a manifestation of the entrenched imbalance of power between these neighbors.

A dilemma that has confronted every leader in Nepal now challenges its newly elected prime minister, K.P. Oli. A Communist Party member, he relies on a coalition of minor parties when boldness and confidence are needed.

Nepal, although never occupied by a foreign power and enjoying the largesse of nations across the globe, has allowed itself to become perilously dependent on India for basic commodities.

Every few years its vulnerability to Indian interests becomes painfully apparent.

Today, without India-supplied fuel, life across Nepal has been brought to a halt. Factories are shut, children and teachers cannot get to school; without propane gas businesses are idle, and intercity travel is impossible. Tourism (customarily at its peak during autumn months) is thwarted and projects designed to repair earthquake damage are suspended.

Why should India be unhappy with this harmless northern neighbor? Nepal poses no serious challenge to India. Barely a year ago, its people applauded Prime Minister Narendra Modi as a hero on his visit to Kathmandu, and following the earthquake Modi pledged $1 billion in relief aid.

But commentators on both sides of the dispute see Delhi's hand in thiscrisis.

It is seen as siding with a major block of Nepal's inhabitants unhappy with the constitution. They are the Madhesi who populate the lowland strip of Nepal along its 1000 mile border with India. They'd wanted the constitution to demarcate a distinct Madhes province and to define Nepali citizenship to favor them.

Most Madhesi originated in the adjacent Indian provinces and they enjoy benefits from both countries. Moving freely across the frontier, they share more with India, including language, religion and economic interests than they do with Nepal's hill people and Kathmandu residents.

With the fall of Nepal's Hindu monarchy and the rise of democratic freedoms over the past decade, regional, religious, gender and language differences became the basis for ethnic awakenings across the country and these sentiments evolved into political interest groups, each demanding special rights constitutional rights. Indeed, competing interests of these communities was a major factor delaying the work of the constituent assembly.

Madhesi leaders, arguing that the new constitution marginalizes them in favor of other 'ethnic' groups, launched the current protest, employing their strategic position along the frontier to impose the blockade. Nepal's Prime Minister (Communist Party) is a compromise candidate relying on a coalition of small parties and it's already apparent that Oli lacks the personality to force a solution. His newly appointed foreign minister (from a small royalist party) returned empty handed from a meeting with India's prime minister.

The United States, so active in fostering democracies across the world, shows little concern for Nepal's struggling democracy. Perhaps that's because of its close ties to India. Also, since the 1990s opposition movement that eventually led to the end of the monarchy and the creation of a republic was Maoist inspired, and with Maoists and Communists still major players in Nepali politics, the US may be less inclined to support this democracy. More reasons for new assertive leadership here.

5

Nepal: Divided by A New Constitution

Nepal, a tiny Himalayan state, has succeeded in ending a seven year long political deadlock by adopting a new constitution on 20th of September, 2015. The new constitution is supported by all the main political parties – Nepali Congress, CPN-UML and UCPN-Maoist. At the same time, the voting was also boycotted by small opposition parties from the Terai region; Even though 507 out of 601 members of the Constituent Assembly (CA) voted in favour of the new constitution, 25 members of Rashtriya Prajatantra Party voted against it along with 60 Madhesi based political parties who boycotted the entire process.

However, it was a watershed moment in the 239 year old history of Nepal, which has witnessed Oligarchy, Monarchy and unstable Democracy in all these years. The last two decades have been a roller coaster ride for Nepal's quest for democracy. A decade long civil war ended in 2006 after a peace deal was signed between government and Maoist group. It was the same year Nepal declared itself a secular state. The work on the new constitution began in 2008 when a Constituent Assembly (CA) was elected after the abolishment of the monarchy, but it could not finish its task despite four extensions. Subsequently, a second CA was elected in 2013 which deliberated the draft constitution for over two years.

New Constitution and Provisions

The new constitution embraces the ideals of a pluralist, multi-ethnic, multi-lingual, multi-religious, multi-cultural society and federal governance. It has 37 divisions, 304 articles and seven annexes. It divides the entire country into seven provinces that will be finalized by a high-level commission within a year. The preamble envisages establishment of sustainable peace, good governance, development and prosperity in a federal democratic republic.

A forward looking constitution must have provisions for the amendment. And the procedure of amendment is laid down so that the needs and requirement of the future generation can be incorporated peacefully. A future Parliament may, by a two-thirds majority, change in part or whole, the federal, secular character of the republic.

Nepal has accepted a presidential form of government. All executive power shall be vested in the cabinet that will be headed by the President. Parliament will be bicameral, with a House of Representatives – 165 members of which will be elected by the first past the post system, and 110 by the system of proportional representation – a third of whose members shall be women, and a National assembly of 59 members.

Madhesi Representation and Women

The transition from Hindu monarchy to secular democracy has been peaceful by and large except for a few protests from ethnic minorities. The ethnic minorities – Madhesi and Tharu expressed their dissatisfaction over some provisions of the new constitution.

Their claim is that the new federal structure leaves them under represented. The new constitution divides Nepal into seven provinces but that hasn't been based on the provisions of the interim constitution. According to article 63 (3) of the Interim Constitution – electoral constituencies were based on population, geography and special characteristics, and in the case of Madhesh on the basis of percentage of population. So, under this provision, Madhesh, with more than 50 per cent of the population, got 50 per cent of seats in Parliament i.e. 83 out 165 electoral constituencies. But the latter part of the provision, related to the Madhesis, has been dropped in the new constitution and that took them to the streets of Nepal.

In addition to this, they are dissatisfied with the provision of citizenship in the new constitution. The citizenship clause discriminates against women. The new clause states that children of Nepali women married to foreign men will not have Nepal's citizenship status by default. The fear is that this provision of the new constitution left Nepali women as a second class citizen in her own country. There are other provisions of the new constitution which too don't represent Madhesis and their concerns and therefore, they want their demand to be reinstated.

India and China: Competing and conflicting interests in Nepal

Sensing the gravity of the situation and the spillover impact of Madhesi protests into bordering Indian states (Bihar and Uttar Pradesh), New Delhi has placed a list of seven amendments to Nepali leadership. Although, these amendments are primarily related to the Madhesi's demand which revolves around Article 84 (electoral constituencies), Article 42, Article 283 (criteria for the higher constitutional post), Article 86 (composition of national assembly), Article 281 (delineation of electoral constituencies), Article 11(6) – acquisition of naturalistic citizenship. New Delhi wants Nepal to address the Madhesi's concerns so that their rightful representation can be ensured in the modern Nepal state.

Geographically, Nepal is sandwiched between the two Asian giants India and China. Diplomatically, it has been struggling to balance their competitive influence that has emerged in the recent past. Beijing, however, is trying hard to get its foot set in Nepal and to an extent it has managed to do so. The huge inflow of Chinese aid and investment in infrastructure and other sectors of Nepal's economy is an example of growing Chinese presence in Nepal.

In order to reduce Nepal's economic dependence on India, Nepal has been included as a dialogue partner in Shanghai Cooperation Organisation (SCO), a China and Russia led regional security organization. It is worth mentioning that India and Pakistan will only be complete members of the SCO by 2016 after certain admission processes are completed.

Beijing wants to reduce New Delhi's influence in Nepal at all levels. And therefore, Beijing has designed a long term strategy to fill in the vacuum created by India. As per reports, Beijing plans to utilize the common border between India and Nepal for accessing the Indian market. China, with its cheap products, wants to access the markets of Indian states bordering Nepal and through them to the rest of the country. So, India needs to be cautious because India and Nepal have a porous border where the volume of informal trade is higher than that of formal trade.

In other attempts to lower New Delhi influence, Beijing is pushing to displace India as the epicenter of Buddhism by promoting Nepal's Lumbini as a Buddhist pilgrimage site. Undoubtedly, it can be said that Beijing is silently spreading its 'zone of influence' in Nepal, which India can't afford to ignore in the long run. Therefore, the need of the hour is that India should work with Nepal to restore peace and install democracy. In addition to the above, what India needs to do is to share its own experience of conflict resolution with Nepal. That would establish India as a benign neighbour.

Conclusion

By adopting the constitution, Nepal has not only done a commendable job but has saved itself from unending eternal conflict. The wave of Arab spring unseated authoritarian rulers and kept alive their hopes of democracy, but most of the states were unable to draft a constitution agreeable to all parties. For instance, Libya tried but failed many times and has been grappling with a bloody civil war. Nepal has decided to travel on the path of democracy which allows for the peaceful disagreement. Madhesh is important for Nepal's economy and polity. Importance of Madhesh can be understood from the fact that it is the backbone of the national economy, containing more than 60 percent of agricultural land and contributing to over two-thirds of the GDP. Therefore, Nepal can't afford to turn deaf ears to their demand for a prolonged time. The beauty of democracy is in peaceful coexistence. Democracy is about inclusion and accommodation of different opinions. Therefore, we hope that Madhesis and Nepali women will get their due place and representation in the new Nepal.

NEPAL ADOPTS DEMOCRATIC CONSTITUTION, ENTERS NEW ERA

Nepal has formally adopted a new democratic constitution amid protests in some parts of the country. President Dr.Ram Baran Yadav promulgated the constitution amidst a special ceremony held in Kathmandu today.

Nepal is a multi-ethnic, multilingual, multi-religious, multi-cultural secular republic divided into seven federal provinces after promulgation of the new constitution.

Nepal's 240-year old monarchy was abolished in 2008, seven years after a palace massacre.The then crown prince Dipendra killed the king and eight members of his family at the height of a Maoist uprising in the country.

The Constitution of Nepal 2072 envisions a federal democratic republican and inclusive prosperous Nepal by institutionalizing the achievements of the democratic movements held in the country.The new constitution expresses the determination to build an equitable society on the basis of the principle of proportional inclusion and participation, by ensuring economic equality and social justice.

The preamble of the constitution mentions people's competitive multi-party democratic system, civic freedom, fundamental rights, human rights, periodic election, voting rights, full press freedom, independent, fair and competent judiciary, building of a prosperous nation with the commitment to socialism based on rule of law, and democratic norms and values, and durable peace, good governance, development through the federal democratic republic.

According to the new constitution, President would be ceremonial head-of-state and the executive rights of the country shall vest on the Council of Ministers.

The 601- member Constituent Assembly (CA) endorsed Nepal's Constitution by more than two-thirds majority. This is the first time in country's history that a constitution has been written by the elected representatives of the people.

Altogether 532 CA members were present in the voting process of the new constitution. Out of them 507 CA members voted in favour of the constitution, with 25 going against it. Some 58 CA members of Tarai Madhes-based parties boycotted the voting process while RPP-Nepal voted against the new constitution.

The promulgation of new constitution has turned 65-year old aspiration of drafting a new constitution through an elected assembly into a reality.

The Constituent Assembly is transformed into Parliament till the next general election as per the provisions of the new constitution.

Travel professionals have expressed happiness over the endorsement of the new constitution by the Constituent Assembly hoping that the new constitution would contribute to achieve political stability and create investment friendly climate in socio-economic sectors including tourism.

THE NEW NEPAL CONSTITUTION

THE landlocked Himalayan state of Nepal, eventually, adopted a new constitution on September 20, 2015, after protracted acrimony, violence and political paralysis. India longs to see enduring peace and tranquility in the new-born Himalayan democracy. Nepal is demographically multilingual, multi-ethnic and has a predominant Hindu majority.

The constitution declares Nepal an independent, sovereign, secular, democratic republic. An India-based Nepal diplomat, in an ecstatic moment, described the Nepalese constitution as "better drafted than the Indian Constitution". The remark is reminiscent of the words of Dr Ambedkar that ring through time: "All constitutions in their main provisions must look similar. The only new things, if there be any, in a constitution framed so late in the day, are the variations made to remove the faults and to accommodate it to the needs of the country." The test of a constitution is whether it accommodates the needs, and fulfils the aspirations of its people.

The constitution of Nepal, containing 302 Articles and 9 Schedules, enshrines the principle of parliamentary democracy with certain innovations and novel features, a Himalayan brand of parliamentary democracy. The President is the ceremonial head of the state. The executive power vests with the Council of Ministers headed by the Prime Minister. The most noteworthy feature of the constitution is (and a cause of upheaval) the provision of a mixed electoral system comprising direct election and proportional representation. The Prime Minister and the Council of Ministers shall be collectively and individually responsible to the Federal Parliament but must enjoy the majority support in the House of Representatives for their survival. A motion of no-confidence or the "Abiswas ko prastab" cannot be brought against the Prime Minister for the first two years after his appointment, and if the motion of no-confidence fails, another motion cannot be tabled within a year of its failure.

The political structure is divided into federal, provincial and local governments. The judicial system is unified with the Supreme Court at the apex, a high court for each state and a district court for each of the districts. The country is divided into seven provinces numbered consecutively. The preamble to the constitution declares Nepal a multi-caste, multilingual, multi-cultural state and resolves to end all forms of discriminations, promote unity in diversity, create an egalitarian society on the basis of the principle of proportional inclusion and participation, and ensure equitable economy, prosperity and social justice. The solemn resolve to establish a multi-party democratic governance system, guarantee civil liberty, fundamental rights, human rights, adult franchise, periodic elections, free press, and an independent and competent judiciary is fortified by explicit constitutional provisions. The national flag, national anthem, coat of arms, national colour, national flower and national animal (cow) are indicated in the constitution. Persons of the same gender and community cannot occupy the post of the President and Vice-President at the same time.

The Federal Parliament comprises the House of Representatives and the National Assembly. The House of Representatives shall consist of 275 members, of which 165 shall be elected through the "first-past-the-post-electoral system" comprising the whole of Nepal, divided into 165 electoral constituencies based on geography and population. As many as 110 members shall be elected through proportional representation, under which the electorates vote for the parties treating the whole of Nepal as a single electoral constituency. The National Assembly, representing the provinces, shall consist of 59, including three nominated, members. The legislative power is divided between the Federal Parliament, Provincial Legislatures and local governments. The constitution provides for the setting up of various commissions for the protection of human rights and for dealing with issues relating to fiscal and natural resources, Dalits, women, language and social inclusion. There are also provisions regarding the constitution, registration and operation of political parties, with the explicit objective of promoting competitive party politics.

The Madeshis and the Tharu, who populate the Tarai and constitute nearly 40 per cent of Nepal's population, are deeply incensed with the manner the boundaries of the seven provinces are proposed to be drawn. The dilution of the element of proportional representation from 58 per cent, as contemplated in the interim constitution of 2007, to 45 per cent, has fuelled further resentment among low-caste groups and the marginalised sections. Women's rights activists are critical of the provision dealing with citizenship being backward and discriminatory against women. They lament that Nepal has not come out of the strong tentacles of a patriarchal society. There is a widespread seething discontent among the Janajatis (hill tribes), Tharus (plains tribes in Tarai), Dalits and Madeshis (majority electorate) that they would be marginalised politically by the new constitution scripted by the ruling clique of high-caste hill elites. They are piqued that the ruling Brahmin-Kshatria (Bahun-Chettri) coalition, comprising less than 30 per cent of the population, will continue to have a dominant control over the state apparatus, as the leadership of the major political parties — NC, CPN (UML) and UCPN-Maoist — belongs to the same minority upper caste clique. Unfortunately, the unrest in the Tarai region is being viewed by vested political interest in Nepal, as though India has played a spoiler. Perhaps democratic politics finds similar ruse — "blame the neighbour for internal failures".

The relations between India and Nepal go to a hoary past, fused together as they are by strong civilisational ties, the legend of the Buddha and the propinquity of blood and kinship. This cannot be allowed to wilt, wither and assume unfriendly overtones. Our close cultural ties and friendship cannot be held hostage by parochial politics. The erroneous perception of "big brother" and the hypothetical view that India is trying to "micromanage their polity" must be dispelled. Nepal and India are civilisational twins. Even the Himalayas did not divide them. The people of Nepal have come out of the throes of monarchy and the Maoists after a long and bloody struggle. Let democracy thrive and prosper in Nepal and let their democratic politics mature and find amicable solutions to redress the legitimate urges and aspirations of all sections of the people, within their own flexible constitutional framework, and resolve the acrimony over geography vs demography in the interest of a stable, peaceful and prosperous Nepal.

A NEW CONSTITUTION FINALLY RATIFIED IN NEPAL AFTER YEARS OF DISPUTES AND DELAYS

President Ram Baran Yadav promulgated the much-awaited new Constitution of Nepal. A few days earlier, the elected representatives inside the Constituent Assembly had approved around 302 articles of the Constitution by an overwhelming two-third majority. The new Constitution is, therefore, the first Constitution which has been finalized by a fully elected sovereign body; the past Constitutions of Nepal were largely a negotiated settlement between elected representatives and a powerful monarchy backed by Nepal's army.

The New Constitution through an elected Constituent Assembly was eagerly anticipated by Nepalese people because it was part of Nepal's recent peace process that led to an end of the ten-year armed conflict. For the Maoists rebels who had waged a protracted armed insurrection since 1996, a new Constitution through an elected Constituent Assembly was the bottom line for giving up their armed struggle. And it was only after the major parties agreed for an election to the Constituent Assembly that the Maoists engaged in the peace process and gave up their armed struggle and came to the democratic fold.

The new Constitution is considered as a remarkable step forward to institutionalize the recent peace process as well as multi-party democracy in Nepal.

Main Features of the New Constitution

The Constitution envisions building an equitable society based on the proportional representation of various social groups, economic prosperity, and social justice. The state features as expressed by the statute are republicanism, federalism and secularism to be headed by the Prime Minster in the executive role and President as the ceremonial head of the state.

For women, the new Constitution guarantees 33 per cent of political representation at federal level and 40 per cent at local level. In addition, the Constitution guarantees proportional representation of women in all the state machineries. The new Constitution has also provided women the right to pass citizenship to children even though women marrying foreigners are still deprived of the equal right as men on this issue.

Engagement in the Constitution-Making Process

Inspired from Denmark on the multi-party collaboration on common issues, the Steering Committee members of JOMPOPS wanted to use that practice in the constitution-making process as well. Accordingly, JOMPOPS members organized a series of multi-party workshops on the most contentious issues of the draft Constitution including re-structuring of the state, election system and the local government.

Representatives of JOMPOPS parties which comprise of major political parties of Nepal worked together to reach an agreement on these contentious issues. The conclusions reached in the workshops were submitted to the top leadership from the respective parties. The findings of the workshop were also shared with the President of Nepal as well as the Chairperson of the Constituent Assembly.

Even though this exercise alone did not result into an agreement among major political parties on contentious issues of the Constitution. It can be said that this exercise of multi-party cooperation definitely contributed positively in the constitution-making process as expressed by top party leadership.

Campaign on citizenship through mother is successful

Since one of the priority areas of JOMPOPS has been promoting gender equality in politics, JOMPOPS members were highly concerned about the provision regarding citizenship in the draft Constitution which openly discriminated against women. More importantly, the draft provision had reversed the achievement of the Interim Constitution which conferred women the right to pass citizenship to their children.

In this context, JOMPOPS collaborated with civil society organizations to lobby for the amendments in the draft Constitution to ensure gender equality in citizenship and equal citizenship rights for mothers. Even though gender equality on the citizenship right could not be fully guaranteed by the new Constitution, it guarantees the right of mothers to pass citizenship to their children as long as they are not married to foreigners.

JOMPOPS members feel that the amendment in the draft provision is a significant step forward. If the provision regarding citizenship right had been passed as in the draft Constitution then it would have created many problems for women including rendering many children stateless. Therefore, JOMPOPS members celebrate the amendment of the draft provision that they actively lobbied for.

New Challenges

The constitution finalization process, despite its advantages, has created new challenges for the functioning of JOMPOPS. Three JOMPOPS' member parties comprising of Madhesi-based parties did not participate in the constitution finalization process. Their differences with the major parties regarding issues of federalism were not addressed by the major parties. Moreover, they were upset by brutal suppression against Madhesi agitators and human rights violations by the state security forces.

There is still hope that the major three political parties will understand and address grievances of agitating parties including three Madhesi parties. If that happens, the new Constitution will mark a new beginning of peace and prosperity for Nepal.

NEW CONSTITUTION TRIGGERS POLITICAL TURMOIL IN NEPAL

Nepal has plunged into another political crisis following the adoption of a new constitution. President Ram Baran Yadav signed the constitution on September 20, after 508 members of the 601-member Constituent Assembly (CA) approved it five days earlier.

Members of the ruling Nepal Congress (NC) and Communist Party of Nepal-UML (CPN-UML) coalition, as well as of the opposition Unified Nepal Communist Party-Maoist (UNCP-M), voted for the constitution, but 25 members of royalist parties opposed it and 66 ethnic Madhesi representatives abstained.

No date has yet been set for the implementation of the constitution, so the interim government led by Prime Minister Sushil Koirala continues in the country of 28 million people, wedged between India and China.

Madhesi parties are demanding greater autonomy for Madhesi and Tharu people in the southern plains bordering India and increased representation in the parliament. Protests called by the ethnic Madhesi Democratic Front (MDF) and Madhesi Janadhikar Forum-Loktantrik (MJF-L) have claimed more than 40 lives so far.

Compounding the crisis, India has effectively backed Madhesi protests, calling on the Kathmandu government to address their demands. New Delhi, though denying any blockade, has imposed an unofficial ban on supplies, including fuel, to Nepal, citing fears of unrest. Landlocked Nepal depends on routes across the Indian border for imports.

The protests have also resulted in a rift within the UNCP-M. Former Maoist Prime Minister Baburam Bhattarai quit the party and the parliament on September 26, expressing sympathy for Madhesis. Though he voted for the constitution, he said Madhesis were "denied a say" in formulating it. Bhattarai is seeking to form a new party to exploit the crisis, under conditions in which the credibility of the established parties, including the Maoists, has sharply eroded.

The Constituent Assembly was established in 2008, two years after the Maoists abandoned their guerrilla war and joined the other capitalist parties to scuttle mass protests against former King Gyanendra's autocratic rule. The monarchy was abolished and an interim government installed, promising a new constitution in the near future.

The establishment parties, however, wrangled for seven years to protect their various interests, frequently postponing the finalisation of the constitution. They hurriedly decided to end the quarrel out of concern for the explosive social situation after deadly twin earthquakes in April and May deepened the misery of workers and the poor. The quakes killed nearly 9,000 people, injured thousands and destroyed many homes and livelihoods.

Under the new constitution, Nepal has been named a "democratic republic," with seven provinces and a federal parliament. The prime minister will exercise executive powers, with the president playing a largely ceremonial role. The constitution seeks to refashion the capitalist state in order to overcome protracted political instability and attract foreign investment.

The document strengthens the state apparatus of the army, police, armed police and other security organs and provides for draconian measures. If a "grave emergency arises in relation to the sovereignty or integrity of Nepal or the security of any part therefore," fundamental rights can be suspended under emergency regulations, with blanket immunity given to the security forces.

Under the monarchy, emergency measures such as the Prevention of Terrorism and Disruptive Activities Act were used to suppress the Maoist insurgency between 1996 and 2006, during which the armed force killed nearly 15,000 people and hundreds more disappeared.

Other reactionary provisions in the new constitution include making religious conversion a punishable offence and denying citizenship rights to the children of women who marry foreigners. Nothing in the constitution addresses the democratic or social aspirations of the working class and rural poor in this poverty-stricken country.

Apart from calling for two autonomous states, the Madhesi parties' other demands include the provision of 83 seats in the 165-member parliament, and reservation of posts for Madhesi and Tharu officials in the administrative, security, judiciary and diplomatic services. They are also calling for an independent commission to inquire into killings and punishments carried out by the security forces.

While the Kathmandu ruling elite systematically discriminates against ethnic minorities in Nepal, the campaign led by the communal parties represents the interests of privileged social layers, not the democratic and social rights of workers and the poor.

The Indian government, seeking to bolster New Delhi's influence in the country, has intervened into the crisis, putting enormous pressure on Nepal to halt the new constitution's adoption until the Madhesi parties are satisfied. On September 19, Indian Prime Minister Narendra Modi sent Foreign Secretary S. Jaishankar as his special envoy to meet Nepal's leaders, including President Yadav and Prime Minister Koirala.

According to media reports, India proposed seven amendments to the constitution, including a clause providing Madhesis with parliamentary seats proportional to their population. The Indian foreign ministry denied suggesting such amendments, but issued several statements warning of widespread protests in Nepal. "We had repeatedly cautioned the political leadership of Nepal to take urgent steps to defuse the tension in these regions," it stated on September 22.

Nepal's Industry Minister Mahesh Basnet has accused India of "an unofficial economic blockade." India has denied any obstruction, saying the halting of goods at border crossings was due to unrest, protests and demonstrations on the Nepalese side.

Nepalese people are increasingly facing a scarcity of essential goods, including fuel and cooking gas. To divert the mounting popular discontent, the government and media have responded with anti-Indian propaganda, encouraging counter-protests and violence. Nepal's broadcast operators have blacked out access to 42 Indian TV channels.

Stratfor, the US-based corporate intelligence service, has drawn attention to the underlying conflicts between China and India, which is aligned with the US. It commented on October 6: "India's active role in the dispute illustrates its broader regional strategy. Since South Asian governments opened to Chinese investment and political outreach at the beginning of the decade, New Delhi has made a concerted effort to regain its footing in the region (excluding Pakistan)."

Statfor said New Delhi was seeking to counter China's influence, citing India's economic pressure on nearby Bhutan on the eve of an election and India's support for the ousting of former President Mahinda Rajapakse in Sri Lanka.

Kathmandu governments have attempted to maintain relationships with both New Delhi and Beijing, which has become the largest donor and investor in Nepal. Washington and New Delhi are determined to undercut Beijing's role in Nepal, in line with Washington's strategic, military and economic "pivot to Asia" to isolate and militarily encircle China. Encouraged by the US, India's intervention is destabilising Nepal, and drawing it into the broader geopolitical tensions developing globally.

NEPAL'S NEW CONSTITUTION: A PATH TO PEACE OR FURTHER CRISIS?

For the first time in history, Nepal has adopted a constitution which is supposed to be representative of the Nepali people. President of Nepal, Dr. Ram Varan Yadav, promulgated the new constitution on 20 September 2015 from the building of the Constituent Assembly (CA). It seems as if the dream of a representative Nepali constitution passed through the CA may have come true, heralding an era of peace and democracy.

The constitution was passed overwhelmingly by 90 percent of votes, after which the CA was converted into a legislative parliament. The Nepali people welcomed the constitution and celebrated by organizing different events nationwide. All over Nepal, people lit candles and greeted each other. The Nepalese people also expressed hope for a better future now that the country has entered into a stable development phase. Much of the international community has welcomed the new constitution. However Nepal's neighbour country, India, has not been so welcoming, issuing only a single statement declaring that India notes the declaration of the new constitution.

The new constitution

Experts have said that whilst the new constitution may not be the best, it does mark progress. They also add that the constitution of Nepal must be judged by its implementation, as well as by what it says in the document. The Nepalese people seem to agree that whilst there are some weaknesses that will need to be amended over time, the new constitution is a positive step for the country.

The constitution is meant to establish Nepal as a federal democratic republic, however demarcation and delineation of federal provinces has become a dominant issue of tension in the wake of the constitution. The concept of a federal structure emerged to try and ensure the rights of disadvantaged communities and bring them into the mainstream of development efforts. Experts are saying that the new constitution has made adequate provisions for the rights of these communities, however there are concerns that the benefits will only reach leaders rather than the Nepalese people as a whole. The principle of federalism has been limited to the demarcation and delineation of the provinces, missing potential steps for further progress regarding issues of inclusiveness and human rights.

Protest in the Terai-Madhes

Political parties based in Terai region of Nepal walked out of the constitution-making process when the 4 major political parties reached an agreement in June to 'fast track' the process and to delineate the federal provinces. Terai-Madhes people have largely objected to the constitution, particularly the new federal boundaries, because they believe it to further marginalize their communities. Since walking out of the process, the Terai-Madhes political parties have been organizing protests opposing the agreement, forming an alliance called the United Democratic

Madhesi Front (UDMF). The UDMF has been protesting to call for nationwide strike against the decision to delineate the provinces in the constitution.

The UDMF's major demands includes (i) the implementation of all past agreements reached between the UDMF and the government, (ii) 2 provinces to be part of the entire Terai-Madhes belt, (iii) an electoral constituency based on population only, (iv) an amendment to citizenship laws, and (v) proportional representation in every state institution. It is becoming harder to understand what the exact agenda of the UDMF is as the protests have been escalating. News of a 7-point agenda has emerged from India, and a 35-point agenda is circulating in the media in Kathmandu. Some UDMF leaders deny these demands to be their own, whilst other are affiliating themselves with them. The Government has registered an amendment bill in parliament to address the UDMF's demands, however the UDMF remain dissatisfied, saying that all demands must be met before they will come to the negotiation table.

Protests have escalated into outbreaks of violence in Nepal. On 24 August, seven police personnel and a child were killed within thirty minutes during protests organized by the Tharu community in the west. After this, an estimated fifty people were killed including protesters and security personnel in the protest in the Terai-Madhes. Some people are saying that internal competition among the parties over which is the most revolutionary is causing non-violent protests to escalate into more violent activity. In the last 2 months, schools, colleges, universities, officers, markets, shops and transportation systems have been closed down in the Terai-Madhes and the day-to-day life of the people has been further jeopardized. The only highway of Nepal that is located in the Terai-Madhes has also been closed down. Millions of children have been prevented from going to school which violates their fundamental right to education.

India and the economic blockade

India has imposed an economic blockade on Nepal in the wake of the promulgation. Nepal, a landlocked country, shares borders with India in the east, west and south, and shares a border with China in the north. The Himalayan mountain range in the north of Nepal prevents easy access to China. Therefore, Nepal depends entirely on India for the importation of goods including fuel, cooking gas, medicines, raw materials, food items, and other necessary goods. India has argued that it has imposed an economic blockade on Nepal due to security concerns caused by the protests, stopping all vehicles coming from India crossing the border carrying the above goods. There is a now a shortage of necessary items nationwide, and the Nepalese people are suffering. The people have not yet recovered from the earthquake which struck in April and May. By imposing the economic blockade, India violates a number of international laws, in particular for a landlocked country. However these treaties and laws have no meaning to a powerful country like India, especially when it comes to Nepal – Asia's second poorest country. Indeed, Chinese President Xi Jinping delivered a speech in the 70th session of the UN General Assembly on 28 September 2015, proclaiming that 'the big, strong and rich should not bully the small, weak and poor, the principle of sovereignty not only means that the sovereignty and territorial integrity of all countries are inviolable and their internal affairs are not subjected to interference'.

In fact, it seems that India may be backing the UDMF leaders, helping their efforts to organize protests and sit-ins in Nepal. Protestors have been frequently using Indian territory to organize their campaigns. The UDMF leaders have been travelling through India to attend protests in different places across the border.The unity in Nepal which was strengthened in the aftermath of the earthquake is being threatened by the economic blockade and continuous strikes in the Terai-Madhes region, particularly between the Pahade (people living in the hills) and the Madhesi (people living in the Terai-Madhes). The issue of ethnicity is becoming deeper and tensions are being brought to the surface, spilling over into the channels of social media. There are also emerging fears of communal violence.

The road ahead

In the face of growing tensions, a number of peacebuilding rallies have emerged, led by Nepalese youth, to maintain harmony, coexistence and peace in the Nepalese society, especially between the Pahade and the Madhesi communities in Kathmandu and in the Terai-Madhes. The newly elected Prime Minister has responsibilities not only to implement the new constitution by also to bring all dissatisfied groups, including the UDMF, into the mainstream of politics. There is no other option left to solve the ongoing unrest in Nepal besides dialogue and negotiation. The negotiation teams formed by the government and the UDMF need to sit at the negotiation table and participate in dialogue to find a common solution. The government have to bring other dissatisfied parties such as Libhuwan in the east and Tharu Communities in the west to the table. Now that long-awaited dream of a Nepalese constitution of the people has come true, it is the responsibility of all to ensure that the constitution is properly implemented.

NEPAL'S LESSON FOR ALL CONSTITUTIONAL GOVERNMENTS

The violence in the Terai plain of Nepal over the last six weeks may not be on your radar screen. Butthe blockade of the Nepal-India border created by armed groups from the Madhesi ethnic minority actually has global significance.

The reason is surprising: On Sept. 20, Nepal ratified a new constitution after a fitful and frustrating eight-year process. You'd think this would be good news, heralding an era of good feelings. Instead, ratification drove the Madhesis into something very like open revolt. Thus, a question of universal relevance: Why do some constitutions work, and others fail? Put another way, what's the essence of a constitutional deal that enables it to succeed?

There is, I think, an intuitive answer to this question. Most people, asked what a constitution is for, would say that it's an agreement among the majority of the people on how they want to be governed. The U.S. Constitution starts with the words "We the people." We know that this doesn't literally mean every single one of the people. So we think that, in a democracy, the constitution reflects the ideal of majority rule.

But that answer is wrong. Constitutions exist as much or more to protect minorities as they do to facilitate majority agreement.

That majority-favoring view certainly drove the constitutional deal reached in Nepal. The odyssey started in 2001, when the crown prince killed his father, mother, siblings, one of his uncles and several aunts before shooting himself. In the aftermath, the new king, a brother of the murdered one, struggled to rule. Maoist rebels traded violence for participation in a significant nationwide protest movement, which ultimately led to the abolition of the monarchy.

Elections for a constituent assembly took place in 2008. The Maoists won a plurality but not a majority. Under an interim constitution, they formed a coalition government, with the Congress Party of Nepal in opposition.

From 2009 until this year, through government turnovers and new elections, the constitutional process failed to produce a document that could garner the agreement of the major political parties. The chief sticking point was that the Maoists and Congress couldn't agree on how to share power, even after 2013 elections gave Congress and other so-called traditional parties a greater position in the assembly than the Maoists.

The terrible earthquakes this past April and May broke the impasse. The major parties finally agreed to adopt a federal system, in principle well-suited to the country's many divisions, which include caste, geography, ethnicity and as many as 100 languages.

One key to the agreement was that the big parties agreed to reduce the degree of proportional representation from the interim constitution. Proportional representation is a way of electing representatives that makes it easier for small groups to get their favored candidates into office. The big parties therefore had a common interest in reducing its effects, because they anticipated that their share of the total of elected representatives would go up even if their number of votes didn't change.

From the standpoint of majoritarian democratic politics, the new constitution should've been a winner. Not all Nepalis liked it — but a big majority did.

One hotbed of opposition was the Terai region, along the border with India. Madhesis there objected to the reduction in proportional representation. They also didn't like a constitutional provision that makes it difficult for the children of a Nepali woman and a foreign man to become citizens. This provision was much more likely to be relevant in a border region, where ethnic and familial ties with India produce mixed marriages.

The majority view was, plausibly enough, that minorities can't get everything they want in a constitutional negotiation. But what the majority parties forgot is that, if you treat minorities too cavalierly in the final constitutional deal, you leave them no option but to respond with violence.

Groups that dissent from a constitutional deal by creating disorder are known in the constitution-making business as "spoilers." They take a big risk when they resort to violence, because the majority may respond with force, as the Nepali government has done. Typically, spoilers judge that, having failed to exert their will democratically, they can gain permanent concessions by demonstrating their capacity to freeze the system.

In the case of the Madhesis, that spoiling capacity is significant. India is Nepal's largest trading partner. With the border to India blockaded, Nepal must look to China for energy and other supplies. Prices will inevitably rise.

Eventually, one of two things will happen. Either the state will suppress the Terai blockade and the Madhesis will be forced to knuckle under, or the state will make constitutional concessions to the spoilers. The spoilers think that in the first scenario they will be no worse off than they already were. In the second scenario, they will be better off.

The upshot is that constitutions aren't just about effectuating the will of the democratic majority. To a large extent, they're also about placating minorities and protecting them

Minority protection can range from morally desirable — like protecting equal rights and free political participation — to payoffs for spoilers who make lots of trouble. In U.S. constitutional history, the first minority that thought it needed protecting was property-holding creditors, who feared wealth redistribution.

The second major minority that sought and got constitutional protection was Southern slaveholding whites. It was only in the post-World War II era that American constitutional law started seeing the protection of religious and racial minorities as a key task.

A constitution that can't produce peace will soon become a failed constitution. Nepal's new constitution has a relatively short window to work. Those who drafted it should settle on a strategy soon. And if history is any guide, their best bet will be to make concessions to the spoilers, and protect their interests — even if it's more than they deserve.

6

Constitution of Nepal: India and China

The forty-first most populous country in the world, neighboring the two emerging powers of Asia, China in the north and India in the rest of its sides became a republic on 20th of September 2015. The transition into a federal republic state has its own reverberations across the country that has killed 40 so far in the protests. The reason for the protests is a widespread opposition to the newly adopted constitution that some believe is not inclusively beneficial to a diversified Nepal that has people speaking 100 different languages.

SOME HISTORY

With these protests, an episode of a forgotten civil war fought by Maoists for a decade-long period from 1996 to 2006 demanding a republic state seem to have been reinvigorated. The civil war led by Maoist Communist Party of Nepal began on 13th February 1996 for being denied permission to contest the elections.

The civil war was ended by a Comprehensive Peace Accord in the year 2006 when the then Prime Minister Girija Prasad Koirala and Maoist leader Prachanda agreed to sign a deal. An interim Constitution came into effect in 2007 that aimed at drafting a permanent constitution by 2010, which didn't happen due to a lack of unanimity and disagreements.

The dates get extended until the Constituent Assembly was dissolved in 2012, and fresh elections were conducted for the second Constituent Assembly of Nepal in 2013. The new assembly pledged to draft a permanent constitution by Jan 22, 2015, but was delayed by disagreements over a number of issues involving judicial and federal systems. Finally, a permanent Constitution was drafted in August 2015, after the country went through a disastrous earthquake in April.

The new document was drafted without subjecting it to much public debate and was rushed in by the political parties representing a few Maoists and politicians from the upper caste, claims those who oppose the constitution. Some of the left out Maoists feel betrayed with the passing of the Constitution.

What does the new Constitution say?

As per the new charter, provisions are made to divide the country into seven states, which some ethnic communities feel threatened to share their state with a more dominating section of the society. The question of whether to demarcate the seven federal states based on ethnicities remains undecided.

Moreover, under the new Constitution only 45% of the members of the Parliament are elected through a Proportional Representation system, which was 53% in the interim constitution. The 53% helped marginalized people being represented in the legislature previously, which will become lower under the current Constitution.

The new Constitution also keeps Nepal's patriarchal dominance intact by denying some women's rights. For instance, a child born to a Nepali mother and a foreign father will not inherit the country's citizenship unless the father becomes a Nepal citizen, whereas a child of a foreign mother becomes a Nepal citizen if born to a man from Nepal.

India & China: Contradicting Views

Two major powers in the region have contradicting opinions about the new republic state.

Along the border of India, in Terai, the minority ethnic communities of Madeshis and Tharu that constitute 40% of the total population in Nepal feel threatened by this division of provinces as they feel becoming politically marginalized. This is where India feels a bit trouble.

People move freely across the 1751 kilometer border between India and Nepal that has resulted in human trafficking, drug peddling, etc. along with infiltration of extremists from Pakistan. There have been a number of instances where a lot of terrorists have crossed the Nepal border to enter or leave India and have got arrested along these boundary lines.

Hence, stability along the Indo-Nepal border region is pivotal for India's national security and hence the grievances of the ethnic communities in Terai should be resolved before passing the Constitution, asserts India. Once this border becomes instable, it will be a task for India to monitor these boundaries to prevent infiltration.

China, on the other hand, looks welcoming the new Constitution saying that the condition including the division of the states can be improved in future with further amendments.

China should necessarily understand that a completely stable and functional Nepal is essential in making an emerging modern Asia one of the stable regions in the world.

NEPAL'S CONSTITUTION AND LESSONS FOR INDIA

On September 20, Nepal's President Ram Baran Yadav announced that his country had a new constitution. The promulgation of the constitution is significant because it paves the way for the establishment of a democratic political system in the country. The constitution itself is the result of eight years of deliberation, including the failure of the first Constituent Assembly in 2012. It is the seventh constitution to have been adopted by Nepal in the last 67 years and the first by democratically elected representatives.

India's Overreaction

The adoption of Nepal's constitution has triggered alarm bells in India. According to reports in the *Indian Express*, a day after the constitution was promulgated; India expressed its displeasure about the content. New Delhi has reportedly asked Nepal to make as many as seven amendments to address the concerns of the Madhesis and Janjatis (minority groups in Nepal). These amendments, the report suggest, have been "conveyed to Nepal's leadership through official channels."

In the last few months, these communities have strongly protested against provisions of the constitution which they fear will impinge on their cultural identities. Prominent among the concerns are provisions related to the reorganization of provinces. The Madhesis largely inhabit the plain regions that border India. The protest has reportedly claimed 40 lives so far and New Delhi fears that violence may spill over to the Indian side if corrective measures are not taken.

The constitution was passed by a clear majority with 507 of the 598 constituent assembly members voting in favor. However, around 60 members from the Madhesis and Janjatis community boycotted the vote. India views the constitution as unrepresentative of a significant fraction of the population.

New Delhi's response to the constitution has come as a surprise to many. As a democratic country itself, India has arguably overstepped the limits of suggestion and rather tried to impose its views on its much smaller neighbor. In various international forums, India has repeatedly advocated for a country's right to self-determination. Unfortunately, this seems not to apply to Nepal.

The concerns that India has raised may well be real. The Madhesis and Janjatis may indeed be fearful of their future at the hands of the three big political parties in Nepal. As a friendly neighbor, it is certainly not unreasonable for India to suggest concerns. However, asking the country to made seven amendments to its constitution the day after it was promulgated goes well beyond suggestion. India must respect the will of the Nepali people and the democratic process through which the constitution was drafted and adopted.

Responding to the report in *Indian Express*, the Ministry of External Affairs has issued a statement stating, "The article is incorrect. Government of India has not handed over any list of specific Constitutional amendments or changes to the Government of Nepal...we continue to urge that issues on which there are differences should be resolved through dialogue in an atmosphere free from violence, and institutionalized in a manner that would enable broad-based ownership and acceptance." The newspaper maintained that it "has confirmed from its sources that these amendments/changes were communicated by New Delhi to Katmandu. It stands by the report."

A review of India's response to the constitution support the *Indian Express*. Indian Foreign Secretary S Jaishankar was sent on a diplomatic mission to ensure that India's concerns are amicably addressed. His visit was a failure. Immediately after Nepal adopted its constitution; India recalled its ambassador in Katmandu for a briefing. New Delhi has expressed its displeasure (and also here) without much impact. It is likely to perceive this as its weakening grip over the Himalayan state, notwithstanding its humanitarian aid in the wake of the recent earthquake and Prime Minister Narendra Modi's visiting the country twice.

Lessons for Democracy?

India may praise itself as the "world's largest democracy" but there are important lessons it can take from the new constitution of Nepal.

With the promulgation of this constitution Nepal has become the first Asian country to explicitly recognize the rights of the Lesbian, Gay, Bisexual and Transgender (LGBT) community. The provisions under Right to Equality clearly state that "no discrimination shall be made against any citizen in the application of general laws on grounds of religion, colour, caste, tribe, sex, sexual orientation, bodily condition, disability, status of health, marital status, pregnancy, financial status, origin, language or region, ideological conviction or any of these."

The constitution also states that nothing shall prevent the state from the "making of special provisions by law for the protection, empowerment or advancement of [among others] gender-based and sexually oriented minorities."

In contrast, same-sex relationship is a crime in India under Section 377 of the Penal Code, which awards punishment of "imprisonment for life or with imprisonment of either description for a term which may extend to ten years and shall also be liable to fine." The Supreme Court in 2013 upheld Section 377 but left it to the wisdom of the parliament to decide whether to retain or repeal the draconian law.

The present Narendra Modi government recently informed parliament that it has no plans to repeal Section 377. The party in the past has welcomed the apex court verdict and also termed homosexuality as "anti-India."

Recognizing the rights of women, the constitution of Nepal explicitly states that "women shall have equal ancestral right without any gender-based discrimination." India has yet to introduce a similar right for women from all faiths. Moreover, ancestral property rights for women are not a fundamental right in India. Apart from this, the principles of positive discrimination and proportional inclusion have been employed in Nepal's constitution to give women the right to participate in all agencies of State mechanism and in health, education, employment and social security. While India has implemented positive discrimination in various fields, it has a long way to go to ensure proportional inclusion of women in state mechanism.

Nepal also has become the second country after Bhutan in South Asia to abolish the death penalty. The Supreme Court of India in the past has accepted the fact that on various occasions innocent people have been executed. Since 1996, around 15 people have been erroneously given the death penalty. Two of them were hanged.

Under the new constitution, victims of environmental pollution or degradation in Nepal now have the fundamental right to receive compensation from the polluter. In India the "right to a clean environment" is not explicitly mentioned in the constitution, but the Supreme Court has interpreted it be included under the right to life. However, unlike Nepal, the victims of environmental pollution or degradation in India are not entitled to any compensation as a fundamental right. The state may impose a penalty on polluters but this does not necessarily mean that the affected will be compensated. The state gets richer; the victims poorer. Similarly, while advocating for a fundamental right to education, the constitution makes special provisions for the empowerment of the differently-able citizens. It states, "Citizens with disability and economically poor conditions shall have the right to free higher education." On the other hand, in India no such provisions are available under fundamental rights for the differently able to access free higher education. Provisions for free education are limited only to the primary level.

What Next?

A constitution can be a living document; India must desist from taking a strong position prematurely. Indian must acknowledge the fact that after years of political uncertainty, Nepal finally has a constitution which on the whole is progressive. Like any other constitution, it has loopholes. The Indian constitution itself is full of them. Yet India would baulk at another country trying to force change upon it. Suggestions are welcome, dictation is not.

Writing for *The Hindu*, senior Nepali journalist Kanak Mani Dixit says, "Perhaps the most welcome aspect is that amendments can be adopted with relative ease over the next two years and four months, as the Constituent Assembly enjoys a kind of afterlife as a Parliament with the same party based configuration. Everything except sovereignty and national integrity are open to amendment... it is important for India to let the neighbor sort out its challenges on its own."

Given the deep historical, cultural and religious links the two countries share, careful employment of soft power diplomacy would very likely be a better way for India to express its concerns.

NEPAL'S NEW CONSTITUTION: INDIA HOPES 'DIFFICULT DAYS' WILL NOT AFFECT INDO-NEPAL TIES

With Indo-Nepal ties witnessing unease after the promulgation of the newConstitution in Nepal, India hoped that "difficult days" would not affect their friendship as it welcomed the Nepalgovernment's move to hold talks with agitating groups.

"We welcome the recent steps taken by the government of Nepal to hold dialogue with the agitating groups to end the existing political crisis in a peaceful manner," Indian Ambassador to Nepal Ranjit Rae said. He said India wants stability in Nepal and it was not against the new Constitution.

"We see the Constitution as the culmination of violence and end of very brutal insurgency Nepal had gone through. Nepal has come out of a very difficult situation and we don't want that it return to another difficult situation," Rae said during an interaction programme here.

"Nepal-India friendship is very old, solid and very much stable, and it doesn't depend on any specific issue or incident," he said, adding "I am confident even after these difficult days our friendship will be stronger."

On his part, Nepal's Ambassador to India Deep Kumar Upadhyaya hoped that there would be ease in supply of essential commodities from India soon as efforts are being made at diplomatic and political level in this regard.

Asking people from both countries to observe tolerance and have a positive attitude towards dealing with the issue, the Nepalese envoy said, "India has always played an important role during the hardship faced by Nepal in the past which was evident during the recent earthquakes.

"Let's not speak irresponsible things and develop negative attitude towards each other at this sensitive time which might damage the centuries old friendly relations."

"We should maintain peace, stability and move towards economic prosperity and I hope India will extend support to our endeavour as a peaceful, stable and prosperous Nepal will also be in the interest of India," he said.

Rae also cautioned that if Nepal does not take every one along while drafting the Constitution then it will be sowing the seeds of future conflict as well as opening the door of instability that will also affect India.

"Therefore, the only solution to the current problem is talk," the Indian Ambassador added. Meanwhile, Nepal's major parties yesterday started talks with the agitating Madhesi parties to find a solution to the Terai problem through peaceful means.

Madhesis are Indian-origin inhabitants of the Terai plains bordering India who are opposed to splitting Nepal into seven provinces.

"The friendship of India is not confined to a particular region, or southern plains, but we have the same family relations between Uttarakhand and Far-western Nepal as well as relations of eastern Nepal with our states in eastern India like Sikkim and West Bengal," the Indian Ambassador said.

The three major parties — Nepal Congress, CPN-UML and UCPN-Maoist — yesterday formed a three-member committee to hold dialogue with the parties and groups agitating against the new Constitution. Nepali Congress leader and Forest Minister Mahesh Acharya and CPN-UML Chief whip Agni Kharel and Narayankaji Shrestha from UCPN-Maoist are the members of the committee.

"We have already started dialogue with the Joint Madhesi Front and other agitating groups of the southern Nepal and the talks are moving towards a positive direction," Acharya told PTI.

Mahanta Thakur, president of Terai Madhes Democratic Party and Bijaya Gachhadar, president of Madhesi Peoples Rights Forum Democratic, among others are taking part in the talks. The agitation in the southern Nepal has entered 45th day and the country is reeling under scarcity of essential goods including petroleum products and cooking gas due to the blockade along the border areas with India.

Shortage of petroleum products have created panic among the people in Kathmandu, who are queuing for hours to fill petrol and diesel in their vehicles. Normal life has been severely affected due to the growing tension in the border areas. More than 40 people have been killed in over a month-long violence.

MOST NEPALIS ARE NOT CELEBRATING THEIR NEW CONSTITUTION

An ambitious warrior from the tiny Gorkha principality in the mid-mountains of Nepal founded the country with a combination of trick and treachery in the late-eighteenth century. Kathmandu has remained a hotbed of conspiracies ever since, where the ruling elite scheme against each other almost on permanent basis. With the ruler's command as the only law, there was no way to break this vicious cycle that harmed almost everyone.

It was at the urging of Jawaharlal Nehru that the kingdom got its first statute in 1947 when Prime Minister Maharaja Padma Shamsher promulgated a constitution to confer political legitimacy upon the Rana oligarchy. The statute didn't last. Padma was ousted in a bloodless coup soon afterwards and the country returned back into the hands of the more autocratic Ranas. It was only after the overthrow of the Ranas and the restoration of a Shah King into power in 1951 that a proper constitution was made – once again under the influence of Nehru – which sought to lead the country towards democratic rule. Perhaps to make up for the lost time, Nepal has given itself a fresh statute once every decade on an average. That must be the highest turnover rate of constitutions anywhere in the world.

The new constitution

The supreme law of the land that President Ram Baran unveiled on September 20, 2015 in a somber ceremony inside the Constituent Assembly hall is this the latest in the series. Of course, it is a much awaited document, but it merely replaces the existing statute rather than fills a constitutional vacuum. And that's the reason the current constitution is being contested so fiercely: Its critics insist that the statute seeks to turn the clock back, specially on issues related to minority rights. Proponents of the document, however, claim that it's the best constitution in the world.

It is possible to take a reformist view and consider the constitution to be a dynamic document where changes can be introduced in a gradual and legitimate manner. The problem with that position is the intransience of the dominant majority in Nepal that has refused to entertain voices of dissent. There is yet another reason that has made opponents of the new constitution desperate – Nepal's experience shows that those in power never amend any constitution to address the aspirations of the marginalised. Without hitting the streets, minorities have never got their aspirations addressed in a legitimate manner. That could be one of the reasons behind the desolation of the Madhesi population in the southern plains of Nepal, where protests have continued for more than one-and-half months, and nearly four dozen people have lost their lives, including eight policemen, in a brutal crackdown by the security forces.

When the constitution was being inaugurated in Kathmandu, nearly half the population of the country was reeling under voluntary shutdowns, police prohibitory orders, and a state of curfew being enforced by the Nepal Army.

Terai-Madhes – the southern plains of Nepal – is home to over half of Nepal's population, two-thirds of them being ethnic Madhesis who are incorrectly described as 'people of Indian origin' due to their family and cultural affiliations across the border.

The presence of Madhesis in the security forces of Nepal is negligible. The ethnic composition of the security forces during times of crisis is a sore point everywhere. Madhesis perceive soldiers and police personnel as oppressors rather than protectors. The security forces, on the other hand, act as if they were keeping order in occupied territories where they have no emotional involvement. Protests have turned violent in response to brutalities by law enforcement agencies and vice-versa, perpetuating a vicious circle of violence. The complete absence of politicos of the dominant majority in Terai-Madhes has further aggravated the situation.

Grievances galore

Nepal adopted parliamentary democracy and an independent judiciary in 1990 with the restoration of the multiparty system. It became a secular country after the success of the spring uprising in 2006, that sidelined the Hindu monarch from mainstream politics. Concepts of federalism, proportionate representation and proactive inclusion were incorporated into the interim statute after prolonged Madhes uprisings in 2007 and 2008 through two separate agreements signed between the-then head-of-state and the head-of-government Prime Minister Girija Prasad Koirala and Madhesbadi parties.

The monarchy was abolished and Nepal was declared a Federal Democratic Republic on May 28, 2008 with the unanimous decision of the first siting of the Constituent Assembly. All these democratic dimensions have been retained in the new constitution. What the new statute adds is the demarcation of federal boundaries. That, and the emasculation of existing provisions, have enraged different population groups in Nepal.

Women are unhappy that they have been scorned. Implementation of their rights enshrined in the interim constitution was bad enough due to antiquated laws and the patriarchal mindset of majority of bureaucrats; the new statute makes it worse by creating different classes of citizenship that will bar mothers from conferring their nationality upon children.

The Janjatis are disappointed as the new constitution has failed to recognize their community rights and delineation of federal units has discarded principles of identity and viability. It violates several agreements that the government had signed with groups such as the Tharus and other indigenous communities in the past. The creation of federal units to pacify Brahman-Kshetris of the hills – the dominant caste groups – has rubbed salt over the wounds of the marginalised.

The dalits had been promised positive discrimination as a form of reparation to end discriminatory practices of the past. The new statute has reneged on the relevant provision of the interim constitution and provided for enactment of laws to regulate such issues. With the credibility of the ruling community – the high-caste Hindus – at all time low, dalit activists are not ready to barter concrete provisions of the existing constitution with a vague promise of enacting liberal laws in the future.

The redefinition of secularism in the constitution – obligating the state to protect and promote Sanatana religious and cultural practices, retention of the Holy Cow as the national animal, and proscription of proselytisation – imply that Nepal will no longer be a equal country for religious minorities. Voices of protest from Nepalese Christians and Muslims are feeble, but their discontent isn't hard to understand.

But there is a reason opposition to the new statute has been the fiercest in Terai-Madhes. The people there have to suffer the consequences of all these provisions in addition to enduring the indignity of being considered second-class citizens in their own homeland.

Frenzied Madhes

With new statutory provisions that seek to conflate citizenship rights with the nationality of the person, the rights of Madhesis who marry across the border will be severely jeopardised. The voices of the women protestors in Kathmandu thus resonate in Terai-Madhes that dread the creation of separate ancestral, naturalised and acquired categories of citizenship. Bearers of the last category of citizenship will be barred from holding several high public posts.

Creation of one, or at most two, provinces in Terai-Madhes was promised to ensure that Madhesis and Tharus will be empowered through a sizable presence in major units of the federation. The constitutionally-mandated fragmentation of Madhes implies that they shall forever be at the mercy of the dominant community from hills and mountains. Had the record of the ruling community been inspiring, such fears might have seemed unfounded. But when raised by communities historically externalised as "the other" in the national discourse, their concerns begin to appear fully justifiable.

The need for proportionate representation in the legislature through delineation of population-based constituencies should have been a self-evident element of a democratic constitution. Fearful of Madhesis getting their due share, which may challenge the hegemony of the dominant community, the new constitution puts geographic representation as the main element of formation of parliament. Such blatantly communal features are unlikely to go unchallenged in Terai-Madhes.

Proportionate inclusion in employment is yet another feature that had made the interim statute of Nepal a progressive document. These provisions have been retained in name, but their effectiveness severely curtailed. For example, the most dominant community has been added to the list of intended beneficiaries – thus reducing opportunities for minorities. Besides, laws will have to be enacted for implementation, making the future of these promises uncertain, and the possibility of making the security forces inclusive through group recruitments from 'externalised' communities such as Madhesis has been closed. In this manner, the assertion that the new constitution is regressive in comparison to the interim statute is perhaps correct.

Little wonder, most Madhesi politicos and activists have refused to own it. Even lawmakers from ruling party representing constituencies in Terai-Madhesh signed on the dotted lines due to party whips but complain bitterly about it in private – fueling protests on the ground.

This is where New Delhi comes into the picture. Several times in the past, Indian interlocutors have acted as agents of pacification to cool down protests in Terai-Madhes with third-party guarantees of agreements signed with the government. India is now discovering that its role is no longer recognised, let alone valued. This has further complicated the constitutional wrangle. Perhaps it will take a while for everyone to realize that such pointless contests end up harming everyone in the end. Meanwhile, the unrest in Madhes continues unabated as the ruling regime rejoices in Kathmandu over its success in promulgating a contested constitution.

CRAFTING A CONSTITUTION FOR NEPAL - AND THE ROLE OF INDIA

In Nepal, there are hurdles to the constitution drafting that have to be resolved urgently if the radical leftists and the royalist right are not to blow away hard-won freedoms. As a player in Nepal politics, the best support India can provide is by staying outside the convention of constitution writing

Nepal is trying to write a constitution for the second time, after the first Constituent Assembly (CA) of four years collapsed in May 2012. The entire polity and economy of the country have suffered a state of suspension since 2006, when the People's Movement and the end of the decade-long internal conflict promised peace and prosperity.

For a land richly endowed by nature, Nepal's lot has been poverty and marginalisation since the unification two-and-half centuries ago down to the present, through oligarchy, monarchy, and obstinately unstable democracy. The ongoing attempt is to erect the newborn republic on a strong foundation of pluralism and representative politics, and make Nepal an exemplary democracy of South Asia, which its size and sensibility allow.

But these are precarious days. There are hurdles to the constitution drafting that have to be resolved urgently if the radical leftists and the royalist (Hindutva) right are not to rear up and blow away hard-won freedoms. India has been a player on the complex Nepal chessboard, recently leaning towards micromanagement of internal affairs, and the best support it can provide is staying outside the *laxman rekha* of constitution writing.

Passionate discourse

There are three main pending issues before the second CA, more or less the same ones that brought down the earlier one — secularism, electoral process and definition of federalism. On secularism, there is a rising undercurrent to redefine Nepal as a Hindu state, and a whole phalanx has taken energy from the Bharatiya Janata Party's electoral success in India However, such a definition would be incompatible with the range and layers of Hindu belief and practice in Nepal, plus the fact that 20 per cent of the population is non-Hindu.

The term "secularism", on the other hand, is imported from the Indian Constitution (as amended) and, translated as "*dharma nirpekchhata*", carries an exclusionary denotation that rankles many. All else remaining the same, the framers can probably agree on declaring Nepal "*dharma bahool*" (with religious pluralism) or do away with mention of religion altogether, to respect all and injure none.

On the electoral scheme, the tussle is between those favouring the first-past-the post system for effective governance and others who maintain that only proportional representation can reflect Nepal's diversity of marginalised communities. The effort is on to find the acceptable proportional-to-direct elections ratio, and a compromise will probably be reached between half-half and 70:30.

It is the demarcation of federal provinces that has the hackles up on all sides, and it is here that communal passions could flare up, particularly on the hill-and-plain dimension. The resulting polarisation would set the country back by another decade, and impact variously the neighbouring States of India as well.

Demarcation debate

Nepal was officially declared a federal democratic republic in 2008, but the debate on federalism has yet to mature to the level of allowing demarcation. There is a bewildering web of positions and demands that the CA has failed to address; some have not even made it to the table.

At its core, the argument is between those who believe (as does this writer) that provincial division should follow the logic of economic geography, to bring prosperity to all communities in a country of mixed habitation, and especially those of the plains where there is a disproportionate volume and density of poverty. Others argue forcefully for demarcation by identity, to make up for historical wrongs committed by the Kathmandu-centric state. The heightened rancour of today has mainly to do with the parcelling of the Terai, with the Madhesi Morcha combine of parties seeking exclusive plains-only province or provinces.

In the CA, the Nepali Congress (NC) and the Communist Party of Nepal (Unified-Marxist-Leninist)-UML can come up with the two-thirds majority required for promulgation. However, they have not been able to generate momentum for constitution drafting, laid low by the lacklustre performance of their coalition government. More importantly, the two parties have not been able to effectively counter the position of the Maoist-Madhesi Morcha, which is that the November 2013 election results ("*mataadhesh*") do not reflect the people's will ("*janaadhesh*"), an argument that is anti-political as much as it is anti-people.

Truth be told, the roadblock to constitution writing is not on the matter of principle, but the political careers of a dozen or so senior opposition leaders. In the case of both Maoist Chairman Pushpa Kamal Dahal ('Prachanda') and senior leader Baburam Bhattarai, their instigation of the 'people's war', the stonewalling on accountability for war crimes, as well as the economic devastation wrought by their party's actions make them fearful of the future.

Seeking collapse

Mr. Dahal is pursued by several personal demons — the possibility of investigation into alleged loot of the exchequer, international jurisdiction for conflict era crimes, and the collapse of his ambitions of emerging as directly elected president. Mr. Bhattarai, for his part, has remained deputy to Mr. Dahal for too long and is desperate to get the party chairmanship. He recently visited New Delhi in early March hoping to reinforce his known image of being "India-friendly" for political advantage back home.

Both leaders suffer under the knowledge that there is another two-and-half years remaining in the life of the second CA (also serving as Parliament). Meanwhile, the Supreme Court has just confirmed that grave human rights abuse of the conflict era must undergo criminal procedure, striking at the heart of the political aspirations of Mr. Dahal and Mr. Bhattarai. Under the circumstances, without a plan at hand, the Maoist leaders would like to foment political chaos hoping that something, somewhere will collapse to their advantage.

Others who lost badly in the 2013 elections were the stalwarts of the Madhesi Morcha, when the Terai (the plains) voters opted for the NC, the UML and the Hindutva-oriented Rastriya Prajatantra Party (Nepali) party of Kamal Thapa. And yet the Madhesi Morcha's line against Kathmandu's "*pahadiya*" (hill-dweller) elites resonates among the restless Madhesi youth, giving it traction.

While the sense of alienation provides a level of unity against Kathmandu, however, the plains are not as homogeneous as the Morcha leaders (mostly from the east-central belt of the Terai) would like to suggest. Beyond the division by language (Awadhi, Maithili, Bhojpuri, etc), there are many permutations of identity among the citizens of plains origin, with cross-cutting layers including the Madhesi (incorporating the Dalits from the plains as the most marginalised nationally), Muslim, Tharu and other plains ethnicities, as well as a significant number of *pahadiyas*.

The demography of the plains is thus rather intricate, and it would be unwise to concede on any proposed federal arrangement out of sheer exasperation, whether identity-based or on economic geography. We need a way to hold off on a decision, to allow a more considered approach in which the protagonists do not talk past each other. Simultaneously, it is vital to satisfy the Madhesi and ethnic activists that the deferral of decision on federalism does not at all mean abandoning it.

The India hand

By some believable accounts, the plains-specific province(s) idea was thought up by Indian diplomats and intelligence operatives, with the Madhesi Morcha leaders made to carry the burden as a kind of ideology. If the plan is to create a geopolitical buffer for India astride the open border, that itself is objectionable for seeking to render the Terai plains and its Nepali citizens as some kind of bulwark for India.

With the arrival of the Narendra Modi-led government in New Delhi, there seems to be second thoughts, at least in some quarters, about the viability of the proposed plains-specific provinces. Some strategists in India are now wondering whether this prescription is not geopolitically fraught, with dangers of making Nepal a stomping ground for international adventurism.

From this writer's perspective, however, the most important concern is that nothing should be done to further impoverish the Terai population, the likely result of a plains-only province when the concentration of investment in the coming years is likely to be in the hills.

Last week, the Maoists and Madhesi Morcha, unlikely collaborators, announced agitations against the attempt by the NC-UML to take forward the proper procedure of constitution drafting, leading ultimately to a vote on provisions. The upcoming protests could well lead to a collapse of the second CA, and the people's opportunity to write their own constitution wrested by the very leaders who claim to have birthed the idea of both the Constituent Assembly and federalism.

The best option for now is to promulgate a constitution that confirms a democratic, federal, non-denominational Republic of Nepal, while leaving the matter of federal arrangement to parliament or to a credible, high-level commission. If the country finds itself without a constitution after eight years of trying, the politicians and political parties of Kathmandu will be the first to be held accountable. But history will also ask New Delhi about its role in the debacle.

INDIA AND NEPAL: A CONSTITUTIONAL CRISIS?

Very few bilateral ties have seen the kind of personal investment of time, energy and resources by Prime Minister Narendra Modi as the one with Nepal.

The PM made one of his first bilateral visits to India's neighbourhood in August last year to Nepal — within a week of External Affairs Minister Sushma Swarajvisiting Kathmandu.

He returned to Kathmandu in November last year — to attend the SAARC summit — and had a detailed bilateral engagement with the entire spectrum of Nepal's political leadership.

When the earthquake shook Nepal in April this year and the Himalayan country's PM could not be contacted — he was overseas — Modi did not stand on ceremony and called up Nepal's President to offer him unconditional assistance for rescue and relief. Within hours, the Indian disaster management machinery was set in motion to assist Nepal, followed by a joint briefing sometimes with as many as four secretary-rank officials to give an update on the rescue ops.

Nepal's New Constitution Most Progressive But An Open Document : Nepal's Ambassador To India

While, this looked like chest-thumping of sorts which led to criticism of India and its media focusing on only the Indian rescue operations, the alacrity of the response received overwhelming gratitude and kudos from all.

So, when on Sunday, Nepal promulgated its Constitution — ignoring all the advice from the Indian government which had been patiently engaging all top political leaders in Nepal — it came as a huge disappointment to the Modi government. Modi had repeatedly asked the Nepalese political class to be "flexible" and "broad-based" in its approach, and to not bulldoze its way through with the brute strength of a majority.

It has now asked the Nepalese government to make seven changes in its Constitution. New Delhi has put its weight behind the Madhesi and Janjati population which it says has been ignored and whose aspirations as "equal citizens" have not been fulfilled in the newly-promulgated Constitution. The impact of the new Constitution is already being felt in the violence, curfew, protests and loss of lives in the last few weeks.

With an apparent stand-off on the issue between the two countries, much will now depend on the sagacity and wisdom of the top Nepal's political parties. While some argue that the current Indian attitude will only harden anti-Indian sentiments and make it closer to China, Nepal's geography and history point to India's major role in the development of Nepal.

The Indian establishment too must remain calm and patient at this hour, since dictating terms will only worsen the situation. It has to move in quickly and quash fears of "blockade" or "recall of ambassador" and other such rumours doing the rounds in Kathmandu for the last few days.

Both sides need to give each other political space so that the current deadlock is resolved.

POST-CONSTITUTION SHIVERS IN NEPAL AND INDIA'S RESPONSE

After seven years of debate and discussion to iron out differences among various political parties, the Constituent Assembly (CA) of Nepal promulgated the new Constitution on September 20. There was a grand celebration in and around Kathmandu immediately after the country's president signed the draft. However, more than half the population, especially the Janajatis, the people living in the Terai region, *Dalits* and women rights groups, opposed the new Constitution.

The Protests

The Terai region witnessed violence protests when the Constitution was promulgated. In fact, the region has been witnessing violent protests since August 9, 2015 and over 46 persons including 10 security personnel have so far been killed in various incidents. According to media reports, around 2,000 Madhesis have taken political asylum in Bihar and Uttar Pradesh and the

Nepal Armed Police has been resorting to excesses to quell the protests. Normal life has been badly hit and many parts of Nepal have been witnessing a shortage of essential goods due to prolonged protests and road blocks by the Samyukt Loktantrik Madhesi Morcha (SLMM), the Tharus and the Janajati groups. As part of the protest, some of the elected members from the Terai region have either resigned from the CA or boycotted the Constitution making process.

The marginalized groups of Nepal – the Madhesis, the Tharus and the Janajatis — argue that the Constitution promulgated by the CA has failed to accommodate their long standing demands. These include: demarcation of provincial boundaries on ethnic lines, establishment of two Madhesh provinces, proportional representation of ethnic groups in State agencies and Parliament, equal political rights to persons to acquire citizenship by naturalisation, and implementation of previous agreements between the State on the one hand and Janajatis and Madhesis on the other. Later, the SLMM has also demanded the withdrawal of the Army from the Terai region as one of the pre-conditions for negotiations. Even after the promulgation of the Constitution by nearly 85 per cent of CA members, the agitating groups are continuing their protests.

According to media reports about 1,000 Madhesi have so far taken political asylum in Sitamarhi and Madhubani districts of Bihar. There were reports that some of them might go underground if the Constitution does not accommodate Madhesi demands. Some reports also indicated that the Madhesi leaders had lost control over the agitators and there was an unforeseen spontaneity in the way the people in the Terai poured out into the streets and went ahead with their protests.

Instead of putting Nepal together, the draft has in fact divided the Nepalese people into two deeply polarised sections — the so-called Pahadis, and the non-Pahadis comprising the Madhesis, the Tharus and the Janajatis.

Initial External Reactions

Despite mixed domestic responses, congratulations have poured in from the International Community. China, the European

Union and Japan were the first to congratulate Nepal immediately after the promulgation of the Constitution. Norway, the United States, the United Kingdom, Russia and the United Nations followed.

India's Cold Response

India neither 'welcomed' nor 'congratulated' Nepal on this occasion. Rather, there was a press release titled "Statement on the situation in Nepal", which stated: "We note the promulgation in Nepal today of a Constitution. We are concerned that the situation in several parts of the country bordering India continues to be violent ...We urge that issues on which there are differences should be resolved through dialogue in an atmosphere free from violence and intimidation, and institutionalized in a manner that would enable broad-based ownership and acceptance."

India's cold response indicated that Nepal's southern and most important neighbour was not happy with the way the Constitution was drafted. India has been following a 'hands-off' policy, i.e., not interfering in the Constitution drafting process and encouraging a 'Nepali grown model' to generate consensus, ever since the process was set in motion in May 2010. However, in the immediate aftermath of the finalisation of Nepal's Constitution and especially with the increase in violence and political asylum seekers entering Indian Territory, India has found itself embroiled in Nepal's domestic issues. As informed observers have noted, Nepal's political leadership has ignored India's concerns and suggestions which have been periodically shared ever since Prime Minister Modi visited Nepal in August 2014. In this backdrop, the Indian reaction appears quite natural because prolonged conflict in Nepal is certainly not in India's interest. Anticipating a Sri Lanka like situation on its northern border and genuinely concerned about the durability of the Constitution which has already become embroiled in controversy, India did not welcome Nepal's new Constitution.

Second, India has felt that it has been let down by Nepal's leadership. Apparently, top Nepalese leaders — including K. P. Oli, Prime Minister Sushil Koirala, P. K. Dahal (Prachanda) and Sher Bahadur Deuba — had, during private meetings with Modi and other senior Indian officials, assured them that the Constitution would be promulgated on the basis of consensus. In fact, India had all along hoped that Nepalese leaders would keep their promise. When that did not happen, it was but natural for the Indian government to feel betrayed.

Thirdly, although many Nepalese commentators linked India's reactions to its traditional support to the Madhesi cause over the years, the aversion of the present government to the word secularism in Nepal's constitution and its apprehensions about the spill-over effect of the Terai violence on the upcoming Bihar elections, the fact of the matter is that the Indian foreign office has been particularly worried about the growing 'united front' among the left political parties of Nepal — especially between the Maoists and the Communists —against India, backed by external powers opposed to Indian influence in Nepal. India had already apprehended such an alignment of forces against it when it was kept in the dark about the 16-point deal signed in June 2015 among the top four political parties.

India had reflexively interpreted this development as a major strategic challenge for it in its Himalayan backyard. Its suspicions were further confirmed when the three-party alliance ignored India's suggestions about preparing a broad-based document by accommodating the demands of the marginalised groups. Even India's suggestions during Foreign Secretary Jaishankar's visit to Nepal on September 18, to delay the Constitution making process by 10 to 15 days and initiate dialogue with the agitating groups, was rejected by the top leaders.

Deepening distrust

Trust deficit and mutual suspicion between India and Nepal have deepened further after India issued its third note on Nepal on September 21, which said: "We are deeply concerned over the incidents of violence... Our freight companies and transporters have also voiced complaints about the difficulties they are facing in movement within Nepal..." This note gave rise to fears in Nepal that India might resort to an economic blockade like it had done earlier in 1988-89. Anti-India elements took full advantage of the growing fear of Indian retribution in Nepal. Most significantly,

India was surprised to see the level of anti-India sentiments posted on Nepalese print, electronic and social media.

The Indian reaction has, in the meanwhile, led to notes of caution by some of the major international actors. China, which had welcomed and congratulated Nepal over the new Constitution, has now suggested to Nepalese leaders that they should make the Constitution broad based so as to accommodate the voices of the marginalised groups. A press briefing by the Chinese foreign office on September 21 stated: "China sincerely hopes that all political parties in Nepal can bear in mind the fundamental interests of their country and the people, address the differences through dialogue and consultation, realize enduring development of the country and bring happiness to the people." The observation by the United States was also along similar lines.

'Caution' is the need of the hour

The present slump in India-Nepal relations could have been avoided had Nepalese leaders adopted caution and pragmatism in their approach. They should not have promised India that they would finalise the Constitution on the basis of 'Consensus' in the first place. Secondly, they could have clarified their position to India before taking the final step of proceeding with a majority decision to promulgate the Constitution, rather than decrying India's role after the promulgation of the Constitution. Moreover, in the face of prolonged protests, the leadership in Nepal has to find a way of bringing the dissenting voices on board, thrash out mutual differences, and initiate necessary revisions in the Constitution to satisfy the groups feeling marginalised by provisions in the constitution. On the Indian side, rather than moving swiftly from its policy of "hands off" to a state of "panic reaction", India has to proactively engage all concerned and ensure that the new Constitution is suitably amended to accommodate the demands of the marginalised groups in Nepal.

HOW INDIA WAS BOTH RIGHT AND WRONG ON NEPAL

As Prime Minister Narendra Modi's special envoy, foreign secretary S Jaishankar delivered a blunt message to Kathmandu's political leadership: He told them India is unhappy about the manner in which they have gone about adopting the country's new Constitution.

India has been concerned that the Constitution is being adopted even as half the country – the Terai region – is paralysed by protests, curfew has been imposed in many parts and the army has had to be called out.

The Nepali political leadership, India feels, has not exercised the flexibility to bring on board all regions and sections of society. This, Delhi fears, could sow the seeds for future instability, right across the open border. Jaishankar pointedly asked Nepal's leaders how they expected India to welcome such a Constitution.

Jaishankar's message has gone unheeded. Nepal's top three political parties are doing little to address concerns of dissenting groups of the Terai region, and are going ahead with the Constitution's promulgation on Sunday.

This throws up important questions. Was India right in taking a public position, even at the cost of inviting a Nepali "nationalist" backlash? Why was it ineffective in getting Nepali leaders to heed its message? And what lies next?

The message of inclusion

Jaishankar's visit was the culmination of a series of Indian public pronouncements on Nepal, underlying all of which was an appeal to the Kathmandu leadership to be inclusive in its approach.

Last year, when Prime Minister Narendra Modi addressed the Constituent Assembly in Kathmandu, he said the Constitution should be such that people from Himal, pahad and Terai can own it. He reiterated this message during a second visit, and categorically gave a call for a consensus-based Constitution.

At the end of August, soon after violence in western Terai, Modi spoke to his Nepal counterpart Sushil Koirala and urged him to find the "widest possible agreement" for the Constitution and initiate dialogue. Last Monday, external affairs minister Sushma Swaraj issued a statement encouraging Nepali leaders to draft a Constitution which was owned by, and accommodated the aspirations of, all regions and sections of Nepali society.

Indian Ambassador Ranjit Rae explained the import of the statement and told Nepali editors that unless concerns of Madhesis and Tharus – two social groups in the Terai agitation for revised federal boundaries, inclusion and political representation – were taken on board, there could be instability. He said India would like Nepali leaders to fulfil their assurances that they would be flexible, for only this could lead to a durable and resilient Constitution.

And on Saturday morning, Jaishankar concluded his visit by noting the completion of the Constitution-making process was meant to be an occasion for "joy and celebration, not agitation and violence".

The message was clear. Pause, negotiate with dissenting forces, make the process inclusive, draw out a wider consensus on the substance of the Constitution and then adopt and promulgate it. If this happened, all of Nepal would celebrate. India then would be happy to join in.

Creating a nation

Make no mistake. What India said was absolutely correct and history will judge it to be the right position.

The need to take all communities on board, all regions into confidence while drafting the Constitution in a staggeringly diverse country like Nepal cannot be over-emphasised. There is overwhelming literature to suggest that while Nepal is an old state, it has never been a nation in the true sense of the term.

The Constitution was meant to bring together its diverse "nationalities" into one common fold: It was to bring the people of pahad and Terai together. In a country bereft of common symbols, the Constitution was to be the defining national document. India instinctively understood this, based on its own democratic constitutional experience.

Delhi was well within its rights to articulate the policy position it did. It was no "interference", if you glance through the history of this special relationship.

As a facilitator of the peace process of which this Constitution is the climax, India could not suddenly wash its hands off developments in Nepal. As the force behind the conduct of the two Constituent Assembly elections in 2008 and 2013, India could feign apathy about the manner in which the Constitution was being adopted.

As a guarantor of a 2008 pact between the Nepal government and Terai forces – when then Prime Minister GP Koirala went out of his way to seek Indian help – it could not turn deaf when one set of signatories complained provisions of the pact on creation of provinces and inclusion were not being implemented.

As a democracy, it could not turn a blind eye to violence and killing of peaceful protestors at its doorstep. As a federal polity, it had to take into account concerns of states like Bihar whose people share close links with Terai and whose legislators had been pushing the Centre to act against state brutality in Terai. As a country sharing an open border, it could not brush aside deep and legitimate strategic interests when it could see clearly the Constitution, far from addressing roots of the past conflict, was creating conditions for deep ethnic polarisation.

And as a neighbour, it could not ignore the fact Kathmandu's political establishment was deliberately stoking "anti-Indianism". The perception was being manufactured that India had instigated the Madhes movement – when this was far from the truth.

Indeed, one of the triggers for the strong message by Jaishankar in his meetings was an article written by Koirala's press advisor in a local daily which was directly critical of India and Modi. This was seen as an open act of hostility straight from the Nepal PMO, and a gross violation of all diplomatic norms. Jaishankar is understood to have flagged the issue strongly with Koirala.

The mixed signals

So when Indian advice was correct, and India was right in delivering it, what went wrong?

It is first important to recognise the limits of any external role.

The balance of power in Nepal is currently in favour of the hill elite-led establishment. With the Maoists turning their back on the agenda of social justice for marginalised and excluded groups, this tilt has become more pronounced. Hill leaders have displayed rare unity in institutionalising a political order which helps consolidate their power. The structural limitation of party-based representative democracy is that even MPs from minority communities toe instructions from party bosses against their conscience for fear of losing their positions – which is why even Terai MPs of bigger forces were reluctant to rebel. Once Kathmandu decided to launch brutal suppression of the movement in the plains, and not listen to domestic dissenting voices, India's space to act shrunk.

But there were two broad problems from Delhi's end – internal divisions which generated mixed signals, and a costly delay in waking up to the crisis.

The immediate Nepal crisis has been brewing for at least 45 days. The parties had drawn up a federal map, which had led to the Terai backlash. The Indian embassy in Kathmandu had consistently warned the headquarters about the possibility of the bigger parties ramming a Constitution through, ignoring Terai concerns, which in turn would lead to unrest and instability. But there was a view within the external affairs ministry that India should stay away, for as long as Delhi got the bilateral cooperation it sought from Kathmandu, there was no reason to alienate the powerful hill-led establishment.

This was a historical view, which underestimated how domestic political developments and bilateral relationship were closely intertwined. The anti-Terai sentiment could very easily spin off into an orchestrated anti-Indian campaign. That is what happened eventually.

It also ignored the fact that the India-Nepal relationship cannot be reduced to a transactional one – a deal here and a deal there may make some mandarins happy but this is too deep and multifaceted a relationship for that to be the sole determinant.

There are also too many freelance political operators who navigate the India-Nepal maze, from mid-level BJP and RSS leaders to businessmen. They go around pretending in Kathmandu to speak for the Indian government, and leaders are quick to lap up what they say if it suits them.

This ended up giving the ruling elite the confidence that it could ram through the document it wanted and a divided India would come around. In fact, Hindustan Times has learnt that one of the top leaders the foreign secretary met told Indian interlocutors that he would be happy to meet all of India's interests on the bilateral front once he became Prime Minister.

This exposes their public pretence of being champions of Nepali "nationalism". But it gives a glimpse into thinking at the top in Nepali polity – that India can be managed with a few sops. This thinking has been encouraged by petty Indian bureaucratic thinking in Delhi.

Too little, too late

By the time the Indian political leadership and the bureaucracy at the highest levels woke up to the crisis, it was too late.

National Security Advisor Ajit Doval spoke to Nepali leaders on September 12 to put off the Constitution vote by a few days and use the time to bring Terai parties on board when voting was scheduled for Sunday. He should have exerted this pressure at least ten days earlier. Swaraj issued a statement late on Monday night – in fact so late that all Indian papers missed it the next morning. This could have come out before the voting process began.

Modi sent his special envoy on Friday, when the vote was over and Constituent Assembly members were signing on to the Constitution. This was a much needed step – and showed that Delhi's political establishment was not comfortable with the manner in which the Constitution was being written. But it should have happened at the beginning of the week. Many Nepali interlocutors told Jaishankar he had come too late.

And even when Delhi woke up, there was a reluctance to use all tools at its disposal.

Top diplomatic sources in Delhi have confirmed that India recently blocked a discussion at the UN Security Council on Nepal. This may have stemmed from the "Nepal is our backyard mindset". But it was counterproductive for it would have helped generate pressure on Kathmandu and the Terai killings would have become subject to international scrutiny. India was reluctant to use the leverage it has with Nepali security institutions and political parties

– for fear of being labelled interventionist. This diffidence is a bit inexplicable. Once it had taken a public position, India should have followed it through with action on all fronts.

India now stares at lose-lose proposition. The Kathmandu establishment is convinced Delhi is behind the Terai unrest and was actively sabotaging the constitution, while the Terai feels India did not invest all its political might in pushing for a fresh constitutional settlement and political deal.

What next?

India is expected to issue a statement on Sunday after the Constitution's promulgation – but while this will note the promulgation, it is unlikely that Delhi will welcome the development.

The triangular dance between Kathmandu, Terai and New Delhi will now determine events.

The gulf between Kathmandu and Terai will only increase in coming weeks and months. As the capital welcomes the Constitution with Diwali-like celebrations, the plains will observe it as a black day. Clashes are expected as ruling parties deploy their foot soldiers to counter protestors. Politically, all of Terai's parties remain outside the process. They are likely to make it clear that they will neither accept this Constitution, nor participate in any of the political processes that take place within the constitutional framework, unless there is a major review. Emboldened with their victory, Kathmandu's leaders will probably turn even more conservative.

The gulf between the two national capitals will also grow. A new government is expected in Kathmandu soon, as a part of a power-sharing deal which drove this Constitution through. This government will probably make overtures to Delhi to soothe ruffled feathers. But India is miffed at the manner in which events have unfolded. And there is little appetite to invest energy in improving the relationship when Nepal has been so obstinate. There is a sense in Delhi that despite Modi's personal investment in the relationship, two visits and an effort to allay Nepali insecurities, the generous support after the earthquake, the blank cheque to Nepali leadership on contentious issues like the 1950 treaty, Kathmandu's leaders neither listen to Indian advice nor do they shy away from the old game of stoking anti-Indian ultra-nationalism. India will turn indifferent to the relationship, at least for a while.

The Terai-India relationship is sensitive. India has a Nepal policy, and not necessarily a Kathmandu policy and Terai policy for Nepal. That is why it was keen to see a harmonious constitutional settlement. But as the gulf between the two parts of Nepali polity increases, the Terai will increasingly look to India for help and support. Constituencies in Bihar will speak up for rights for Madhesis. And India will find it difficult to ignore these voices.

As Nepal promulgates its Constitution, one cannot but regret how an opportunity for defining a new nation was lost. What should have inaugurated a golden period could well be the harbinger of tougher times. India will be watching, as it enters a challenging period in ties with Nepal.

INDIA 'NOT HAPPY' WITH NEPAL'S NEW CONSTITUTION

New Delhi finds itself looked down upon as a villain in Nepal even as the agitation against the constitution, promulgated on 20 September 2015 engulfs the Terai region that borders India. Its fault is that it merely took 'notice' of the draft statute and wished to see some 'flexibility' but the political elite in Nepal, mostly from the hill region, has reacted strongly.

As against India's *"lukewarm"* response, China and Pakistan, the two most hostile neighbours of India, have warmly welcomed the new constitution which has come nearly eight years after the end of the monarchy following a long and bloody civil war, and after missing several deadlines.

"Stop interfering in Nepal's internal affairs," the Indian critics in Kathmandu have said. The mainstream Nepalese media as well as the social media have gone after the South Block hammer and tongs. No one is willing to concede that India may have some genuine concerns over the new constitution that has served to polarize the people.

Dissatisfaction With the New Constitution

Arrayed against the elite, especially from the hills, are the people from the Terai, called the Madhesis, and the Janjaatis (tribes), and Dalits - all of whom say that the new constitution was unfair to them, downgrading their representation in the decision making process. What it means is that nearly 40 per cent of population is dissatisfied with the new constitution. Of the 22 districts in the plains, 20 are said to be on the boil. One of the contentious issues is denial of citizenship rights to children of a Nepali woman who married a foreigner.

It is natural for India to be disappointed to see Nepal opt for a constitution that rejected inclusiveness. New Delhi had played an important role in ending the more than a decade of Maoist insurgency and then putting the country on track for a monarchy-free democracy. Moreover India has traditionally been a key partner in Nepal's development notwithstanding the penchant of the Palace first and then of the Maoist leadership to play the China card.

Resentment Against India

The reasons behind Nepal's resentment against India are not difficult to fathom. Many in that country have always seen India as the meddlesome Big Brother who likes to take the tiny Himalayan country for granted. The tribe of the anti-India Nepalese has risen a great deal ever since the Chinese paid full attention to Kathmandu, and see its potential to create trouble for India.

What is of immediate concern is the fact that much of the trouble in Nepal is taking place close to the Indian province of Bihar which is about to face its own battle of the ballot, a situation fraught with law and order problems. India shares more than 1700 km of open border with Nepal which is notoriously used by smugglers, traffickers and Pakistan-trained terrorists to enter India in large numbers.

Many Things Blamed on India

Indian transporters are said to be reluctant to enter Nepal owing to the strife there, especially in the areas close to the borders. Any hardship that it may cause to the Nepalese will be, of course, blamed on India.

Sections of Nepalese leaders are not impressed by whatever India does to help their country, one of the poorest in the world, to develop into a modern nation. Recently when Nepal was hit by a severe earthquake that took a heavy toll of human lives, India was the first country to rush with help and succour. That failed to please a vocal section of Nepalese elite; and they went to the town alleging that it was done to get favourable notice.

Barring the troublesome duo of Pakistan and China, India under Prime Minister Narendra Modi is enjoying good relations with most foreign governments. As of now Nepal is certainly not among the countries where Indian diplomacy has worked well. Modi sent foreign secretary S. Jaishankar as his special envoy to Kathmandu in the hope that he would be able to persuade the Nepalese leaders to take everybody on board before the constitution was adopted by the Interim Parliament.

Jaishankar met Nepali leaders when the new statute had almost crossed the last lap. Yes, he could have visited Kathmandu a little earlier but it is possible that the Indian leadership did not feel the necessity. When Modi was in Kathmandu for the SAARC summit in November 2014, he made the Indian stance clear.

"Outstanding differences (amongst the Nepali parties) should be resolved through dialogue, and widespread consultation so that it could create the basis of a united, peaceful, stable and prosperous Nepal," he told the Nepalese media.

New Delhi voiced the same view after the constitution was promulgated as well. *"Contentious issues should be resolved through dialogue in an atmosphere free from violence and intimidation, and in an institutionalized manner that would enable broad-based ownership and acceptance. This would lay the foundation of harmony, progress and development in Nepal,"* the Indian Foreign Office said extending *"our best wishes to the people of Nepal."*

Turn of events show that voices of reason have to come to prevail in Kathmandu. As of September 25, the Nepal Government has agreed to hold *"decisive"* talks with parties agitating over the new Constitution. It also has agreed to *"withdraw"* the army from the violence-hit Terai region bordering India, which is one of the major pre-conditions for talks set by the protesting groups notably

Madhesi Peoples Rights Forum-Democratic led by Bijaya Kumar Gachhadar and Tharuwan Struggle Committee.

Three major political parties - Nepali Congress, CPN-UML and UCPN (Maoist) are parties to the initiative of Prime Minister Sushil Koirala to break the new logjam. Forest Minister Mahesh Acharya will be the government's interlocutor with leaders of protesting groups. War time British Prime Minister Winston Churchill used to say that there is a solution to any problem; Nepal's own experience shows that dialogue helps to cool tempers and to arrive at some consensus. In this sense, the Nepal government can be said to have hit the right buttons.

India: Next Step

What India should do? It should encourage the new dialogue. And continue what it is doing now namely holding Nepali sovereignty as paramount, and underscoring the unique relationship the two countries share.

Nepalese ambassador to India, Deep Upadhayay has told Times of India, *"India has not prescribed any changes in the Nepali constitution."* This policy must continue.

And as Shiv Shankar Mukherjee, India's former ambassador to Nepal (2004-2008) said in a recent newspaper opinion piece, India should ignore *"the fulminations of armchair analysts, and parachute pundits."*

Instead New Delhi should *"continue engaging with leaders on both sides."* Because political stability is sine qua non for Nepal's march towards development.

Nepal is a *"youthful"* country with more than 25 per cent of the population below 25-years of age. For them Nepali nationalism is not anti-Indianism nor is India a favourite punching bag since six to eighty lakh Nepalis live and work in India; yes, they don't want to be short changed and this concern of theirs can be addressed not in street corner protests but across the table in the spirit of understanding.

On its part, India must remain conscious of its unique relationship with Nepal. It is not a villain but a true friend who always stands by its Himalayan neighbour with its open borders.

NEPAL CONSTITUTION CRISIS: INDIA LOST PRECIOUS TIME DURING DRAFTING

There used to be a time when one heard a phrase that was often cited in conversations in Kathmandu. It described Nepal as a yam plant caught between two rocks. The rocks in question were India and China. These days, they do not talk about the two rocks anymore. Instead, they speak about one hard place that is currently proving too hard to handle. That hard place, in the eyes of many Nepalese, is their big neighbour to the south.

Despite Prime Minister Modi's energetic attempts to reach out to India's immediate neighbours, one place where that policy appears to be coming unstuck is here. The sharp deterioration in relations between New Delhi and Kathmandu in recent weeks tells one something about the sloppy manner in which New Delhi has handled the relationship.

The point at issue is about the Madhesis' grievances regarding the new constitutional dispensation. The Madhesis are Indian origin Nepalese who inhabit the Himalayan foothills, commonly known as 'terai'. The new Constitution— while seeking to turn Nepal into a secular democratic Republic— does not adequately address the concerns of the Madhesis. There is some merit in what these people are saying. It is just the manner in which New Delhi has chosen to handle it that has given rise to tensions in the relationship.

The distrust with which Madhesis have been traditionally viewed by the Valley Nepalese has a history of its own. Sometimes even their nationalism is questioned. One has heard, for example, senior Nepalese politicians in Kathmandu citing the Madhesis' *dhoti-kurta* dress as proof of their not being Nepali enough. It is equally true that these people of the terai look towards India—much like the Tamils in Sri Lanka—as protector of their interests.

Understandably, New Delhi has been concerned enough to convey the Madhesis' feelings regarding the new Constitution to the Nepalese leaders. Equally, it was important to impress upon the Nepalese leaders the need to build a national consensus so that everybody was on board in a pluralistic polity that Nepal was trying to be. This should have been done while the draft constitution was still under preparation. It would have taken some quiet and efficient diplomacy to make that point without ruffling any feathers.

Instead, the high profile visit of Foreign Secretary Jai Shankar as the Prime Minister's special envoy to Kathmandu did not achieve that end. Moreover, it was a bit late for any course correction. Even assuming that the Nepalese leaders had wanted to accommodate the Indian viewpoint, they would have been open to the charge of acting under foreign pressure.

No student of Indo-Nepalese relations can be unaware of the fact that there are huge Nepalese sensitivities regarding its big neighbour to the south. Equally, there are enough India-baiters in Kathmandu who would pounce upon any opportunity to show India in a poor light. That is exactly what has happened. Today, Madhesis are agitating, and supply lines to the north have been blocked by the agitators. And yet, India is getting the blame for forcing an economic blockade on her land-locked Himalayan neighbour. Whipping up the anti-India sentiment, telecast of 42 Indian TV channels has been blocked in Nepal in retaliation to the imagined economic blockade.

The pity is that it is not for any lack of goodwill on India's part that the relations have been dipping so low. It is just the shoddy manner of conducting the diplomatic discourse that has landed New Delhi's relations with her Himalayan neighbour in the current mess.

The situation is somewhat reminiscent of an earlier experience of similarly hamhanded handling of India's relations with Sri Lanka. In Sri Lanka then—as Nepal now—public opinion was sharply polarised. India sought to ensure Sri Lanka's territorial unity and integrity by proposing that the Tamil aspirations be accommodated through a scheme of devolution. This was seen as bias favouring the Tamils by the majority Sinhalese in that country.

Similarly in Nepal, India has been trying to ensure that the Madhesis concerns are addressed in Nepal's own long-term interest. It is easily understood that when domestic opinion is polarised—in Nepal now as in Sri Lanka earlier—it takes a lot of diplomatic tact and circumspection to handle the situation. That apparently has not happened in the instant case. Today, armed commandoes have to guard the Indian Embassy in Kathmandu as Black Cats used to protect the Indian High Commission in Colombo. Obviously, there is something amiss about New Delhi's way of handling the situation. Do our South Block mandarins need to be reminded that in international relations one is judged by the results, and not by intents?

CHINA BACKS NEPAL ON CONSTITUTION AMID INDIA CONCERN

In recent years, China has become the biggest source of foreign direct investment in Nepal, overtaking India.

In comments that will ease the pressure on Kathmandu amid concerns from New Delhi on the process, the Chinese Foreign Ministry called on "all political factions" in Nepal to "bear in mind fundamental interests of the country and people", suggesting that all groups should come together behind the government.

New Delhi had in a strongly-worded statement on Sunday said it was "concerned that the situation in several parts of the country bordering India continues to be violent".

In contrast, Chinese Foreign Ministry spokesperson Hong Lei in a positively-worded statement said "China sincerely congratulates Nepal on promulgating the new constitution". "It is hoped that Nepal will seize the opportunity to realise national unity, stability and development," he said at a regular press briefing on Monday.

Hong said China would continue providing economic support to Nepal. In recent years, China has become the biggest source of foreign direct investment, overtaking India. "China values its relations with Nepal," he said, "and is willing to further deepen mutually beneficial cooperation, and provide assistance to economic and social development of Nepal as our capacity allows."

With reports of violence amid concerns, especially in the Terai region, that the constitution did not adequately represent all groups, the Ministry of External Affairs in New Delhi had in its statement called for dialogue in an atmosphere "free from violence and intimidation".

Beijing, however, suggested that for now at least, groups should keep in mind the "fundamental interests" of the country. Asked how it viewed the concerns expressed by some groups and reports of violence, the Foreign Ministry said, "China sincerely hopes that all political factions in Nepal will bear in mind fundamental interests of the country and people, resolve relevant differences through dialogue and consultation, realise enduring development of the country, as well as happiness of the people."

CHINA FACTOR IN NEPAL CONSTITUTION CRISIS CANNOT BE IGNORED

The Constituent Assembly of Nepal delivered a new Constitution on 20 September this year, the eighth Constitution since 1948. It comes after seven years of heartburns, intransigence and delays, primarily owing to the Maoists. If the birth pangs are any indicator, the endurance of this Constitution is debatable. Half of Nepal is unhappy and in the throes of violence. The Terai — or the plains of Nepal, home to nearly 50% of the population — has witnessed more than 40 killings.

The Constitution has provoked the Terai (plains)-Pahari (hill) divide to new levels. The consequent instability is impacting India and, not in the least, China. The two countries share 1,751 kilometres and 1,414 kilometres of boundary with Nepal, respectively. Not only the people of Nepal are split over the Constitution on demographic lines, the document has divided the country into pro-India and pro-China segments.

The Chinese took unprecedented interest in influencing the framing of the document. In August, even as the Constituent Assembly was debating the new Constitution, very senior ministers from China including Foreign Minister Wang Yi visited Nepal. The other dignitaries, who visited in the same period, were Vice-Minister Chen Fengxiang and Assistant Minister Dou Enyong. The Chinese weight on Constitution making in Nepal became very evident in March, when the Maoist leader Prachanda was invited by China. Prachanda was reportedly asked by the Chinese authorities to back the Constitution. On 26 September, the former Prime Minister of Nepal, and one of the founders of the Maoist party UCPN (Maoist), Baburam Bhattarai resigned over his concern for Madhesis. He not only quit Parliament but also resigned from the primary membership of the party. Bhattarai was, however, chased out in Janakpur by a Madhesi crowd when he refused to burn a copy of the Constitution.

Bhattarai's resignation can have several motives and interpretations. In the Chinese scheme of geopolitical strategy, it is not uncommon to leverage on a target country through various unsuspecting machinations. The Maoists and the CPN(UML) are two distinct and unabashed Chinese leverages in Nepal. The 1962 India-China War served as a fillip to the communists and anti-India forces in Nepal, who began opposing the presence of the Indian Military Liaison Group (IMLG). The IMLG was eventually withdrawn in 1970.

It is rather confounding that the Maoists, who were comprehensively defeated and relegated to the third place in the Constituent Assembly elections in 2013, should have found such a disproportionate voice towards the end of the Constitution making process. All through they held the CA hostage with their intransigence over "unanimity".

Some subterranean leverages were also created and activated by China to ensure the promulgation of the Constitution, despite deep reservations of not only India, but also the President of Nepal. These leverages extended to the Nepali Congress as well. There have been reports to suggest that large sums of Chinese money, ostensibly meant for rehabilitation and relief of earthquake victims were diverted to political parties and personalities. Morally, in the formulation of a sacred document like the Constitution, the members of the Constituent Assembly should be allowed to vote as per the conscience, but tragically, political parties resorted to "whips". Such was the level of intimidation and inducement that out of 598 members, 507 voted "for", and 65 abstained. The 25 members of the pro-Hindu Rashtra party, the Rashtriya Prajatantrik Party voted "against" and most Madhesh based parties boycotted.

India's immediate reach-out to Nepal during the earthquake in April this year was lauded the world over for its promptness and scale. Nepal Prime Minister Sushil Koirala had said: "We are really blessed to have a neighbour like India." The Maoists, however, resented India's popularity and launched a vicious defamation campaign at the behest of China. In those days, a photograph in which Prachanda was seen addressing a rally in the backdrop a banner, "Indian Relief a Threat to Nepal", went viral. This was at a time when the tragedy in Nepal had cost 9,000 lives. Prachanda indeed is inured to such tragedies. After all, he perpetrated a decade long insurgency in Nepal, which claimed 16,000 lives.

The Maoist leadership, it may be mentioned, was protesting against the proposed federal structure and was championing the cause of dividing Nepal in deference to various ethnicities or janjatis, i.e. Rai, Magar, Limbu, Newars, Gurungs, etc. This had the backing of some Western countries, particularly Scandinavian, impelled by the agenda of religious conversion. These countries, with the conversion agenda, have been sympathetic and supportive to the Maoists in Asia. It is engendered by the simple reason that the societal and religious unsettling process unleashed by the Maoists, creates a favourable environment for religious conversions. The phenomenon impacts India as well. Both China and the Western world were, therefore against the continuation of Hindu status of Nepal, constitutionally. Nevertheless, China, as India, was against too many federal units in Nepal, as it felt that it would lead to destabilisation and impact adversely on the security environment in Tibet.

Further, to further tighten its stranglehold on Nepal's polity, China has been on an overdrive, espousing the candidature of the Communist Party of Nepal (Unified Marxist-Leninist) chief, K.P. Oli for Prime Minister.

India did send its envoy, S. Jaishankar to Nepal, to prevail on it for the postponement of promulgation of the Constitution till the Madhesis and the Tharus, who constitute 70% of the Terai population, came onboard and the document had broad-based ownership. It was too late. The vote in the Constituent Assembly by then had been cast, and the major political parties were determined in their intention, override Indian concerns. Also, last minute efforts in this regard by the Indian ambassador in Nepal, Ranjit Rae were spurned.

It is no secret, therefore, that on the chessboard of geopolitics, the first round has gone to China. Complicit in this geopolitical victory of China are the Chinese leverages in India as well. It began during the period of the last UPA dispensation, which had outsourced India's Nepal policy to the leftists. An Indian university dominated by leftists and supporters of the Maoists played no mean role. This university serves as the bridge between the Maoists in India and Nepal. Together, these forces ensured that the historical binding force of Nepal's nationhood, i.e., Hindu moorings, was done away with, even in the absence of a whimper of demand to that effect. This was one of the first things done by the Maoist regime on assumption of power in Nepal. In the same vein, the new Constitution of Nepal has declared Nepal a "secular" state. After much protest and pressure, it has made a small concession in this regard, in that it later included "preservation of dharma sanskriti (religion and culture that has been in existence for generations)". Those opposing the abandonment of Nepal's "Hindu" status are convinced that the term "secularism" in the preamble has been introduced at the behest of China, the Communists and the Church. Some argue that this move has an inherent anti-India bias or even disdain for India.

Compared to China, India has far greater security stakes in the type of federal structure in Nepal. Nepal's border with China is forbidding due to altitude and in-hospitability. On the other hand, the India-Nepal boundary has been a nagging concern for India, serving as a facilitator for terrorists, smugglers, human traffickers and elements inimical to India. Even the Maoist leaders of Nepal in their decade-long insurgency slipped in and out of India at will, notwithstanding Prachanda's hostility towards India. In his underground avatar, he had said in an interview, that he was convinced that one day he will have to fight the Indian Army. Yet, in deference to Nepal's sensitivities — and given the religious, social and cultural bonds — the contemplation of militarising the border has been a revolting proposition for India.

It is a geopolitical truism, by virtue of India's long border, majorly in the plains, the densest demography of Nepal — almost 50% of the population — impacts India. Dense populations pose a variety of security challenges and their destabilisation can cause nightmares to neighbouring countries, as did the East Pakistan crisis. It is, therefore, of critical interest to India that fewer provinces of Nepal have geographical, demographic and security interface. Nepal's Constitution-makers have but done the opposite. The seven provinces have been carved out to cause India's marginalisation in its interface with Nepal and at the same time ensuring advantage to China. The delineation rewards the hill people and perpetuates their domination of politics in the country. Out of the 165 seats in Parliament, the hill and mountain people would have monopoly over 100, while the Terai would be represented by only 65 seats despite having 50% of the population. Only one province, comprising eight districts, has been constituted into a province. The rest 14 districts have been joined with the hill districts, which, in effect, reduce them to a minority.

Although the President, the Vice President and Deputy Prime Minister are from Terai, they had no say in the drafting process. Cleverly, the Constitution was hijacked by the Koirala-Oli-Prachanda combine.

It is also a geopolitical truism that India, due to its geographical interface with Terai, holds the lifeline to a land-locked Nepal. China, with all its infrastructure growth in Tibet, cannot supplant this lifeline on any enduring basis. The Madhesis in Nepal have economically crippled Terai and consequently rest of the country. Nepal, as a substitute, has urged China to open two trade routes, i.e., Barbise-Tatopani-Khasa and Nuwakot-Rasuaghadi-Kerung. These have been out of operation since the earthquake.

The disruption in the lifeline is not on account of India, but because of a blockade by a segment of the Nepalese people of Terai. For Nepal's dispensation, it is no gain blaming India. It is also no gain whipping up "anti-India" sentiments. In the past, this discourse has been mischievously used by pro-China forces in Kathmandu and Delhi to put India on the defensive. The bluff this time must be called. In the worst case scenario, even if 50% of Nepal's population gets anti-India, the remaining half will still be with India. It would still be a reckonable percentage to negate Chinese machinations in Nepal.

Nepal is at an epoch-making juncture. India cannot allow a new Nepal to dilute its sub-continental moorings and fall prey to

Chinese machinations. Our sanctimonious religious and social connect to Nepal has to be reclaimed from China-inspired anti-India forces in Nepal. Indian security interests cannot be sacrificed for the sake of a Constitution prepared through less than transparent, if not subverted, process.

INDIA'S NEPAL POLICY NEEDS CAUTION, NOT GRANDSTANDING

India has reacted strongly to Nepal's new constitution. In India's official statements issued on the subject, the promulgation of the new Constitution has just been "noted", not welcomed. Concern has been expressed over the disturbed situation in the Terai region that borders India. Nepal has been urged to resolve differences "through dialogue in an atmosphere free from violence and intimidation" so as to "enable broad-based ownership and acceptance". India's ambassador in Kathmandu spoke to Nepal's Prime Minister about the difficulties being faced by India's "freight companies and transporters" in "movements within Nepal" due to prevailing unrest. This may, if allowed to persist, result in essential supplies from India to Nepal getting disrupted.

The statements and the underlying warning on the issue of supplies have brought a sudden low in the bilateral relationship which had received a boost after Prime Minister Narendra Modi's first visit to Nepal in 2014.

In some ways, the situation is reminiscent of 1989, when King Birendra's decision to import anti-aircraft guns from China and refuse to reform the Panchayat system in the face of the democratic movement precipitated tensions in India-Nepal bilateral relations. At the same time, the India-Nepal trade treaty lapsed and the Rajiv Gandhi government closed down the special entry points for trade and transit – resulting in the severe shortage of essential supplies in Nepal.

India's objections

India has its reasons to be upset with the way Nepali leaders have gone about the constitution-making process Three of them are obvious and openly stated. First, the constitution as promulgated is not inclusive. It ignores the aspirations and sensitivities of the Madhesis, the janjatis (tribal groups), dalits and women. This is contrary to the spirit of the Jan Andolan-II that created a vision of New Nepal and against the assurances given by the late Girija Prasad Koirala as Prime Minister in 2007 during the Madhes agitation. Janjatis and women had also been repeatedly assured that their concerns would be accommodated. Then, the manner in which the promulgation was effected is clearly in conflict with the principle of consensus adopted in Nepal's interim Constitution. The leaders of the major political parties belonging to the dominant hill social groups have ignored the wishes of the marginalised groups in the new constitution. The marginalised groups are accordingly agitating against the bulldozing of the constitutional process. The use of force by the government to suppress the agitation has resulted in the loss of more than 40 lives, with many more injured. Life has come to a standstill in nearly 20 of the 22 Terai districts of Nepal. There are also agitations in Kathmandu which have been joined by monarchists, Hindutva forces and extremist Maoist splinter groups.

The second reason for India's reaction is that the violence in the Terai region can spill over into the bordering Indian areas. Particulalrly sensitive in this respect is Bihar, which is in the midst of a crucial electoral process. The ruling BJP has very high stakes in the Bihar elections and fears that violence and instability in the Nepal Terai will help its opponents led by Nitish Kumar, Lalu Prasad and the Congress party. It is feared in New Delhi that if the conflict between the Kathmandu authorities and the marginalised groups, particularly the Terai people, is not resolved amicably soon, the persisting turbulence will continue to adversely affect India's bordering region.

The third and most important factor behind New Delhi's displeasure arises from the Modi government's feeling of being ignored in the constitutional process. India had been encouraging Nepali leaders to draft an inclusive and democratic constitution. In his address to the Constituent Assembly in August 2014, Modi had hoped that Nepal's new constitution would be like a bouquet of flowers representing the different shades of Nepal's communities, regions and opinions – and reflecting a broad national consensus. His address had been universally acclaimed in Nepal. He underlined the same theme during his second visit to Kathmadu during the SAARC summit in November last year. He has also done his best to lift Indo-Nepal relations by trying to fulfil pending Indian promises and committing India's support and help in Nepal's development. During the earthquake in Nepal, India went out of its way in extending all possible support. The Nepali leaders, have, however, been unresponsive to Indian concerns regarding the constitutional process.

Modi ignored

Some prominent Nepali leaders like Sher Bahadur Deuba of the Nepali Congress, Madhav Nepal of the Communist Party of Nepal–United Marxist Leninist (UML) and Prachanda of the United Communist Party of Nepal – Maoists, were invited for consultations to New Delhi to make them appreciate India's concerns. All of them endorsed these concerns and assured India that marginalised groups would be accommodated. But there were no signs of this being done as the process started moving towards conclusion.

Barely a week before the promulgation of the constitution, External Affairs minister Sushma Swaraj in a statement on September 14, 2015, recalled "the encouraging voices... from Nepalese leaders" that "the Constitution will carry along all regions and sections".She expressed India's concern "over the ongoing protests and strife in several parts of Nepal" and urged "continuing flexibility on the part of all the political forces so that all outstanding issues are addressed through dialogue and widest possible agreement, in an atmosphere free from violence".

Not only did this not make any difference to the situation in Nepal and the direction of the constitution making process, but instead India was blamed for inciting violence in the Terai and interfering in Nepal's internal affairs. Prime Minister Sushil Koirala's press adviser wrote an article in a Nepali newspaper asking India to desist from such interference.

Finally, the Nepal Constituent Assembly adopted the constitution on September 17, by voting for its remaining clauses but without any accommodation towards the demands of the marginalised groups and India's appeals. This led Prime Minister Modi to send a special envoy, Foreign Secretary S. Jaishankar to see if any last minute effort could be made to redress the situation, but in vain. Therefore, the Indian establishment has felt frustrated and dismayed.

Where India went wrong

The Modi government's frustration with Nepal's constitutional process seems to have been fuelled further by two other factors that have not been publicly and officially expressed.

One is that sections of the ruling party, particularly the Hindutva forces were keen to make Nepal a Hindu state and possibly create space for the future reinstatement of the monarchy. Considerable effort and material support had been extended to Nepali monarchists and Hindutva forces to mobilise support and raise their voices in this regard by the concerned political sections of the ruling party. Nepal's new constitution has only accommodated them to the extent of making the cow a national animal, discouraging cow slaughter and adding a definition of "secularism" that covers respect and protection of all religion, including Hinduism. Second, India feels that the Nepal's major parties have been more accommodative in the constitutional process towards the lobbying efforts of China and the European Union on issues of religion and federalism than to India's concerns.

Notwithstanding the attitude of the dominant social groups which have driven the process of Nepali constitution making, New Delhi ought to have bee cautious and cool in its reactions. It should have welcomed Nepal's first Republican and democratic constitution worked out by popularly elected representatives. This was the promise made by India way back in 1951, when the anarchical Rana system was being transformed, initiating a process of democratisation. India should also realise that the fragmented Terai leadership was unable to throw its proportionate weight in the constitutional process. Many of the Madhesi, janajati and women members of the Constituent Assembly have also voted for the new constitution – though under the pressure of their political bosses.

The new constitution has sharply polarised Nepal along ethnic and regional lines. This polarisation will keep Nepal unstable and turbulent, which is not at all in India's long term interests. To jump into such a polarisation by taking sides is neither a prudent policy or effective diplomacy. India's effort should have been to nudge both sides of the polarised debate through quiet and sustained diplomacy so that an amicable resolution was found. Instead, India's policy unfolded in three different stages within the broad parameters of Prime Minister Modi's Constituent Assembly address in Nepal last year. These stages have moved from being (i) "hands off", to (ii) "having a Constitution is better than no constitution at all" and finally (iii) insistence on specific issues.

India could not sensitise itself adequately to understand the internal dynamics of posturing and power-sharing within and between Nepali political parties, so as to move them in the desired direction. This failure has now landed India in the company of monarchists, Hindu fanatics and left extremists (break away radical Maoists) within the Nepali political spectrum. Some of these disruptionist forces are joining marginalised groups in burning copies of the new constitution and creating turmoil in Nepal. They are exploiting the situation to their advantage at the cost of India. There is need for India to approach the issues involved coolly and carefully so as to get justice for the marginalised groups – rather than reinforcing the already existing forces of anti-Indian pseudo-nationalism in Nepal.

NEPAL'S CONSTITUTIONAL CRISIS: THE FIRST STAGE OF A CHINESE-INDIAN COLD WAR?

The relatively obscure and media neglected topic of Nepal's growing constitutional crisis has the very real possibility of transforming into a larger proxy confrontation between China and India. Neither state stands to gain by falling into this strategic trap, but as their mutual neighbor's destabilization only intensifies, and each Asian giant finds themselves increasingly supporting opposing sides, it might just take another small spark of violence to enflame the country once more in civil war, and with it, bring the continent's two largest countries into a full-blown proxy conflict.

This briefing looks at the recent history behind the latest political crisis in Nepal, and then concisely examines the dichotomies between China and India's approaches to it. Finally, the last part sums up the most probable regional scenario of what would happen if civil war returns to the South Asian state.

The "Blockade"

Nepal's government overwhelmingly passed a new constitution last month which plans to devolve the unitary state into a federal one formed from seven new provinces. The decision was met with immediate consternation by some of the country's minority ethnic groups, most notably the Madhesi and Tharu that live in the fertile Terai region that stretches along the Indian border.

India, too, hasn't been too keen about supporting its neighbor's moves, giving indications that it's worried that friendly ethnic groups like the Madhesi might be underrepresented in the new structure.

India's lack of enthusiasm about Nepal's federalization is occurring at the same time as the growing Madhesi uprising in the south (now joined by the Muslim community) that has stopped border trade between the two countries, leading Kathmandu to accuse New Delhi of implementing a de-facto blockade. India, for its part, denies the accusations, and says that its trucks can't get through the border because of the anti-federalization unrest there.

The crisis is becoming especially acute because fuel supplies are blocked at the border, and Nepal is having difficulty compensating with imports from China because of most of the border checkpoints are still unpassable after the earthquake earlier this year. One of them just reopened , however, and it's already having a positive effect on ameliorating the crisis.

Divergent Paths

What had begun initially as a domestic political issue has warped into one with international dimensions, as it's observable that China and India are now competing for Nepal's loyalty. China has the advantage of taking a hands-off approach to its partner's internal affairs, and combined with its fuel exports to the beleaguered country, this has ingratiated it with the national government. At the same time, however, India exerts a different level of influence that's concentrated along cultural, economic, and ethnic lines. It's the Himalayan state's largest trading partner , and it has strong connections to the country's majority Hindu population and plethora of minority border-region groups. There's thus a certain dichotomy when it comes to China and India's present methods of influence over Nepal – Beijing's are top-down, while New Delhi's are bottom-up.

From Civil War To Proxy War?

At this juncture, it remains to be seen whether the government will budge on amending the internal borders of its proposed federal entities. Kathmandu is afraid that giving in to the Madhesis' demands will grant them too much clout within the new administrative construction, essentially carving out a de-facto state for the pro-Indian ethnicity within Nepal which other minorities might be eager to copy.

On the other hand, failure to work with the Madhesis in calming its agitated protests might lead to the unintentional outbreak of an ethnic-based civil war, which would then have the potential to unravel the country in ways that its ideological precursor never could, and consequently provoke a humanitarian crisis that could predictably spill over into India.

In such an event, India's subtle support of the Madhesis and others would become overt and stated, and it would find itself forced to deal with this (somewhat expected) crisis along its northern borderlands. Forecasting ahead, India's support would be for anti-government ethnic minorities, while China would assist the government. If it gets to the point of both states sending weapons to their preferred side, then the constitutional crisis will formally become the next Asian Cold War (with US-Chinese pan-regional tensions and their subset of Chinese-Japanese insular and ASEAN rivalry being the first one), and the disastrous consequences that this would have for BRICS and SCO unity could drive India even closer into the hands of the US and offset the multipolar zeitgeist that's sweeping the supercontinent.

NEPAL AND CHANGING RELATION BETWEEN TWO ASIAN GIANT INDIA AND CHINA

The two Asian giants have desire to become a super power in global perspective. Before that they have to take a leadership of region. India and China both are trying to get a regional leadership. Fresh long-winded visits of senior leaders from both neighbouring country emphasize Nepal's strategic importance for them. After nuclear deal was signed between India and America, America officially get a place in South Asia politics. The competition has got new dimension. After this nuclear deal the affect is observed between India and China relation have multidimensional effect in Nepal. Effect can be in the trilateral relation between India, China and Nepal. Nepal's political scenario has been changed after the constitutional assembly election. India and America never want to have a communist government in Nepal. For that this nuclear deal has greater importance in triangular relation. Hence, Nepal has to adopt the suitable foreign policy in changed circumstances.

We would like to mention the divine instruction given by Late king Prithwi Narayan Shah before he died 'Southern neighbour (India) as cunning and be aware about the national interest'. He had instructed to his successor to make a balance and try to remain close with northern neighbour (China) for national benefit. If one can analyse this statement then it gives very clear meaning. When Nepal and China established their bilateral relationship since then to until now there is neither border dispute nor other problem. Never trying to hurt the nation's sovereignty and as it promised follows too.

China has clear policy towards that never intend to involve country's internal affairs. And if there somewhere dispute then in friendly environment with positive attitude wants to solve. As Chinese authority has clearly gives the statements regarding the matter of 'Kalapani' issue. It says its matter between India and Nepal and both countries' official has to solve this matter. North neighbour always shows its friendly, cordial image towards Nepal. One can not deny the fact that the topography, language and culture of Nepal makes to become closer to India. He was a real state man and has clear vision about the nation. He dares to give this clear statement before his death. After his death Nepal has got other leader and signed the most unequal treaty in 1950. Because of this treaty Nepal is suffering since then to now. This treaty gives the authority to India political and economical dominance over the sovereign Himalayan country. Prachnada on his first visit to India has expressed 'I think due to our historical, cultural and geographical relation and also due to our whole tradition of interdependence the relation with India is crucial and vital although we also want to develop a relation with China'. This statement shows in competencies of the leadership. Not having sufficient homework on it. Nepal definitely needs both south and north neighbour due to its geographical structure. But first Nepal's leadership have to have clear mindset and lots of homework before visiting any neighbouring country.

During each democratic regime, Nepal's relation with India and China remained inconsistent. Where as China's non intervention policy to other countries internal affairs fuelling and giving opportunity to India to play active role in Nepal's politics. In other hand China want to show that against of their policy to take part in other country's internal affairs. However, India's excessive influence in Nepali Politics makes Chinese involvement in Nepal's politics weaker.

After coming to the government unified communist party of Nepal (Maoist) an immature foreign policy adopted by Nepal regarding India and China has made its foreign policy weak. Lack of confidence and hesitation or excessive India's involvement in Nepal's politics whatever to maintain political as well as economies ties with China. Nepal needs to perform excessive homework to cooperate with difficult and changing scenaric to formulate appropriate policy.

Power greedy countries are eager to exploit resources of their periphery countries for their economic prosperity. Bangladesh and Burma contains huge amount of natural resources (gas). Similarly Nepal is reach in water resources. Around 83000 mega watt hydropower energy can be generated in Nepal. Such aggression and hunger towards natural resources could be the cause to invite the conflict between them in future.

After the Beijing Olympics strategically Nepal's importance for both India and China became immense importance in the region. After the game held in Beijing, vast interest exhibited by the Chinese authority towards Nepal and exhibits strategic importance. Other hand India is intending to show the Nepal has become a safe place for criminal activities in the international arena. For example, India airlines IC-814 had hijacked from Nepal in 1999, recent Mumbai blast and Indian media had alleged that Nepal is safe place for the terrorist group. This can be seen as revenge showing by India. Because China have good relation with its periphery countries (Pakistan, Nepal, and Burma). India and China both can be seen as major opponent and trying take a leadership in South Asia Regarding water resources issues 'Kalapani' is well known issue between India and Nepal. This is about the belongingness. Nepal had raised the voice of necessity of triangular consensus between Nepal, India and China for solution of this issue. China has clearly says on this issue in may 10, 2010 'Government of China has informed the ministry of foreign affairs that there is not concern belonging to Kalapani among the documents signed between China and India during visits of Chinese Premier Wen Jiabao to India'. India needs huge amount of water for the irrigation purpose as well as electricity. Due to lack of homework and negligence of Nepali authority from the past time to until now this issue has not been solved. These shows the roles of Nepal on its resources and raise question about the sovereign country and national interest.

NEW EMERGING RELATION BETWEEN NEPAL AND CHINA, INDIA'S WORRY

Nepal's political scenario has been totally changed after the resignation of Prachanda. His resignation only pushes the Nepal towards the political crisis but also affects the geopolitical vulnerability of the country as it is in between two big Asian giant India and China. India always considers Nepal as a part of its influence which is challenged by China inroads to Nepal.

If Nepal will become the communist country then it would be biggest threats as well as challenge to India. That is why India always wants to influence and involve in Nepal's internal affairs directly/indirectly. India perceives Nepal is facilitating China's security interest in the South Asian region. The statement given by the Chinese ambassador in 2008 makes India to think in that way. The statement was given at council of world affairs by the Chinese ambassador Zheng Xianglin- 'Nepal is situated in a favourable geographical position in South Asia and a passage linking China and South Asia.'

Nepali print media says more than 60 years ago India was playing such game with Nepal. The first elected Prime minister of Nepal and founder member of Nepali Congress Mr. Bisheshwor Prasad Koirala was thrown and with the help of India Late king Mahendra reformed again the king rule in Nepal. It was written in the article that after being elected as first prime minister of Nepal it was fixed his first official foreign visit to China.

But India's Prime Minister Jawahar Lal Nehru had forced him (Bisheshwor Prasad Koirala) to make his first visit to India and not to visit China. This shows India's cunning behaviour as well as clearly seen that India thinks Nepal is literally its sphere of influence. India has feared that if his first visit would be China, it means to India that Nepal wants to build its bilateral relation stronger with China rather than India. And if it goes like that then India's influence to Nepal would be less and can not use Nepal in monopoly way.

At the time when Bisheshwor Prasad was Prime Minister Jawahar Lal Nehru gave the statement that 'India's border will starts from the Himalaya.' India did it intentionally because when India forced him not to visit China. He refused the proposal. It's other way to make a Nepal's political situation unstable. It seems very well planned game to put Bisheshwor Prasad in Jail and after that in Nepal there will not be any more democracy.

It happened and again king rule has been reformed. Further more articles say that Chief of the Indian army came to Nepal and met late king Mahendra and advised him to do so. Nepal seems like independent and sovereign country but in reality not like that. Nepal's national interest is in always in the shadow. What India or other foreign country says the political leaders are following.

It means leaders are not capable or if someone wants to follow the national interest then foreign power forced not to do so or otherwise he/she can get death penalty.

For example of Leaders from Nepal communist name as Madan Bhandari. His death still mystery. Nepali citizens are not ready to accept as just a car accident. But investigating committees report says it's just an accident. Similarly the case of late king Birendra, he was trying to make sound bilateral relation with both the neighbouring country and he seems nationalistic and always thinking about the national interest that is why he easily transform the 237 long king rule history into the democracy in 1991.

To neutralise India's influence he was trying to increase the relation with China which India does not like. In 2001 in Nepal royal massacre occurred and the mystery until now has not been solved. Late king Birendra was proposed the proposal about Nepal has to be recognized as peace country in the world. Except India, Nepal got 112 countries support including China and Pakistan.

Similarly Maoist led government only was in the government for 9 months and after that their government also fell down due to their advocacy on integration of Maoist rebel army into Nepal army. There has few official visits been done to India from the Nepal's side and India was against of this. China is always in favour of integration rebel army to Nepal army. Indian Army chief also advised to Nepal's army Chief it should not be happened. Due to this there was huge politics was going and finally Maoist led government fell down. Since then Maoist are trying to be in the government again but could not succeed.

According to Abanti Bhattacharya, China has laid down a four folded policy with the aim to strength its bilateral relations with Nepal. First accommodate each others political concern, second is enhance the economic cooperation on the basis of mutual benefits third is boos people to people culture exchange and last one is strength the cooperation and coordination in international and regional affairs. China wants to develop the relation with Nepal in a way that it would serve as a model for bilateral ties between small and big countries. Normally there is saying that big fish eats small one but China wants to prove this proverb not always. China in one hand wants to show that Nepal's is independent and sovereign country and will be. Also other hand to get Asia's powers its necessary to marginalise the growing India's involvement in Nepal and other periphery country.

According to Bhim Prasad Bhurtel, executive director of the Nepal South Asia Centre, Kathmandu, there are 33 China study centres have already been established adjoining to India border in the south. Further more he concluded with the aim of close contact with Nepal, China has launched a local FM radio station in Kathmandu. With the aim to strengthen the diplomatic relations between both countries in 2005 Nepal-China Mutual Cooperation Society (NCMCS) has been established which is funded by Chinese embassy, Nepal. So due to Nepal's geopolitical structure and culturally and linguistically also Nepal is very close to India. That is why also what ever is going India always keep its eyes on it. Especially after Maoist Rebel came to the political main stream.

7

Politics of Nepal

The politics of Nepal function within a framework of a republic with a multiparty system. Currently, the positions of President (head of state) and Prime Minister (head of government) are occupied by Ram Baran Yadav and Madhav Kumar Nepal, respectively. Executive power is exercised by the Prime Minister and his cabinet, while legislative power is vested in the Constituent Assembly. Until May 28, 2008, Nepal was a constitutional monarchy. On that date, the constitution was altered by the Constituent Assembly to make the country a republic.

POLITICAL CONDITIONS

1990–1996: Parliamentary monarchy

Until 1990, Nepal was an absolute monarchy running under the executive control of the king. Faced with a people's movement against the absolute monarchy, King Birendra, in 1990, agreed to large-scale political reforms by creating a parliamentary monarchy with the king as the head of state and a prime minister as the head of the government.

Nepal's legislature was bicameral consisting of a House of Representatives and a National Council. The House of Representatives consisted of 205 members directly elected by the people. The National Council had 60 members, 10 nominated by the king, 35 elected by the House of Representatives and the remaining 15 elected by an electoral college made up of chairs of villages and towns. The legislature had a five-year term, but was dissolved by the king before its term could end. All Nepalese citizens 18 years and older became eligible to vote.

The executive comprised the King and the Council of Ministers (the Cabinet). The leader of the coalition or party securing the maximum seats in an election was appointed as the Prime Minister. The Cabinet was appointed by the king on the recommendation of the Prime Minister.

Governments in Nepal have tended to be highly unstable; no government has survived for more than two years since 1991, either through internal collapse or parliamentary dissolution by the monarch.

In the first free and fair elections in Nepal in 1991, the Nepali Congress was victorious.

The 1994 election defeat of the Nepali Congress Party by the Communist Party of Nepal (Unified Marxist-Leninist) (CPN(UML)) made Nepal the first communist-led monarchy in Asia, with Man Mohan Adhikary prime minister. In mid-1994, parliament was dissolved due to dissension within the Nepali Congress Party. The subsequent general election, held 15 November 1994, gave no party a majority and led to several years of unstable coalition governments. As of the May 1999 general elections, the Nepali Congress Party once again headed a majority government. There have been three Nepali Congress Party Prime Ministers since the 1999 elections: K.P. Bhattarai (31 May 1999–17 March 2000); Girija Prasad Koirala (20 March 2000–19 July 2001); and Sher Bahadur Deuba (23 July 2001–2003). The final distribution of seats in Parliament gave the Nepali Congress 113; the CPN(UML) 69; the RPP 11; the RJM 5; the NSP 5; the Workers and Peasants Party 1; and the United People's Front 1. Nepali Congress Party has divided to Nepali Congress Party led by G. P. Koirala and Nepali Congress (Democratic) led by Sher Bahadur Deuba. Amongst the elected MPs, 39 MPs belong to Nepali Congress (Democratic). Former Prime Minister and Influential Leader Krishna Prasad Bhattarai has expressed his support for Nepali Congress (Democratic). Both Congress parties regard Krishna Prasad Bhattarai as their main leader. King Gyanendra discharged Sher Bahadur Deuba and on 4 June 2003 appointed Surya Bahadur Thapa as Prime Minister.

1996: Maoist Insurgency

In February 1996, the Communist Party of Nepal (Maoist) began a violent insurgency in more than 50 of the country's 75 districts. About 13,000 police, civilians, and insurgents have been killed in the conflict since 1996. In July 2001 Prime Minister Deuba announced a cease-fire, which the Maoists pledged to observe, as part of a government effort to seek a negotiated solution to the conflict. Although Maoist-instigated intimidation and extortion continue, the killings have largely subsided since the cease-fire was announced. The government and Maoists held talks in August and September 2001.

Political parties agreed in 1991 that the monarchy would remain to enhance political stability and provide an important symbol of national identity for the culturally diverse Nepali people. The King exercises limited powers, including the right to declare a state of emergency in the event of war or armed revolt, with the advice and consent of the Council of Ministers and the Prime Minister. According to the constitution, the King's declaration of a state of emergency must be approved by a two-thirds majority of the lower house of the Parliament.

2001: Royal Massacre

On June 1, 2001, Crown Prince Dipendra was officially reported to have shot and killed his father, King Birendra; his mother, Queen Aishwarya; his brother; his sister, his father's younger brother, Prince Dhirendra; and several aunts, before turning the gun on himself. Although he never regained consciousness before dying, Crown Prince Dipendra was nonetheless the king under the law of Nepalese royal succession. After his death two days later, the late King's surviving brother Gyanendra was proclaimed king.

2005–2007: Suspension of parliament and Loktantra Andolan

On 1 February 2005 King Gyanendra suspended the Parliament, appointed a government led by himself, and enforced martial law. The King argued that civil politicians were unfit to handle the

Maoist insurgency. Telephone lines were cut and several high-profile political leaders were detained. Other opposition leaders fled to India and regrouped there. A broad coalition called the Seven Party Alliance (SPA) was formed in opposition to the royal takeover, encompassing the seven parliamentary parties who held about 90% of the seats in the old, dissolved parliament.

The UN-OHCHR, in response to events in Nepal, set up a monitoring program in 2005 to assess and observe the human rights situation there

On 22 November 2005, the Seven Party Alliance (SPA) of parliamentary parties and the Communist Party of Nepal (Maoist) agreed on a historic and unprecedented 12-point memorandum of understanding (MOU) for peace and democracy. Nepalese from various walks of life and the international community regarded the MOU as an appropriate political response to the crisis that was developing in Nepal. Against the backdrop of the historical sufferings of the Nepalese people and the enormous human cost of the last ten years of violent conflict, the MOU, which proposes a peaceful transition through an elected constituent assembly, created an acceptable formula for a united movement for democracy. As per the 12-point MOU, the SPA called for a protest movement, and the Communist Party of Nepal (Maoist) supported it. This led to a countrywide uprising that started in April 2006. All political forces including civil society and professional organizations actively galvanized the people. This resulted in massive and spontaneous demonstrations and rallies held across Nepal against King Gyanendra's autocratic rule.

The people's participation was so broad, momentous and pervasive that the king feared being overthrown. On 21 April 2006, King Gyanendra declared that "power would be returned to the people". This had little effect on the people, who continued to occupy the streets of Kathmandu and other towns, openly defying the daytime curfew. Finally King Gyanendra announced the reinstatement the House of Representatives, thereby conceding one of the major demands of the SPA, at midnight on 24 April 2006. Following this action the coalition of political forces decided to call off the protests.

Twenty-one people died and thousands were injured during the 19 days of protests.

On 19 May 2006, the parliament assumed total legislative power and gave executive power to the Government of Nepal (previously known as His Majesty's Government). Names of many institutions (including the army) were stripped of the "royal" adjective and the Raj Parishad (a council of the King's advisers) was abolished, with his duties assigned to the Parliament itself. The activities of the King became subject to parliamentary scrutiny and the King's properties were subjected to taxation. Moreover, Nepal was declared a secular state abrogating the previous status of a Hindu Kingdom. However, most of the changes have, as yet, not been implemented. On 19 July 2006, the prime minister, G. P. Koirala, sent a letter to the United Nations announcing the intention of the Nepalese government to hold elections to a constituent assembly by April 2007.

December 2007 to May 2008: Abolition of the monarchy

On 23 December 2007, an agreement was made for the monarchy to be abolished and the country to become a federal republic with the Prime Minister becoming head of state. Defying political pundits, who had predicted it to be trounced in the April 2008 elections, the Communist Party of Nepal (Maoist) became the largest party amidst a general atmosphere of fear and intimidation from all sides.

A federal republic was established in May 2008, with only four members of the 601-seat Constituent Assembly voting against the change, which ended 240 years of royal rule in Nepal. The government announced a public holiday for three days, (May 28—May 30), to celebrate the country becoming a federal republic.

Current (2008 onwards)

Major parties such as the Unified Communist Party of Nepal (Maoist), Communist Party of Nepal (Unified Marxist-Leninist) and the Nepali Congress agreed to write a constitution that replaces the interim one within the time limit of 2 years.

However, incooperative and "selfish" behaviour of the political parties has been cited as the major cause behind the derailing of the peace process. The Maoists, as the largest party of the country, took power right after the elections were held and named Pushpa Kamal Dahal or Prachanda as the Prime Minister of the country.

CPN UML also joined this government but the Nepali Congress took part of the main opposition. People soon saw that the country's situation deteriorated and political turmoils were in store. Prachanda soon fell into a dispute with the then army chief Rookmangud Katwal and decided to sack him. But the President Ram Baran Yadav as the supreme head of military power in the country revoked this decision and gave the army chief additional time in office. An angry Prachanda and his party quit the government, majorly citing this reason and decided to be the main opposition to the government headed by CPN UML and co-partner Nepali Congress afterwards. Madhav Kumar Nepal was named the Prime Minister.

The Maoists have been to this date demanding superiority of civilian supremacy to army supremacy. This created turmoils in the country and showed vividly that development was a dream far away and the political leaders were just wrangling for power. The Maoists have been forcing closures or commonly known as *bandhs* in the country and have also declared autonomous states for almost all the ethnic groups in the country, seen as a part of revenge against the action that foiled their decision to sack the army chief. Political leaders are discussing plans to end this turmoil, but none of the talks have been successful. Rising inflation, economic downturn, poverty, insecurity and uncertainty are the major problems. Many analysts opine that this freedom has brought anarchy to the country. Many don't even believe the political parties will be successful on writing a constitution.

LEGISLATIVE BRANCH

Pre-2006

From 1991 to 2002 the Parliament (*Sansad*) had two chambers. The House of Representatives (*Pratinidhi Sabha*) had 205 members elected for five year term in single-seat constituencies. The National Council (*Rashtriya Sabha*) had 60 members, 35 members elected by the Pratinidhi Sabha, 15 representatives of Regional Development Areas and 10 members appointed by the king. Parliament was subsequently dissolved by the king in 2002 on the pretext that it was incapable of handling the Maoists rebels.

From Loktantra Andolan to the Constituent Assembly

After the victory of Loktantra Andolan in the spring of 2006, a unicameral interim legislature replaced the previous parliament. The new body consists both of members of the old parliament as well as nominated members. As of December 2007, the legislature had the following composition.

Party	Seats
Nepali Congress	133
Communist Party of Nepal (Maoist)	84
Communist Party of Nepal (Unified Marxist-Leninist)	83
Rashtriya Prajatantra Party	9
Nepal Sadbhavana Party (Anandi Devi)	5
Janamorcha Nepal	4
Nepal Workers Peasants Party	4
Rashtriya Jana Morcha	3
United Left Front	2
Communist Party of Nepal (Unified)	2
Rashtriya Janashakti Party	1

The first democratic elections: the Constituent Assembly

In May 2008 the first democratic elections made the Communist Party of Nepal the largest party in the Constituent Assembly, which will have a term of two years.

Party	Seats
Communist Party of Nepal (Maoist)	220
Nepali Congress	110
Communist Party of Nepal (Unified Marxist-Leninist)	103
Madeshi Jana Adhikar Forum Nepal	52
Tarai-Madhesh Loktantrik Party	20
Sadbhavana Party	9

Rashtriya Prajatantra Party	8
Communist Party of Nepal (Marxist-Leninist)	8
Janamorcha Nepal	7
Communist Party of Nepal (United)	5
Rastriya Prajatantra Party Nepal	4
Rastriya Janamorcha	4
Nepal Workers Peasants Party	4
Rastriya Janshakti Party	3
Sanghiya Loktantrik Rastriya Manch	2
Nepal Sadbhavana Party (Anandidevi)	2
Rastriya Janamukti Party	2
Nepali Janata Dal	2
Communist Party of Nepal (Unified)	2
Dalit Janajati Party	1
Nepa Rastriya Party	1
Samajbadi Prajatantrik Janata Party, Nepal	1
Chure Bhawar Rastriya Ekta Party, Nepal	1
Nepal Loktantrik Samajbadi Dal	1
Nepal Parivar Dal	1
Independents	2
Not yet determined	26

Judicial branch

The judiciary is composed of the Supreme Court of Nepal|Supreme Court (Sarbochha Adalat), appellate courts, and various Trial court|district courts. The Chief Justice of the Supreme Court was appointed by the monarch on recommendation of the Constitutional Council; the other judges were appointed by the monarch on the recommendation of the Judicial Council. Nepal's judiciary is legally separate from the executive and legislative branches and has increasingly shown the will to be independent of political influence. The judiciary has the right of judicial review under the constitution. The king appointed the chief justice and all other judges to the supreme, appellate, and district courts upon the recommendation of the Judicial Council. All lower court decisions, including acquittals, are subject to appeal. The Supreme Court is the court of last appeal. The king could grant pardons and suspend, commute, or remit any sentence by any court.

International organization participation

AsDB, CCC, CP, ESCAP, FAO, G-77, IBRD, ICAO, ICFTU, ICRM, IDA, IFAD, IFC, IFRCS, ILO, IMF, IMO, Intelsat, Interpol, IOC, IOM, ISO (correspondent), ITU, MONUC, NAM, OPCW, SAARC, UN, UNCTAD, UNESCO, UNIDO, UNIFIL, UNMIBH, UNMIK, UNMOP, UNMOT, UNTAET, UPU, WFTU, WHO, WIPO, WMO, WToO, WTrO (applicant).

POLITICAL DEVELOPMENTS IN NEPAL 2002

The year 2002 remained highly turbulent for Nepal. Nepali politics suddenly took a new turn when King Gyanendra on October 4, sacked elected Prime Minister Sher B. Deuba for his "incompetence" to hold parliamentary elections. On May 22 Prime Minister Deuba had recommended the king for the dissolution of the 34-month old House of Representatives followed by a fresh election on November 13. Deuba took this decision on ground of his difference with his party president G. P. Koirla who was reluctant to endorse the state of emergency and maneuvered to remove him from power. On the eve of election date, Premier Deuba, on the advise of six parliamentary parties, suggested the king to postpone election for 14 months on security grounds contrary to the constitutional provision of holding it within six month.

On October 9 the meeting of six parliamentary parties—Nepali Congress (NC), Communist Party of Nepal-Unified Marxist Leninist (CPN-UML), Rastriya Prajatantra Party (RPP), Nepal Workers and Peasants' Party (NWPP), Nepal Sadbhavana Party (NSP) and People's Front Nepal— asked for a collective audience with the King to talk about the formation of an all-party government and suggest him to "rectify the unconstitutional steps" while dismissing the elected government and assuming all executive powers. As the king refused to provide collective audience they met him individually. On October 11 the king nominated a royalist politician and leader of RPP Lokendra Bahadur Chand (63) to head a nine-member interim government with a mandate to restore law and order, hold mid-term elections and election of the local bodies which were dissolved on July 15, solve Maoist insurgency, implement development works and stop the economy sliding further downhill. The king nominated Badri Prasad Mandal, the acting President of NSP as the Deputy Prime Minister and picked other ministers from smaller parties and independents.

Ministers	Portfolios
Prime Minister Lokendra Bahadur Chand	Royal Palace Defense
Deputy Prime Minister Badri Prasad Mandal	Agriculture&CooperativesLocal Developments
Ramesh Nath Pandey	Information&CommunicationsGeneral Administration
Devi Prasad Ojha	Education & Sports
Dr. Badri Prasad Shrestha	Finance
Narendra Bikram Shah	Foreign Affairs
Dharma Bahadur Thapa	Home, Law, Justice and Parliamentary affairs
Gore Bahadur Khapange	Women, Children and social welfare
Dr. Upendra Devkota	Health, Science and Technology
Narayan Singh Pun	Physical Planning and Construction
Badri Narayan Basnet	Land Reforms & Management Forest and Soil Conservation
Kamal Prasad Chaulagai	Labour & Transport Management Population and Environment
Kuber Prasad Sharma	Culture, Tourism & Civil Aviation
Mahesh Lal Pradhan	Industry, Commerce & Supplies
Deepak Gyawali	Water Resources
Assistant Ministers	**Portfolios**
Anuradha Koirala	Women, Children & Social Welfare
Gopal Dahit	Population and Environment
Rabi Bhatka Shrestha	Culture, Tourism & Civil Aviation
Jagat Bahadur Gurung	Industry, Commerce & Supplies
Rabindra Khanal	Education & Sports
Dr. Asharfi Shah	Local Development
Prakash Chitrakar Pariyar	Land Reforms & Management

While the leaders of RPP and NSP welcomed the king's step, NC, CPN-UML, NC (Democratic) of ex-premier Sher B. Deuba and leaders of small left parties showed their disinterest in joining the government. CPN-UML asked the king to form a new government comprising major parliamentary parties as per the Article 128 of the Constitution. NC wanted the restoration of parliament, NC (Democratic) favored the revival of Deuba government and smaller parties wanted an all-party government. Home Minister Dharma Bahadur Thapa, however, said, "Article 128 of the Constitution is dead in the present context, as it was made to give legitimacy to the interim government, formed immediately after the people's movement in 1990." Dissimilar political positions taken by the parties and distrust among them have weakened their bargaining position.

On November 19 the CPN-UML issued an ultimatum to the King to correct his "constitutional mistakes and asked him to declare the dates for national and local elections. Otherwise, it said, "they would plunge into nationwide struggle." The party also suggested the king to act as per the "consensus of all political forces in the country." In contrast, the king, on November 18, expanded the Chand cabinet by adding eight ministers and five assistant ministers. On December 8, after the two months of the formation of government the King instructed the Council of Ministers to deliver and do not denigrate the political parties. He also asked them to implement reforms set for the Chand government at the time of its formation, remain clean and not to make incoherent speeches.

GOVERNMENT-MAOIST DIALOGUE

The seven years old Maoist insurgency and counter-insurgency operations by the security forces has claimed the lives of over 7,000 Nepalese and over 4000 were killed after the imposition of emergency in November 2001 (which lasted nine months). 6,011 Maoists and 873 policemen, 773 civilians, 97-armed policemen and 219 army personnel were killed. Fifty-five percent of Village Development Committee buildings have been destroyed along with several bridges, police posts, telecommunication towers, hydroelectric projects and district administrative offices. On October 22 Home Minister Thapa said, "the government will consider a "give and take" measure. If the Maoists choose peaceful ways, we will welcome them. The government is committed for talks with the rebels but they should put a precise agenda." This indicated a ray of hope for political dialogue but due to lack of good intermediaries understanding between the king and the main political parties, between the main parties and the Maoists and between the Maoists and the king has not been reached for the resolution of national problems.

On October 22 National Human Rights Commission (NHRC) asked the government to declare cease-fire to create an atmosphere for talks, bring the Maoists to negotiation table, halt killing people in "fake encounters," follow minimum norms of human rights and stop the use of excessive force to suppress Maoists. It demanded an independent probe into the cases of mass killings reported during the security operation against Maoists, penalties for the wrong doers and compensation for the victims. Accordingly, it sent a letter to the Maoist leader Prachanda urging him to stop all sorts of killings including unarmed security personnel and personnel on leave, kidnapping and torture of captive persons, and follow the principles mentioned in Article 3 of the Geneva Convention and observe the minimum norms of international human rights practices.

On October 24 the UNDP Resident Representative to Nepal, Dr. Henning Karcher expressed the UN's readiness" to assist in the peace talks between the rebels and the government." But he said that neither of them has sought such assistance. The same day, the European Union Heads of Mission urged the government to hold negotiations with the Maoists. The EU team also "reiterated the need for accelerated reforms in the key areas of the government, vigorous action against corruption and human rights abuse, and effective action to tackle the underlying cause of the on-going conflict."

Responding to these appeals, on October 25 Maoist leader Puspa Kamal Dahal (Prachanda) revealed two ways of exit from the current crisis: "first, formation of the constituent assembly and new constitution through talks between our party, and all the other major political parties of the country including the intellectuals and the king. Second, the people at large would be left with no option but to go ahead with our decisive and historical struggle if the king continues with his reactionary stubbornness and deploys Army to suppress the people instead of making them sovereign in real sense, strengthen national unity and pave the way for progressive development." He also warned that they would come out with fresh mode of reprisal and protest program if their demands were not favorably responded.

The government also showed some flexibility. On November 7 it freed five journalists who were regarded as pro-Maoists and Home Minister Thapa indicated that the government is serious about resuming dialogue with the Maoists and even said that it is not his government but the Congress government that decided to call the Maoists as "terrorists" and affixed price tags on the heads of its leaders. He said, "these terms are not acceptable to the incumbent government as his government is preparing for dialogue with them. The current government cannot own all the decisions of the earlier governments."

On December 3 in a statement signed by Prachanda said, "For a peaceful, positive and progressive political outlet, the meeting has formed a central level high level committee to hold talks with the old regime (the government), provided that a conducive environment is ensured." He, however, did not disclose the names of the committee members. Newspapers speculate that the committee is headed by no.2 Maoist leader Dr. Baburam Bhattarai. The party has also decided to stop the targeting of political leaders of other parties and development infrastructure directly linked to the people's welfare. He, however, warned the cadres of other parties to stop spying against them.

Anti-Corruption Measures

On April 14 the House of Representatives passed four crucial bills— the Commission for the Investigation of the Abuse of Authority (CIAA) (2nd Amendment) Bill 2002, Corruption Control Bill 2002, Impeachment (Regulate Working Procedure) Bill 2002, and Special Court Bill 2002 seeking to empower CIAA, set up Special Court and allow Impeachment. Accordingly, a high-level committee to investigate properties of public officials since the political changes of 1990 has been established under the chairmanship of an officiating judge of the Supreme Court B. P. Lamsal.

On the recommendation of CIAA State Minister for Forest and Soil Conservation, Surendra Hamal, and minister Gopal Man Shrestha were fired for taking bribe for approving a file of Khanal-Rojin and Turpentine Ltd. The CIAA also filed a case against 51 persons for embezzling Rs. 213.9 million while granting loans to a private party. It carried out overnight raids against 22 government employees and found millions of rupees without any reliable sources of income. On August 22 the government formed a Special Court under the chairmanship of judge Tapa Bahadur Magar to look after the cases of sedition and corruption filed by the CIAA.

The Lamsal Commission asked banks to furnish details of account held by 19 ex-ministers including G. P. Koirala and his daughter Sujata Koirala since April 2000. The CIAA equally interrogated former ministers Jaya Prakash Gupta, Khum Bahadur Khadka and R.K. Mainali, raided the houses of R. Chaturbedi of Royal Nepal Airlines Corporation (RNAC) and Joint Secretary Anand Khanal— for amassing huge property and took into custody former ministers Khadka and Gupta and two engineers Narayan B. Thapa and Amodananda Mishra. Gupta has been accused of making huge amounts of money while issuing permit for the import of celluar mobile phone sets. Khadka and others were accused of corruption in Bakraha River Control Project in Sunsari district. On December 18, CIAA filed a charge sheet against former minister Chiranjibi Wagle at the Special Court for amassing over Rs. 32.9 million through illegal means. The government also registered an impeachment bill in the parliament secretariat proposing a probe committee to investigate the charges against the Supreme Court judges and the members of the constitutional bodies with the signature of at least 25 percent of Lower House MPs and also created a National Surveillance Centre under the chairmanship of Mohan Bahadur Karki, to curb corruption and irregularities.

Reforms in Gender Laws: On March 7, the government constituted eight-member high level women's commission under

Dr. Durga Pokhrel to redress women's problems. On March 14 the House of Representatives passed a Civil Code Amendment Bill guaranteeing equal property rights and conditional abortion rights to women. The Bill seeks to empower women by providing the unmarried ones equal rights to parental property, provides for share from husbands' property to those who are divorced and those who are widowed, besides banning the age-old practices of child marriage and polygamy. It legalizes abortion of foetus up to 12 weeks under any circumstances. But that should be done with the husband's consent and with the help of officially authorized paramedics or surgeons. It also allows the victims of rape or incest to abort the foetus till 18 weeks.

Formation of National Dalit Commission: On March 19 the government formed a ten-member National Dalit Commission under the Chairmanship of Padma Singh Bishwokarma aiming to ensure active participation of Dalit castes in the development of the country. The Commission will, inter alia, focus on areas requiring changes in legal and policy areas for Dalit rights, make recommendations to implement international documents to which Nepal has been a party, monitor and coordinate NGOs on dalit upliftment, launch programs on social awareness to end social discrimination and untouchability, receive petitions, act as per the existing law and draft a bill to make legal arrangements. Code of Ethics Bill for MPs: On March 19 parliament passed the Bill related to the code of conducts for political parties stipulating a provision for stating the name, place and address of any organization or individual donating more than Rs. 25,000 to any political parties, mandating political parties submit their annul reports including the "income and expenditure" to the Election Commission (EC) within six month of the completion of the fiscal year and releasing the report publicly. The parties should audit their account of income and expenditure through the auditors recognized by the Auditor-General, state the election expenditure, elect at least 50 percent of the total members of the acting committee of the party in every five years, and refrain from accepting donation from any international organizations, foreign government, individual and the institution. The Bill bans to issue party membership to any person below 16 years and the acting civil servants. The parties contesting elections should also present their manifesto and attested program to the EC within seven days of the announcement of the election date. There is also a provision of cancellation of the registration of the political party if it is found to be issuing party members on the basis of caste, sex, group, community, religion and area.

Party Politics

Nepali Congress (NC): Factionalism and split gripped NC from the beginning of 2002. In February while president of ruling NC Party Girija Prasad Koirala argued that his idea of "Broader Democratic Alliance" (BDA) was meant to solve the country's social, political and economic problems, premier Deuba's faction smelled it as a ploy to remove him from power. Koirala pressurized Deuba to reduce the size of cabinet by 10 percent of the total of MPs, establish a commission to investigate on the assets of the public officials collected after the restoration of democracy and formulate laws to confiscate the assets of those failing to disclose the source of income. He also constituted a five-member committee headed by party treasurer Mahanta Thakur to give suggestions on the amendments of the present constitution. Despite opposition from Deuba, G. P. Koirala arbitrarily constituted a Parliamentary Committee and Central Works Performance Committee on February 26 manned mostly by his followers. The disciplinary action taken by NC against three cabinet ministers and one Central Working Committee member for their remarks against the party president's decision to form the party's Parliamentary Committee further widened the rift with Deuba's faction. Factionalism became acute as Central Disciplinary Committee (CDC) of the party expelled Minister for Information and Communication Jaya Prakash Gupta from the party's general membership for a period of one year for supporting the remarks of Army Chief against the "bad governance" of political parties and politicians.

On April 11, 33 ministers asked Koirala to immediately revoke the decision against Gupta. As the government extended the state of emergency for three more months and dissolved the Lower House, Koirala expelled primer Deuba from the party for three years. Ex-premier K. P. Bhattarai's efforts to bridge the differences too failed as Koirala asked Premier Deuba to revive the dissolved House. Koirala viewed that crisis in the party is the product of a "grand design." On June 16, Premier Deuba summoned all the NC general convention members for discussion in Kathmandu and also accused Koirala of breaking the party. Out of 1502 General Convention members 873 members attended the meeting. The meeting spelled out the preconditions for party unity—revocation of the expulsion of Deuba and others, reorganization of the party's powerful Central Working Committee, parliamentary board, and the party's Central Disciplinary Committee.

As Koirala seemed adamant on his stand fifty-six years old NC suffered a vertical split on June 18. The Convention removed the incumbent president G. P. Koirala from the party and a day later elected Deuba as the new president. Deuba faction accused Koirala of perpetuating "a dynastic rule." The Party elected Chiranjibi Wagle as vice-president, Khum Bahadur Khadka as the General-Secretary and Bijaya Gachhedar as the Joint General Secretary. Deuba nominated Bhim Kumari Budamagar, Amar Raj Kaini, Duryodhan Singh, Krishna Bahadur Gurung, Sheikh Zahir, Hom Nath Dahal, Gopal Man Shrestha, Chitra Lekha Yadav, Narendra Bikram Nembang and Krishna Prasad Bhattarai as CWC members in the 27-member Central Committee.

The Election Commission (EC) on September 17 recognized the pro-Koirala NC as the official party and entitled it to party flag and symbol. At the same time, the EC asked Deuba's faction to register a new party within seven days to facilitate its participation in the mid-term polls. The EC, however, said that it was only an "interim" order conceding that both the factions had more or less equal number of general convention members. On September 23 Premier Deuba registered a new party at the EC called Nepali Congress (Democratic) and received Kalash (a water jar) as the party's election symbol.

After Deuba's removal from power, NC president G. P. Koirala concentrated his attack on the King. On October 27 he said that King Gyanendra's assumption of executive power has blown away the notion of "king can do no wrong." The nation was caught in a "grand design." The Royal Massacre of June 1 last year was part of a grand design." On November 18 in a press meet organized at Birgunj, he said, "NC, which has long been in favor of constitutional monarchy, could change its stance in favor of a republic set up. But this would be decided by the party's general convention and not me alone." On December 18 speaking at the mass awakening campaign, NC President G. P. Koirala also demanded that the army should be made accountable to parliament.

Left Politics: Left political parties showed a trend towards unity and accommodation in politics. In the beginning of January Communist Party of Nepal-Unified Marxist-Leninist (CPN-UML) and CPM-Marxist-Leninist (CPN-ML) drafted their unity proposal. After four years of split, the splinter faction CPN (ML) merged into the CPN-UML on February 15. A senior CPN (ML) leader, C. P. Mainali has, however, denounced the merger and re-organized the party with the same name. Mainali forwarded a concept of "Broad Left Democratic Alliance" to resolve the present crisis in the country.

On January 11 CPN-UML parliamentary task force, constituted to monitor post-emergency situation, informed the government of various "unfortunate" incidents in the country and demanded to stop them. On February 12, all the left parties opposed the Terrorist and Disruptive Activities (Prevention and Control) Ordinance (TADO) 2001 and Financial Ordinance 2001 (First Amendment) in the parliamentary secretariat alleging the government for "introducing the ordinances and bypassing the parliament." The Finance Ordinance has been issued to channel extra funds to meet its skyrocketing security expenses. In doing so, it has slashed the annual budgets allocated to the country's 3913 Village Development Committees by 50 percent, 58 municipalities by 10 percent and parliamentarian development fund by 25 percent. The government allocated additional budget of Rs. 500 million to buy arms and recruit more security personnel to fight against the Maoists. On February 28 the House of Representatives passed the TADO Ordinance 2001 and Finance Ordinance 2001 introduced after the state of emergency despite opposition from smaller left parties. The new legislation empowers the security forces with the right to conduct search operations and house arrest of suspected individuals.

On April 22 CPN-Masal and CPN-Unity Centre announced their merger stating: "Since the country is moving backwards, it is the responsibility of left parties and other people-oriented forces to come together for safeguarding the achievement of people's movement." The joint statement was signed by respectively by two secretary-generals—Ram Singh Shris (CPN-M) and Narayan Kaji Shrestha (CPN-UC). Similarly, on July 10 two other left parties—the United People's Front (UPF) and the National People's Front (NPF) formally announced their unification and constituted the People's Front Nepal.

On October 31, NC, CPN-UML and United Front Nepal (UFN) announced protest programs against the October 4 Royal proclamation to "safeguard the achievements of the 1990s people's movement, to meet the challenges against the nation and democracy, and to protect constitutional norms and democratic values." The UML also announced month-long public awareness program against what they call "conspiracy." The program began at national meet in the capital on November 19.

Just on the eve of UML's protest program, King Gyanendra discussed current political deadlock with Nepal. Nepal suggested the king to form the government under the Article 128 (2) of the Constitution which mentions that "His Majesty shall constitute a new Council of Ministers consisting of representatives from the main political parties" if the existing cabinet is dissolved. A day earlier NC President G. P. Koirala who had asked the king to revive the parliament suggested the king to form the government under Article 128 (2) of the Constitution. On December 14 addressing its crowd CPN-UML leader Madhav Kumar Nepal said, "The king does not have the right to sack or appoint a Prime Minister. The king has done both. October 4 move was unconstitutional and illegal. CPN-UML leaders warned the king to correct his constitutional mistakes otherwise "we will be forced to launch a decisive battle against the king, which will ultimately uproot the monarchy."

Leadership conflict in Nepal Sadbhavana Party: On November 25 in a move aimed to control the party, acting president of Nepal Sadbhavan Party, Badri Prasad Mandal removed his vocal critic and general-secretary, Hridayesh Tripathi, from the central working committee of the party and reconstituted 28-member CWC.

RPP Calls for Effective role for the King: The Central Working Committee (CWC) meeting of RPP held on July 23 in Kathmandu pointed out that no single party could relieve the country of the crises. It also highlighted the need for "consensus" and "alliance" among different political parties. The December 11 Third General Convention of RPP in Pokhara elected a new leadership for the next four years. The convention elected 18 central committee members including its Chairman Pashupati S. Rana. Rana garnered 735 votes where as his nearest rivals Dr. Prakash C. Lohani secured 320 and Rabindra Nath Sharma got 134 votes. The RPP concluded its meeting saying, "The king's cooperation is a must to get rid of the present problems including the Maoist one."

NEPALESE CIVIL WAR

The Nepali Civil War (labelled People's War by the Maoists) was a conflict between government forces and Maoist rebels in Nepal which lasted from 1996 until 2006. The war was started by the Communist Party of Nepal (Maoist) on 13 February 1996, with the aim of overthrowing the Nepalese monarchy and establishing the "People's Republic of Nepal." It ended with a Comprehensive Peace Accord signed on 21 November 2006 which is now monitored by United Nations Mission in Nepal.

Overview

More than 12,800 people were killed (4,500 by Maoists and 8,200 by the government) and an estimated 100,000 to 150,000 people were internally displaced as a result of the conflict. This conflict disrupted the majority of rural development activities and led to a deep and complex Left Front which, together with the Nepali Congress, was the backbone of the broadbased movement for democratic change. However, communist groups uncomfortable with the alliance between ULF and Congress formed a parallel front, the United National People's Movement. The UNPM called for elections to a Constituent Assembly, and rejected compromises made by ULF and Congress with the royal house. In November

1990 the Communist Party of Nepal (Unity Centre) was formed, including key elements of constituents of UNPM. The new party held its first convention in 1991, the adopted a line of "protracted armed struggle on the route to a new democratic revolution" and that the party would remain an underground party. The CPN(UC) set up Samyukta Jana Morcha, with Baburam Bhattarai as its head, as an open front ten contest elections. In the 1991 elections, SJM became the third force in the Nepali parliament. However, disagreements surged regarding which tactics were to be used by the party. One sector argued for immediate armed revolution whereas others (including senior leaders like Nirmal Lama) claimed that Nepal was not yet ripe for armed struggle.

In 1994 CPN(UC)/SJM was split in two. The militant sector later renamed itself the Communist Party of Nepal (Maoist). The Maoists labeled the government forces and included in this accusation the monarchy and the mainstream political parties. The armed struggle began soon afterwards with simultaneous attacks on remote police stations and district headquarters. Initially, the Nepali government mobilized the Nepal Police to contain the insurgency.

The Royal Nepal Army was not involved in direct fighting because the conflict was regarded as a matter for the police to sustain control. Furthermore, controversy grew regarding the army not assisting the police during insurgent attacks in remote areas. The popularly-elected prime minister resigned his post, due to the refusal of the Royal Army to take part in the conflict. This situation changed dramatically in 2002 when the first session of peace talks failed and the Maoists attacked an army barracks in Dang District in western Nepal. Overnight, the army was unleashed against the insurgents. At the same time, the king of Nepal maintained a puppet democratic government which depended upon him for their status to remain legitimate. Under the aegis of the global War on Terrorism and with the stated goal of averting the development of a "failed state" that could serve as a source of regional and international instability, the United States, European Union, and India, among other nations, have provided extensive military and economic aid to the Nepali government. This material support to the Nepali government dried up after King Gyanendra seized full control in February 2005 to get rid of civil war for once and all.

The government responded to the rebellion by banning provocative statements about the monarchy, imprisoning journalists, and shutting down newspapers accused of siding with the insurgents. Several rounds of negotiations, accompanied by temporary cease-fires, have been held between the insurgents and the government. The government has categorically rejected the insurgents' demand for an election to the constituent assembly; it would result in the abolition of the monarchy by a popular vote. At the same time, the Maoists have refused to recognize the installation of a constitutional monarchy. In November 2004, the government rejected the Maoists' request to negotiate directly with the King Gyanendra rather than via the Prime Minister Sher Bahadur Deuba; their request for discussions to be mediated by a third party, such as the United Nations was dismissed.

Throughout war, the government controlled the main cities and towns, whilst the Maoist dominated the rural areas. Historically, the presence of the Nepali government has been limited to town and zonal centers. The only state apparatus present in most small villages, where most of the inhabitants of Nepal live, were a health post, a government school, a village council, and a police booth. Once the insurgency began, the schools were all that remained, indicating that the Maoists had seized control of the village. The Royal government powerbase is located in the zonal headquarters and the capital Kathmandu. Unrest reached Kathmandu in 2004 when the Maoists announced a blockade of the capital city.

Intense fighting and civic unrest continued well into 2005, with the death toll rising to 200 in December 2004. On 1 February 2005, in response to the inability of the relatively democratic government to restore order, King Gyanendra assumed total control of the government. He proclaimed, "Democracy and progress contradict one another... In pursuit of liberalism, we should never overlook an important aspect of our conduct, namely discipline."

On 22 November 2005, the joint CPN(M)-United People's Front conference in Delhi issued a 12-point resolution, stating that they

"...completely agree that autocratic monarchy is the main hurdle" hindering the realisation of "democracy, peace, prosperity, social advancement and a free and sovereign Nepal." In addition, "It is our clear view that without establishing absolute democracy by ending autocratic monarchy, there is no possibility of peace, progress, and prosperity in the country."

An understanding had been reached to establish absolute democracy by ending monarchy with the respective forces centralizing their assault against monarchy thereby creating a nationwide storm of democratic protests. This marked a departure from the previous stance of the CPN(M), which had so far vehemently opposed the gradual process of democratization advocated by the UPF.

As a result of the civil war, Nepal's greatest source of foreign exchange, its tourism industry, suffered considerably. iExplore, a travel company, published rankings of the popularity of tourist destinations, based on their sales, which indicated that Nepal had gone from being the tenth most popular destination among adventure travelers, to the twenty-seventh.

The conflict has forced the young and able to seek work abroad in order to avoid the Human Rights Violations committed by the Government forces and the crimes committed by the Maoists. These labourers work predominantly in the Gulf (Qatar, Saudi Arabia, etc.) and Southeast Asia (Malaysia etc). The regular flow of remittances from these labourers has permitted the country to avoid serious economic crisis or economic bankruptcy. The economy of Nepal is heavily dependent on the infusion of foreign income from the labouring class (similar to the Lebanese economy during its civil war).

Use of child soldiers

To achieve their goals of removing the king and establishing a secular communist republic, the Maoists resorted to underage recruitment, particularly of young students, usually between 12 and 16 years old.

At the conclusion of the war, an estimated 12,000 Maoist soldiers were below 18 years of age, and Human Rights Estimates that the majority of the current militia joined as minors. The

United Nation Mission in Nepal (UNMIN) has verified nine thousand child soldiers currently in Maoist cantonment training camps.

Maoists used children as soldiers, messengers, cooks, porters and suppliers. Regardless of role, all children received rudimentary military training concerning explosives, so they would be able to recognize and avoid land mines. The Maoists, however, continue to deny that any soldiers were less than 18 years of age. They claim that they have cared for orphans of adult soldiers killed in the war, and that these children were not placed in danger.

Children, including girls, were deployed in combat situations, often to help provide ammunition or assist with evacuating or caring for the wounded. A 16-year-old boy from Dang district in Western Nepal reported that he was forced to carry wounded Maoist combatants to India for treatment. He revealed how he and six others of the same age managed to run away. A 14-year-old girl explained how arms training took place by torchlight during the night.

Timeline

1996

- 13 February: Initiation of "the people's war" by the Communist Party of Nepal (Maoist)
  - o Kathmandu: A soft-drink bottling factory owned by a multi-national company is attacked and the building torched.
  - o Gorkha District
    - — A foreign liquor factory is completely destroyed.
    - — The office of the Small Farmer's Development Programme of the state-owned Agricultural Development Bank in Chyangli VDC (Village Development Committee) is ransacked.
  - o Kavre District: A moneylender's house is raided at night, properties and cash reportedly worth 1.3 million rupees seized, and loan documents worth several million rupees reportedly destroyed. 7 members of the moneylender's family are killed, all shot to death.

- o Rolpa, Rukum & Sindhuli Districts: One police outpost raided in each district. The outpost at Holeri, Rolpa has its stores seized, including a substantial amount of high explosives. Athbiskot-Rari, Rukum is also raided. The Sindhuligarhi post in Sindhuli is reportedly raided without. 17 Police personnel are killed in total, and only one Maoist guerilla is killed in retaliation.

2001

- January: The government creates the Armed Police Force to fight the insurgents.
- 28 May: Chairman Prachanda gives an interview with the Communist journal *A World to Win*.
- 1 June: Crown Prince Dipendra reportedly kills King Birendra and most of the royal family in the Nepali royal massacre. Dipendra, comatose after a failed suicide attempt or assassination attempt by palace guards, is crowned king, according to tradition. He dies on 4 June, Gyanendra is crowned King.
- 3 August: The first round of peace talks begin.
- 23 November: Peace talks collapse when the Maoists withdraw and launch a ferocious attack Police and Army posts in 42 districts, in which 186 Army and Police personnel and 21 Maoists are killed.
- 26 November: The government of Sher Bahadur Deuba declares a Nationwide State of Emergency and employs the Nepal Army in attacking the Maoists.

2002

- The United States Congress approves US$12 million to train Royal Nepal Army officers and supply 5,000 M16 rifles.
- May: Peace talks collapse.
- May: Large battle fought between Army and Maoist forces at Lisne Lekh along boundary between Pyuthan and Rolpa districts.

- 11 May: A photograph is discovered by Nepal government soldiers in western Nepal. The photograph depicts Nepal's Maoist rebel leaders Baburam Bhattarai, Hisila Yami, Ram Bahadur Thapa (alias Badal), and Pushpa Kamal Dahal (alias Prachanda).
- 22 May: King Gyanendra, acting on the advice of Prime Minister Sher Bahadur Deuba, dissolves Parliament and orders new elections. The reason given for the dissolution is opposition to the state of emergency.
- 11 July: Information leaks out that the Belgian weapon manufacturer FN Herstal is allowed to deliver 5,500 M249 *Minimi* rifles to the Nepali monarchy, a decision made by all coalition parties. Minister of External Affairs Louis Michel speaks of "a country in a pluralistic democracy."
- 4 October: King Gyanendra deposes Prime Minister Deuba and the entire Council of Ministers, assumes executive power, and cancels the elections for the dissolved House of Representatives, which had been scheduled for 11 November.
- 11 October: King Gyanendra appoints Lokendra Bahadur Chand as Prime Minister.

2003

- January: The United States hold exercises with the Nepali army. Maoist insurgents kill the Inspector General of Armed Police, Krishna Mohan Shrestha, his wife and his bodyguard, Head Constable Subhash Bahadur Gurung of the Armed Police Force Nepal, while on their morning walk, as they used to do on Sunday mornings, intending to represent general safety to fellow citizens. The Inspector General and his wife, who was a teacher at an international school in the capital, were both unarmed. They were riddled with bullets from Type 56 Rifles and G3 rifles used by the Maoists.
- 29 January: A second ceasefire is established and peace talks begin.

- 13 May: Code of conduct jointly declared by the government and the Communist Party of Nepal (Maoist) for the mutually agreed period of cease-fire
- 17 August: Nepali Military and Police forces kill 39 Maoist rebels in the Ramechhap District of central Nepal during an offensive launched jointly by the Army, Police, and Air Force of Nepal. 7 Soldiers of the Nepali Army and 5 Constables of the Armed Police are also killed in the operation.
- 24 August: The Maoists set an ultimatum, threatening to withdraw from the cease-fire if the government does not agree within 48 hours to include the question of the Maoists participating in the Constituent Assembly.
- 26 August: The Maoist ultimatum expires.
- 27 August:
    - o Strike: The Maoist call for a three-day strike to denounce the Army's attacks on their cadres
    - o The Maoists unilaterally withdraw from the 29 January cease-fire. Prachanda's statement revives the rebels' demand for an end to monarchic rule in favour of a people's republic, stating, "Since the old regime has put an end to the forward-looking solution to all existing problems through the cease-fire and peace talks, we herein declare that the rationale behind cease-fire...and peace process has ended."
- 27 September: "Fifteen people including 8 Rebels and 4 Policemen were killed on Saturday and suspected Maoists bombed five government utilities despite the guerrillas' plans for a nine day truce from 2 October, officials said. Eight Maoists were killed in a gun battle with security forces at Chhita Pokhara in the Khotang District, 340 kilometres east of Kathmandu, a police officer said. 4 Policemen were also martyred. Elsewhere in eastern Nepal, the Maoists killed two Policemen,Constable Purna Prasad Sharma and Head Constable Radha Krishna Gurung, and a woman selling beetle nuts, Kali Tamang, in the Jaljale-Gaighat area, an official said. 'A group of seven Maoists

descended from a public bus when police were checking the passengers and suddenly opened fire from automatic pistols, killing the three and wounding two others,' said Sitaram Prasad Pokharel, the chief administrator for the region. In Janakpur, an industrial hub on the Indian border 260 kilometres south-east of Kathmandu, the Maoists under the direct command of Prachanda carried out five early morning bombings that disrupted telephone service and power, police said. No one was killed directly by the blasts but an elderly man died of a heart attack after hearing the explosions, Police Deputy Superintendent Bharat Chhetri said. He said the sites that were bombed included the offices of the roads department and the Nepal Electricity Authority and a telecommunications tower. Police personnel and Maoists traded fire for nearly 40 minutes after the blasts but the rebels escaped and 37 people were injured, Mr Khadka said."

- 13 October: At least 42 Police Recruits and 9 Maoists are killed when an estimated 3,000 Maoists attempt to storm a Police Training Centre in Bhaluwang. "'The rebels had snapped telephone cables, set up roadblocks by felling trees or blowing up highway bridges to prevent reinforcements from coming,' a witness, Krishna Adhikary, told Reuters."
- 27 October: " Colonel Adrian Griffith and six Nepali nationals were freed last week 42 hours after being taken captive in Baglung, 300 km (190 miles) west of Kathmandu, while on a drive to recruit young Gurkha soldiers to serve in the British army." Party chief Prachanda said, "We are sorry for the incident that took place against the policy of the party."
- 11 November: The government Defence Ministry accuses the Maoists of abducting twenty-nine 9th-and 10th-grade students from Riva Secondary School in Mugu District, western Nepal during the previous week.
- 19 November: According to a Nepal army official, four people were caught at the Chinese Khasa border point, 114

kilometers northeast of Kathmandu, smuggling weapons from Tibet into Nepal. The official named Hirala Lal Shrestha and Gyaljen Sherpa and said they were taken for interrogation in the Tibetan town of Xigatse.

2004

- 5 February: An Army raid is carried out by the Bhairavnath Battalion on a village in Bhimad, Makwanpur District. Reports emerge that 45 suspected Maoist rebels and two civilians were executed after being captured. Amnesty International later wrote a letter to Prime Minister Surya Bahadur Thapa and Brigadier-General Nilendra Aryal, Head of the Royal Nepal Army (RNA) human rights cell, demanding an immediate inquiry.
- 10 February: Two central committee members of Communist Party of Nepal (Maoist), Matrika Yadav and Suresh Paswan, are reported to have been handed over by India to Nepal. They were reportedly arrested in Lucknow after Nepal provided information.
- 13 February: Ganesh Chilwal leads an anti-Maoist protest on this day, the ninth anniversary of the commencement of the revolution.
- 15 February: Ganesh Chilwal is shot dead in his Kathmandu office by two suspected Maoists.
- 15 February: Fighting erupts at a Maoist jungle base in Kalikot District, 360 km west of Kathmandu. The base is said to hold 5000 Maoist troops. On 17 February, a security official says that a private helicopter flying troops to Kalikot was hit by Maoist fire but that it returned safely to Kathmandu. On 18 February 65 Maoists are reported to have been killed, though this conflicts with other reported death tolls of 35 and 48.
- 15 February and 16: Nepalese state radio reports that 13 Maoist rebels were killed in seven separate small clashes with security forces across the country.
- 18 February: Lawmaker Khem Narayan Faujdar, a member of the parliament dissolved by King Gyanendra in 2002,

is shot dead by two suspected Maoists riding a motorcycle in the Nawalparasi District, 200 km southwest of the capital, according to the police.

- 2 April: The largest rallies since 1990 begin in Kathmandu. They are variously labelled "pro-democracy" and "anti-monarchy."
- 3 April: More than 12 trucks are burnt while waiting at a western Nepal border post to pick up petrol from India. India condemns the attacks and vows to fight terrorism.
- 4 April: "Some 150 demonstrators were struck during a police baton charge" during demonstrations in Kathmandu
- 4 April "Hundreds of Maoist rebels" attack a Police outpost in Yadukuwa, Jadukhola. 13 policemen are killed, 7 wounded, and 35 are listed as missing. 8-9 Maoists are also killed. "Witnesses said more than 500 rebels attacked the Police post and began firing Assault Rifles and RPG-7 rockets. at around 9 p.m. (1515 GMT) on Sunday night. The fighting lasted two to three hours." Other reports state 400 rebels.
- 4 April: In the west of the country three Indian traders are shot and injured and have their vehicles burned.
- 5 April: A three day national strike begins, called by CPN(M) and opposed by an "alliance of five political parties" who are protesting in Kathmandu against the monarchy and say the strike will hamper the movement of demonstrators in Kathmandu. Prachanda said, "The time has come to win a united struggle against the feudal forces as the king is trying to take the nation back to the 18th century."
- 5 April: In the morning, 3 soldiers are killed and 7 injured by a CPN(M) landmine activated by their vehicle at Dhalkhola, 50 km east of Kathmandu.
- 5 April: At least 140 people are injured in clashes in Kathmandu as "about 50,000" demonstrators confront the police. Demonstrators try to break through a police barricade close to the royal palace. The police respond with tear gas and protesters are reportedly injured by

police batons. Rocks and bricks are thrown by both sides. Demonstrations also occur in Lalitpur and Bhaktapur. Meanwhile, king Gyanendra has reportedly been away touring villages in western Nepal.

- 5 April: The Indian government announces that it will no longer provide police escorts to Indian officials shopping in Nepal, as a means to discourage such trips. Fears are based on the CPN(M) targeting Indians. "We are worried about possible reprisals here if the Maoists continue to target Indians inside Nepal," said a senior police official.
- 16 August: The Soaltee Hotel, a popular luxury hotel in Kathmandu, is bombed, after refusing a demand from the Maoists that the hotel close.
- 18 August: A bomb explodes in a marketplace in southern Nepal. The blast kills a 12-year-old boy and wounds six others, including three policemen. In addition, Maoist rebels, demanding the release of captured guerrillas, stop all road traffic near Kathmandu by threatening to attack vehicles. Some Nepal businesses are shut down because of threats.
- 10 September: A bomb explodes at the United States Information Service office in Kathmandu.
- 13 September: U.S. Peace Corps suspends operations and non-essential U.S. Embassy personnel are evacuated from Nepal.
- 9 November: 36 people were injured when suspected Maoist rebels exploded a powerful bomb at a under-construction government office complex,the Karmachari Sanchaya Kosh Office Complex in the heart of Nepalese capital Kathmandu Tuesday.
- 15 December: Twenty government security personnel are killed in the western district of Arghakhanchi when the Maoists mount a surprise attack.
- 16 December: Sixteen Maoist rebels are killed in clashes with Nepali security forces in the western district of Dailekh.
- 23 December: Maoist forces launch blockade of Kathmandu.

- 26 December: Over 15,000 hold peace rally in Kathmandu.

2005

- 2 January: Nepali media falsely reports two children being killed in Dailekh District by a Maoist bomb.
- 4 January: Three government security personnel and between two and twenty-four Maoist rebels reported killed in fighting.
- 8 January: Maoists detain and later release 300 passengers from six buses that defy their blockade of Kathmandu.
- 10 January: Prime Minister Deuba said he would increase defense spending to fight the Maoists unless they come forward for talks with the government.
- 11 January: Protests and blockades over the government fuel price increases of between 10% and 25%.
- 15 January: Maoists allegedly detain 14 Indian Gurkhas from Chuha village in Kailali.
- 1 February: King Gyanendra dissolves the Deuba government and bans all news reports. The army begins arresting senior political leaders, journalists, trade unionists, human rights activists and civil society leaders. All telephone and internet connections are cut.
- 6 June: Badarmude bus explosion: Some 38 civilians are killed and over 70 injured after a packed passenger bus runs over a rebel landmine in Chitwan District.
- 9 August: Maoist rebels kill 40 security men in midwestern Nepal.
- 3 September: The Maoists declare a three-month unilateral ceasefire to woo opposition political parties.
- 19 November: After negotiations, the Maoist rebels agree to work with opposition politicians in a common front against the rule of King Gyanendra of Nepal.

2006

- 2 January: Rebels decide not to extend a four month ceasefire saying that the government had broken the ceasefire with numerous attacks on Maoist villages.

- 14 January: Maoists launch coordinated attacks of five military and paramilitary targets in the Kathmandu Valley. The first demonstration of their ability to organize violence within the Valley, prompting curfews at night for the next several days.
- 14 March: Nepali rebels extend road blockade; nationwide strike called for 3 April.
- 5 April: General strike begins with Maoist forces promising to refrain from violence.
- 6 April 7: Protesters clash with police, hundreds arrested, dozens injured.
- 8 April: A curfew is imposed in Kathmandu from 10 p.m. to 9 a.m. The king orders protesters violating the curfew to be "shot on sight."
- 9 April: General strike scheduled to end. Government extends curfew, BBC reports. Three dead in two days of unrest, as thousands of demonstrators defy curfews.
- 27 April: Maoist insurgents, responding to a demand by the newly appointed Prime Minister Girija Prasad Koirala, announce a unilateral three-month truce after weeks of pro-democracy protests in Kathmandu, and encourage the formation of a new constituent assembly tasked with rewriting the nation's constitution.
- 3 May: Nepal's new cabinet declares a ceasefire. The cabinet also announces that the Maoist rebels will no longer be considered a terrorist group. Rebels are also encouraged to open peace talks.
- 21 November: Peace talks end with the signing of the Comprehensive Peace Accord between Prime Minister Girija Prasad Koirala and Maoist leader Prachanda. The deal allows the Maoists to take part in government, and places their weapons under UN monitoring.

2007

YCL kidnap the doctor and medicall college Directors Dr. Gyanendra Giri, Nawaraj Pandey, Umesh Pandey, Aditya Khanal/ Janak Rizal and Santosh mani Neupane lucklyly save other two partners Hari R.Acharya and Asha Bashat.

NEPALESE CONSTITUENT ASSEMBLY

The Nepalese Constituent Assembly is a unicameral body of 601 members formed as a result of the Constituent Assembly election that was held on April 10, 2008. The Constituent Assembly is tasked with writing a new constitution, and it will act as the interim legislature for a term of two years. 240 members were elected in single seat constituencies, 335 were elected through proportional representation, and the remaining 26 seats were reserved for nominated members.

The Communist Party of Nepal (Maoist), or CPN (M), is the largest party in the Constituent Assembly, having won half of the constituency seats and about 30% of proportional representation seats. The Constituent Assembly declared a republic at its first meeting on May 28, 2008, abolishing the monarchy.

In late June 2008, the parties agreed to divide the 26 nominated seats in the Constituent Assembly between nine parties: the CPN (M) was to receive nine of these seats, while the Nepali Congress and the Communist Party of Nepal (Unified Marxist-Leninist) (which respectively placed second and third in the election) would each receive five, the Madhesi Janadhikar Forum would receive two, and the Sadbhavana Party, the Nepal Workers and Peasants Party, Janamorcha Nepal, and the Communist Party of Nepal (Marxist-Leninist) would each receive one nominated seat.

Opening of the Constituent Assembly, declaration of the Republic

The official and final list of members elected under the PR system was released on 8 May 2008; this meant the first meeting of the CA (which has to be held within 21 days of the publication of the final result) would be held before the end of May 2008. On 12 May 2008, it was announced that the first session of the CA would be held on 28 May 2008. The members of the CA were sworn in on 27 May 2008.

At the first session of the Constituent Assembly on 28 May, it voted to declare Nepal a federal democratic republic, thereby abolishing the monarchy. 564 members of the Constituent Assembly voted on this motion, with 560 in favour and four opposed. Of all the parties represented in the Constituent Assembly, only the Rastriya Prajatantra Party Nepal (RPP-Nepal) opposed the motion. Koirala said that Nepal was entering a new era and that "the nation's dream has come true", while celebrations took place in Kathmandu; May 29 and May 30 were declared to be public holidays by the government. The Constituent Assembly also decided that Gyanendra should leave the Narayanhity Palace within 15 days.

Earlier on 28 May, the major parties agreed on the creation of the position of President, while the Prime Minister was to hold executive powers; however, they reached no agreement on exactly what powers the President should have or who should become President, and these deliberations led to a delay in the opening of the Constituent Assembly.

On 29 May, the royal standard was removed from Narayanhity Palace and replaced with the national flag. Gyanendra reportedly said on 2 June that he accepted the Constituent Assembly's decision.

Power-sharing discussions

13 parties, including the CPN (M), the NC, and the CPN (UML), met at the Ministry of Peace and Reconstruction on June 1; no agreement was reached regarding power arrangements. The CPN (M) pressed its demand for both the positions of President and Prime Minister, but the NC and CPN (UML) were unwilling to accept this. The NC wanted these positions to be chosen through a simple majority vote in the Constituent Assembly.

Addressing a rally in Gorkha district on June 1, Prachanda gave Koirala an ultimatum to present his resignation to the Constituent Assembly within two or three days, warning that if he failed to do so, the Maoist members of the government would resign and the party would lead street protests. After Gyanendra requested that the government make arrangements for his residence on June 1, the government decided on June 4 to give another palace, the Nagarjuna Palace, to Gyanendra. Also on June 4, Prachanda and Koirala met; at this meeting Prachanda demanded that the government step aside by June 5 and again threatened street protests. On the same day, the three main parties held a meeting at which they again failed to reach an agreement, but the parties agreed on the need for a few more days and the CPN (M) postponed its deadline for the government to step aside to allow for this period.

On June 5, the CPN (M) softened its position, deciding at a meeting of its Central Secretariat that it would not press its claim to the presidency and that it would instead favour having a member of civil society become President. The party expressed continued opposition to a proposal that would allow the Prime Minister to be dismissed by a simple majority vote of the Constituent Assembly. Despite the Maoist desire to have a neutral figure as President, the Nepali Congress proposed Koirala for the position.

The Constituent Assembly held its second sitting on June 5; due to the three major parties' deadlock, this sitting was very brief, lasting less than a half hour, and took no major decisions.

On June 11, Gyanendra gave a brief press conference at Narayanhiti, stating his acceptance of the republic and promising cooperation. He also said that he intended to stay in Nepal, asserted that he held no property outside of Nepal, and expressed his hope that he would be allowed to keep his property. He left Narayanhiti on the same evening and went to his new residence at Nagarjuna.

Shortly after another meeting between Prachanda and Koirala, the CPN (M) ministers announced their resignations and sent a joint resignation letter to Prachanda on June 12. According to the CPN (M) Minister for Local Development, Dev Gurung, the purpose of the resignations was to "accelerate the process of formation of a new government and bring an end to the current transitional period". However, some considered the resignations to be a means of increasing pressure on Koirala. The resignations were not immediately submitted to Koirala by the CPN (M), and therefore were not made effective. Gurung said that he expected a coalition government to be formed by June 18.

Also on June 12, CPN (UML) General Secretary Jhala Nath Khanal asserted that a member of his party should become President. On June 14 he blamed the CPN (M) for the deadlock. At a meeting with Communist Party of Nepal (Marxist-Leninist) General Secretary C. P. Mainali on June 14, Koirala stressed the importance of power-sharing according to the popular mandate and consensus. Mainali expressed the view that the Maoists should be allowed to lead the government, while the post of President should go to someone from the Nepali Congress and the post of Chairman of the Constituent Assembly should go to someone from the CPN (UML). Meanwhile, Prachanda rejected the possibility of Koirala becoming President, saying that this would be a "dishonour to the people's mandate"; he also expressed concern that having Koirala as President could cause the development of a separate power centre from the government, in addition to noting Koirala's advanced age and health problems. Prachanda said that the President should come from a smaller party rather than from the Nepali Congress or the CPN (UML).

Koirala said on June 15 that he would not "run around pleading" for the presidency. Prachanda, meanwhile, said that he expected the new government to be formed imminently, calling on other parties to support this and warning that anyone contravening the people's mandate would have a "heavy price" to pay. Another meeting of the three main parties on June 16 ended in continued disagreement on the key issues, and the CPN (M) said that it would submit the resignations of its ministers to Koirala if the next meeting on June 17 did not produce an agreement.

CPN (UML) General Secretary Khanal said on June 17 that it was important for the left-wing parties to work together. While saying that the CPN (UML) and the CPN (M) would cooperate in the future, he noted that it would be necessary for the parties to improve their difficult relationship. The CPN (M) Central Secretariat met on the same day and approved the decision to hold firm on the key issues and for its ministers to resign if an agreement was not reached later in the day. The party chose to support Ramraja Prasad Singh for the presidency. Upendra Yadav, the Coordinator of the Madhesi Janadhikar Forum, also said on June 17 that his party would not participate in the government and would instead be an opposition party, and he stressed the importance of cooperation among the Madhesi parties. Although he criticized the three main parties for focusing on their power struggle, he endorsed the Maoist claim to lead the government, while asserting that some of the key portfolios should be given to other parties.

The Constituent Assembly went into indefinite recess on June 18. The three main parties continued their discussions on that day, but did not reach an agreement. However, CPN (M) spokesman Krishna Bahadur Mahara said that they were getting closer to an agreement, and he said that the party had postponed its deadline to June 19.

On June 19, the three main parties reached an agreement providing for a constitutional amendment that would enable a government to be formed or dismissed by a simple majority vote of the Constitutent Assembly, rather than the previously required two-thirds majority vote. An agreement was also concluded on the issue of integrating Maoist fighters into the national army. However, the parties did not yet agree on a way to resolve the question of power-sharing. Later that day, the Seven-Party Alliance held a meeting at which Koirala said that he was prepared to resign at any time.

The CPN (M) and the CPN (UML) leadership met early on June 20, and afterwards Khanal said that the CPN (M) had "responded positively" to the CPN (UML)'s proposal to have someone from the CPN (UML) as President. A leading member of the CPN (UML) said that the two parties had agreed on the candidacy of Madhav Kumar Nepal, the former General Secretary of the CPN (UML). However, a leading member of the CPN (M) disputed this, saying that the two parties were closer to an agreement but that their party had not agreed to support a CPN (UML) candidate; he said that both Nepal and Sahana Pradhan (whose name was proposed by the CPN (M)) had been discussed as candidates.

The Nepal Federation of Indigenous Nationalities (NFIN) met with Koirala on June 20, seeking a recommendation that indigenous peoples not already represented in the Constituent Assembly be included in it through the 26 nominated seats. Koirala, who was supportive of the NFIN's request, also sharply criticized his rivals on this occasion, saying that they were practicing petty politics and were not respecting the people's mandate to work on a consensus basis. The Maoist ministers submitted their joint resignation at a meeting of the seven parties on June 20.

Ṡher Bahadur Deuba of the Nepali Congress said on June 24 that the CPN (M) was responsible for the deadlock and claimed that it was working to divide the Seven-Party Alliance. He also said that Koirala would resign after the election of a President and that the CPN (M) had no authority to demand his resignation before then. Also on June 24, the seven parties agreed on the introduction of a constitutional amendment providing for the election of a President and the formation of a government through simple majority votes.

There was, however, disagreement over the Nepali Congress proposal to include a member of the opposition on the National Security Council; the CPN (M) and the CPN (UML) described this as undemocratic. There was also a proposal to include members of each of the seven parties on the National Security Council.

Despite the failure to agree about the opposition's inclusion on the National Security Council, it was agreed to give the opposition a place on the Constitutional Council. The parties also reached agreement on a number of issues related to peace, disarmament and reintegration.

A decision was also reached with to divide the 26 nominated seats in the Constituent Assembly between nine parties: the CPN (M) was to receive nine of these seats, while the Nepali Congress and the CPN (UML) would each receive five, the Madhesi Janadhikar Forum would receive two, and the Sadbhavana Party, the Nepal Workers and Peasants Party, Janamorcha Nepal, and the Communist Party of Nepal-Marxist Leninist would each receive one nominated seat.

Resignation of Koirala, Madhesi demands

The Council of Ministers approved the constitutional amendment late on June 25. At a meeting of the Constituent Assembly on June 26, Koirala announced his resignation, although it will not be finalized until after the election of a President, to whom the resignation must be submitted. Although it was expected that the constitutional amendment would be approved at the same meeting, it was not introduced after Madhesi members of the Constituent Assembly demanded that the amendment be expanded to incorporate a March 2008 agreement between the Madhesis and the government that provided for Madhesi autonomy, among other things. As a result of this, the Constituent Assembly meeting was suspended until June 28. After meeting with Koirala on June 27, Hridayesh Tripathy of the Terai Madhes Loktantrik Party (TMLP) said that Koirala was in favour of incorporating the Madhesi agreement into the amendment and that he asked the Madhesis not to disrupt the Constituent Assembly again.

On June 28, the seven parties met to discuss the Madhesi demands; although no decision was reached, all of the parties opposed the Madhesi demand for a single province. The Constituent Assembly met later that day and was again disrupted by representatives of the Madhesi parties, forcing the cancellation of the meeting after only a few minutes. The next Constituent Assembly meeting on June 29 was also disrupted by the Madhesis and was cancelled. Jaya Prakash Gupta, a leading figure in the Madhesi Janadhikar Forum (MJF), also warned on June 29 that the Madhesi parties would "not only obstruct the Constituent Assembly but also paralyse the entire nation to force [the seven parties] to meet our demands." Prachanda, in an interview on June 30, expressed frustration with the Madhesi parties' disruption, which occurred just after Koirala's resignation, when it appeared the road to forming a new government was clear. He said that he favored Madhesi autonomy, but opposed their demand for all of Terai to become one Madhesi province. Khanal, the CPN (UML) General Secretary, flatly rejected the demand for a single Madhesi province, condemning it as "a game to disintegrate the nation". He said that the demand ignored the wishes of other ethnic groups in the Terai.

The Constituent Assembly met on June 30 but was again disrupted by the Madhesis and the meeting was cancelled. The three main parties reached an agreement with the three Madhesi parties, the MJF, the TMLP, and the Nepal Sadbhavana Party, on July 1, providing for a supplementary amendment bill that would meet the Madhesi demands. Another meeting of the Constituent Assembly was disrupted by the Madhesis and aborted on July 2, while the CPN (M), Nepali Congress, and CPN (UML) met to decide the draft text of the supplementary amendment bill.

The CPN (M) and MJF met on July 3, and the CPN (M) agreed to include a reference to Madhesi autonomy in the bill, while also saying that it wanted the bill to mention other indigenous groups' desire for autonomy. 13 small parties in the Constituent Assembly said on July 3 that they were completely opposed to the Madhesi demand for a single autonomous province, and they criticized the larger parties for the political deadlock that prevented discussion of the issues from taking place in the Constituent Assembly.

Sessions of the Constituent Assembly were attempted on July 3 and July 4, but both were immediately disrupted by the Madhesi members and were aborted. On the latter occasion, Kul Bahadur Gurung, who chaired the session, urged the Madhesi members to respect the right of other members to be heard, but they ignored him. On July 4, the CPN (M), Nepali Congress, and CPN (UML) agreed on a draft supplementary amendment bill intended to satisfy the Madhesi demands. The draft requires the State Restructuring Commission to consider the March 2008 agreement between the government and the Madhesis when drawing up Nepal's federal structure. A meeting of the Seven Party Alliance followed the three-party agreement, and at this meeting, the People's Front Nepal, United Left Front, and Nepal Workers and Peasants Party objected to the draft, saying that it would endanger national unity. The cabinet approved the bill late on July 4; at the same time, it decided to nominate the 26 remaining members of the Constitutent Assembly, dividing the seats between nine parties in accordance with the parties' earlier agreement and the lists of names they presented. The Madhesi parties quickly deemed the supplementary amendment bill to be an unacceptable "betrayal". Khanal, the CPN (UML) General Secretary, said that the bill should satisfy the Madhesi demands, and he warned that opposition to the bill would not be in Madhesi interests or in the interests of any of the peoples of Terai. He called on the Madhesi members to make proposals and engage in discussion in the Constituent Assembly instead of disrupting it.

On July 6, at a meeting between the three main parties and the Madhesi parties, the former agreed to formulate a new bill to replace the one agreed upon two days prior, while the latter agreed to stop disrupting the Constituent Assembly. 23 of the 26 nominated members of the Constituent Assembly were sworn in on July 7; the remaining three were unable to attend the swearing in ceremony. On July 8, the Seven Party Alliance, with the exception of the Nepal Workers and Peasants Party, agreed on the content of a new draft bill, according to which federal structures would be created in line with the wishes of the Madhesis and other ethnic groups.

The Constituent Assembly was able to meet and function on July 9, for the first time since the Madhesis began pressing their demands on June 26. Although they did not disrupt the Constituent Assembly on this occasion, the three Madhesi parties furiously condemned the proposed bill and vowed that their struggle would continue. During the Constituent Assembly meeting, they submitted a protest notice, and when this was rejected, they chose to boycott the Constituent Assembly's proceedings. Narendra Bikram Nemwang, the Minister for Law, Justice and Parliamentary Affairs, tabled the bill regardless.

Koirala said on July 11 that forming a government was the responsibility of the CPN (M). However, the CPN (M) criticized the Nepali Congress on July 12 for "obstructing the process [of forming a government] for the past three months". To protest the amendment bill, the Madhesi parties boycotted the Constituent Assembly meeting held on July 13, at which the amendment bill was considered. The bill was passed on the same day; 442 members of the Constituent Assembly voted for the amendment and seven voted against it. It thus became the interim constitution's Fifth Amendment. The amendment allows for the formation of a government based on a Constituent Assembly majority; it also allows the President, Vice-President, Chairman of the Constituent Assembly, and the Deputy Chairman of the Constituent Assembly to be elected by majority vote if there is no consensus. In addition, the amendment provides for the Leader of the Opposition to become a member of the Constitutional Council, however, the Constituent Assembly rejected a proposal from the cabinet that the Leader of the Opposition be included on the National Defense Council.

In a meeting with the Nepali Congress on July 14, the CPN (M) urged it to participate in the new government. A Nepali Congress leader replied that the party had still not decided whether to participate.

Election of Nepal's first president

An indirect presidential election was held in Nepal on 19 July 2008 with a presidential run-off on 21 July. The Nepalese Constituent Assembly (CA) elected in April 2008 elected a new President and Vice-President after the Fifth Amendment to the Interim Constitution was passed on July 14. This would be the first President to be elected after Nepal became a republic a few months earlier. In the newly passed amendment, the majority party will form the government, the CA will elect the new President on the basis of majority and a new provision that the Opposition Leader will be a member of the Constitutional Council. The leading political parties, Nepali Congress, Communist Party of Nepal (Maoist) and Communist Party of Nepal (United Marxist-Leninist) engaged in discussions regarding who would be the new President. The Nepali Congress wanted Prime Minister and interim Head of State Girija Prasad Koirala while the Communist Party of Nepal (United Marxist-Leninist) wanted its former Secretary-General Madhav Kumar Nepal as President. However, the Communist Party of Nepal (Maoist) wants an independent figure as President rather than party figures such as Koirala or Nepal. The Maoists won the most seats in the CA however needs to form a coalition government with the other parties.

MAOIST THREAT AND POLITICS

The previous issue of the Indian Defence Review carried a letter from a serving air force officer Group Captain RK Prasad to the Home Minister of India. The officer and his family had been mentally and financially tortured by their own countrymen, who like to call themselves 'Maoists'. The younger brother of Gp Capt Prasad was kidnapped in Jharkhand in his and his father's presence. His father and the kidnapped brother had served in the army as well. Overnight, Gp Capt Prasad had to arrange Rs.10 lakh, which the Maoists had demanded as the price for his brother's release. The police expressed its helplessness and the Governor had only sympathies to offer. Incidentally, Gp Capt Prasad was one of the air force officers responsible for coordinating air effort during the 26/11 attack in Mumbai. This is just one story, but there are many more stories about armed forces, para-military and police personnel, both serving and retired, and their families being victims of extortion and kidnapping by the Maoists in the so-called Red Corridor extending from Tirupati to Pashupati.

Not a thought is spared when security personnel are killed in combating the Maoists. The initial stance of the newly elected Jharkhand Chief Minister, wherein he had ordered the security forces to halt all anti-Maoists operations, clearly expatiate the malaise with regard to the criminal neglect and insensitivity to security issues and security forces on part of a large section of our political class and bureaucracy. For them, power and perks of office, and political expediency overrides all other concerns even at the cost of the rapid erosion of the writ of the state. It is for this reason that the Maoists have been able to manipulate our political system and expand their areas of influence that cuts right through the heart of India.

In an earlier article 'The Naked Truth of Naxalism', the nexus between the Maoists and the mainstream political parties. This was clearly evident during the recent assembly elections in the Jharkhand and subsequently from the statements of the Chief Minister. Reportedly, in many seats that the 'Jharkhand Mukti Morcha' (JMM) emerged victorious was due to the hidden support of the Maoists. Press reports also suggested that the state government had issued verbal instructions to the police to not to intercept the mobile phones of Maoists. Also four BSF battalions were diverted to Chhattisgarh as the state government did not give them the green signal to commence operations against the Maoists. Nothing can be more humiliating to security forces. These developments were reported even as the Home Minister P Chidambaram accompanied by high level intelligence and security officials visited Raipur to discuss and coordinate the ongoing joint operations against the Maoists. The meeting was attended by Mr

Raman Singh-Chief Minister of Chhattisgarh, Mr Naveen Patnaik-Chief Minister of Orissa and Mr RR Patil-Dy Chief Minister of Maharastra. Also present in the meeting were the respective DGPs of these states. The Chief Minister of Jharkhand was not part of the meeting even as 18 out of 23 districts of his state, is impacted by the Maoists menace.

Ostensibly, under the pressure of his coalition partner, the BJP, Mr Soren backtracked and issued a statement that he was misquoted and he was not against the special police operation (Green Hunt). Nevertheless, from the posturing of Mr Soren, the Maoists in Jharkhand, have received a major boost. This approach has been atypical of many politicians, who even while paying lip service to the need of curbing Maoist movement, have secret understanding with the Maoist leaders. It is for this reason that the Maoist cadres never have the difficulty in finding safe havens in one or more of the seven worst affected states in the red corridor. Therefore, it would not be misplaced to say that the some of the Maoist affected states are enemies of each-other and in the ultimate analysis are untrustworthy for the integrity of the Union of India.

The Telangana movement, it is well known, is being actively supported by the Maoists by way of militant manpower and financial contributions. Some of the areas in Telangana are virtual Maoist territories for past three decades. The Telangana movement, therefore would acquire even more violent overtones in the future due to the involvement of the Maoists. The Maoists along with the members of CPI (ML) Janashakthi are trying to hijack the Telangana movement and are regrouping in their strongholds of Nizamabad, Karimnagar, Warangal districts. The Maoists are also trying to galvanize people in the interior villages, while the Janashakthi leaders are engaged in mobilization of the masses in urban and semi-urban areas. If the Telangana state were to materialize, the Maoists would have a state to themselves, which would serve as a formidable base for their pan-India aspirations.

The Maoists are not necessarily creations of underdevelopment and neglect. If that was the case, then they would not be destroying critical infrastructure like schools, hospitals, highways, communication towers and railways. If it was a crusade against underdevelopment and for betterment of the people, there would have been no indiscriminate extortions and kidnappings, and their leaders would not have amassed the wealth that they have. And most importantly, if their movement was for positive and benign reasons, the word 'Mao' would have never figured, and if Mao is their inspiration so must be his philosophy: 'power flows out of the barrel of the gun'.

The fact of the matter is that the Maoist movement is aided and abetted by China. A major part of the red corridor lies in India's mineral heartland. It is a deliberate attempt to slowdown or derail India's economic development. The Maoists are engaged in illegal mining with the tacit support of the political dispensations in some areas.

The people of that area have revealed to this author that minerals like iron ore, illegally mined by the Maoists, gain legitimacy through bona fide mining concerns by intimidation and inducement, and are transported to Haldia port in West Bengal from where it is shipped to China. For China, the Maoists are the most reliable tool in the proxy war that it is waging against India.

In the event of an Indo-China armed conflict the Maoists would act as 'fifth columnists'. The nexus of the Maoists in India with Maoists of Nepal is well established. The linkages between the Maoists and insurgent groups like ULFA as well as jihadi terrorist organizations are also known. A Maoist leader has on record said that he supports the growth of Islamic fundamentalism, as it is essentially anti-American.

The Maoist leadership, therefore, are not a bunch of alienated and dissatisfied people. They have a definite agenda, which is scripted outside the country. They have not been averse to being used by the *mafia*, politicians across the political divide and elements inimical to India, even Pakistan's ISI. They have elaborate network. On their payroll are page-3 intellectuals, who surface on the media from nowhere when going gets tough for the Maoists. They also have an elaborate financial, legal and medical network. Some of the ultra leftist political parties, who are overtly in the electoral politics, are actually part of the Maoist network to manipulate the political processes and creation of urban bases.

The Maoists have in effect declared war on India, therefore, the Union of India, must respond not only because of the external dimensions of the problem, but also for the security and well-being of its affected citizens, who for long have endured the Maoist cruelty because of the fear of the gun. If a government of a particular state becomes a burden or distraction in the ongoing war against Maoists, the central government should not hesitate to dismiss that government for the sake of the country.

CEASEFIRE AND DEMOCRACY IN NEPAL

The Maoists in Nepal have once again demonstrated exemplary resilience by declaring a unilateral and indefinite ceasefire on April 3, as proof of their commitment to their understanding with the "democrats". They ceased all military actions in the Kathmandu Valley considering "the requests from the seven-party alliance and from the civic societies". It is too early to assess the exact impact. During their last year's 4-month long ceasefire in the aftermath of the "Royal Regression" of February 1, 2005, they achieved a 12-point agreement with the "democrats", which gravely agonized the Bush regime. The US ambassador and commanders in the Indian Ocean became hyperactive in their words and deed. As reports indicate, the US rulers are eager to renew their military aid to the Big Boy on the Himalayas, which was solemnly withdrawn after his February naughtiness last year. For legitimacy, they are seeking a nod from the "parliamentary" parties. However, it is hard to tell if 'active cooperation' has not yet already started, we definitely have a history behind us, of Reagan's Irangate (Iran-Contra affair) and other covert operations in Latin America, of training and arming fanatic Talibans in Afghanistan.

The spread of the leftist 'menace' in the Global South seems evident, with Peru's forthcoming elections, the Maoists' ceasefire and the interesting possible comeback of the Sandinistas in Nicaragua, against whom the US nurtured narcoterrorism and had a scandalous affair with Iran. The US is at loss for words to characterize this 'scourge', but has begun to realize its deadly vigor. With regional powers in Latin America cooperating among themselves and the increasing Chinese economic support replacing the hollowed and debt-ridden US economy, which survives as the global hegemon only by displaying its militarist pomp and dollar seigniorage, the desperation of the US rulers is evident. They are forced to see the puncturing of the Monroe Doctrine (visualizing the US as the sole power in the Americas), founded on the basis of the self-confidence borne out of the domestic political economic prosperity and stability of the rising US in the 19th century, which ultimately fed on itself, destroying its own basis.

However, as it is well known, a devil is most dangerous when it faces its own death. The Bush administration mentions the threat from the "demagogue" Chavez, the "anti-American dictator" Castro and the "vicious" Maoists in a single breath in its National Security Strategy 2006.

It is not surprising that the US is deploying a Navy Carrier Strike Group "from the U.S. east coast to the Caribbean Sea to conduct Operation Partnership of the Americas from early April through late May 2006". Jorge Martin rightly sees this exercise for "enhancing military-to-military relationships with regional partner nations, improving operational readiness, and fostering good will" as "a strong message to Venezuela and Cuba. The commander of the US Southern Command General Bantz Craddock has on many occasions attacked the Venezuelan government. The decision to send this unusually large force to the Caribbean was announced just two weeks after General Craddok spoke at a US Senate committee hearing in which he called the Venezuelan government a "destabilizing force" because of its moves in the international arena, as well as ongoing efforts to purchase weapons, particularly from China."

On the other side of the Global South, the Commander of the US Pacific Command visited Nepal on the anniversary of the last year's February "royal coup". Since it was an official visit, which could not have happened without the royalty's willingness to meet with him, we must presume the visit as marking the 'celebration' of the "coup". Admiral Fallon called for "national reconciliation" among the "constitutional" forces-parties and the King-to fight the Maoists, who must "not be viewed as a legitimate political actor". To attract the Nepalis, the US embassy time and again advertised this visit with an ostentatious short introduction for the commander-"as PACOM chief, the Admiral commands some 300,000 U.S. military personnel in an area reaching from the west coast of the United States to the east coast of Africa". After that, every significant statement by the US diplomats on Nepal has displayed the US' desperation to renew the military help, begging the parties to break their outrageous alliance with the Maoists. In fact, one needs to just cursorily go through media reports to see US Ambassador Moriarty's daily media interactions, which are heavily concentrated on demonstrating the illegitimacy of this alliance and its dangerous consequences.

In fact there are "unconfirmed" reports in South Asian media about the likely resumption of the US arms supply to Nepal, which has been duly denied by the US embassy. However one needs to just know that there have been such repeated denials many times. Amit Baruah of a leading Indian newspaper, The Hindu (September 29, 2004) while reporting about "a private Bulgarian cargo company, carrying explosives and ammunition to "combat" the Maoists in Nepal"â•¦sitting at an Indian airport", correctly noted, "Given the fact that governments do not want to be seen sending arms and ammunition to other countries, the use of a private charter aircraft would hardly come as a surprise. An element of "deniability" is built into such an arrangement, which governments could easily invoke if and when required."

With the preparation for the 6-9 April showdown by the democrats and the Maoists' exemplary gesture by declaring a unilateral ceasefire, the anxiety among the international players is quite evident. There is definitely a crisis for the US-India imperialist coalition in South Asia. On the one hand, the economic fundamentalist China is busy mobilizing whatever space it can get for its own corporate expansion, unabashedly supplying arms to the King at the wake of the laziness on the part of the Indian counterpart. (However, India recognizes the complementary role of China in this regard, as its Foreign Secretary noted in December 2005, "to the extent that our objectives are the same [to preserve the monarchy], it is better for us to work together".) On the other hand, the EU powers, inconsistent and militarily irresolute as ever, see a good opportunity in the Nepalese "crisis" to aggravate the anxiety of the US-India coalition by giving support, although cautious, inconsistent and largely verbal, to the democratic alliance.

Evidently the ideology of "anti-terrorism" too, which was configured to replace the Cold War ideologies, of the fight against "red menace", is in crisis now. It is on the vehicle of the export of "representative democracy" that Western imperialism under the US has been trying to homogenize the world under its hegemony. This way they can definitely terrorize a few regimes, using democracy as a bargaining chip. In Nepal, even a moderate democrat and, sometimes considered as, a "royalist" among the democrats, ex-Prime Minister G.P. Koirala understands the hypocrisy of the West's "democracy" propaganda. In a recent interview when asked about his reaction to the US ambassador's "warning that the Maoists might take total control with the aid of the [ongoing] movement", he categorically replied, "In order to prevent that from happening. America and all the others have their contradictions here. They say that there is no military solution and we need to find a political solution but why do they fear when we try to bring the Maoists closer to the political solution?"

But it is here that the crisis for global imperialism's post-Cold War ideology of "democracy propagation" lies, with the rise of a 'menace of more democracy' in Latin America and Nepal. Evidently, the democratic appeal of the major revolutionary forces in the world today is more powerful with the elimination of the hegemonist Soviet and Chinese burden. Even the formal bourgeois democratic institutions are increasingly transformed into red flagships. The revolutionaries, like in Venezuela, are aware of the inherent contradiction, as the "democratic representation" in these institutions is founded on the principle of "popular exclusion", of denying the people to directly rule themselves.

However, remarkable is the self-confidence of the post-Cold War revolutionaries that enables them to establish "participatory democratic" practice right in front of the residential palaces and the representatives' talking shops, 'politically competing' with them. This competitive vigor of the 'new' democracy was evident in Venezuela in 2002 during the 2-day-drama around the coup against Chavez, eventually bringing him back to power. In the Venezuelan practice of co-management and in the Argentine "asambleas barriales" and "piqueteros' that openly defy the 'legitimate' political, economic and financial administration we find the heightening of this popular democratic consciousness in Latin America.

The same self-confidence is evident among the Maoists in Nepal, when Prachanda says he is ready for "political competition". This confidence is derived from the heightened political consciousness of the Nepalese poor peasantry, landless, the unemployed, women and the oppressed nationalities/identities, acquired during the decade-long armed struggle. The Maoists have succeeded in drawing this excluded majority to the centre-stage of the Nepalese polity-integrating Nepal in real terms. It is the direct democratic practice of this majority in their daily life that will be decisive in the political competition that Prachanda talks about. Prachanda and other Nepalese revolutionaries question themselves, "What were the negative experiences of the 20th Century in which people who should have been more powerful and should have had more rights, could not get them?" And they stress "that-from the lessons of the 20th Century communist states-we want to move to a new plane in terms of leadership-where one person doesn't remain the party leader or the head of state."

Today, the defiant resistance by Castro's Cuba, the possible comeback of the Sandinistas in Nicaragua and the resolution of the Nepalese 'problem' with an active Maoist participation re-establish the link between the present "Post-Cold War" revolutionary democratic movements and the revolutionary movements of the past. The Maoists' strategy and 'new democratic' program are radically different from what have traditionally characterized the revolutionary movements. However, by refusing to follow the universalist dogmatic voluntarism of radical idealism, they recognize that they are in "a catastrophic new constellation in which the old co-ordinates proved useless". They understand that "the idea is not to return to Lenin [or Mao and others], but to repeat him in the Kierkegaardian sense: to retrieve the same impulse in today's constellation", as Zizek would put.

2006 DEMOCRACY MOVEMENT IN NEPAL

The 2006 Democracy Movement is a name given to the political agitations against the rule of King Gyanendra of Nepal. The movement is also sometimes referred to as Jana Andolan-II ("People's Movement-II"), implying it being a continuation of the 1990 Jana Andolan.

On February 1, 2005 the royal takeover was further advanced as the King appointed a government led by himself and at the same time enforced martial law. The King argued that civil politicians were unfit to handle the Maoist insurgency. Telephone lines were cut and several high-profile political leaders were detained. Other opposition leaders fled to India and regrouped there. A broad alliance against the royal takeover called the Seven Party Alliance (SPA) was organized, encompassing about 90% of the seats in the old, dissolved parliament.

In December SPA signed a 12-point understanding with the Maoists. Within the framework of that understanding, Maoists committed themselves to multiparty democracy and freedom of speech. SPA, for their part, accepted the Maoist demand for elections to a Constituent Assembly.

At the beginning of 2006, the situation became yet more tense as SPA launched agitation programmes around the country. A series of waves of arrests of opposition leaders were conducted. The agitations reached a peak around the February 8 municipal elections, which were boycotted by the SPA and the Maoists. In total, official figures claimed a participation of about 21%. Opposition sources questioned those claims.

April general strike

SPA called for a 4-day nationwide general strike between April 5–9. The Maoists called for a cease-fire in the Kathmandu valley. The general strike saw numerous protests. A curfew was announced by the government on April 8, with reported orders to shoot protestors on sight. Despite this, small, disorganized protests continued.

On April 9, SPA announced that it intended to continue its protests indefinitely and called for a tax boycott. The government announced plans to step up its enforcement of the curfew and claimed that the Maoists had infiltrated the protests. Prachanda, the leader of the CPN(M), had said that "this is no longer a protest by opposition parties... it has become a people's movement," and warned that he himself could lead a revolt in the capital. Protests continued in the following days, with crowds increasing to sizes estimated at 100,000 to 200,000 in Kathmandu in various estimates, more than 10% of the city population. On April 21, opposition sources claim that about half a million took part in the protests in Kathmandu. More conservative estimates talk about 300,000. It is worth noting that a number of the protesters came from outside Kathmandu Valley.

Later the same evening, King Gyanendra announced that he would return political power to the people and called for elections to be held as soon as possible. He called on SPA to nominate a new Prime Minister of Nepal in a speech on a state-owned television station, saying, "We return the executive power of the country to the people. We request the seven-party alliance to recommend a name for the post of prime minister who will have the responsibility to run the government." The position of Prime Minister has been vacant since 1 February 2005 when King Gyanendra removed Sher Bahadur Deuba from office and dissolved the Nepalese Parliament indefinitely. However, the royal proclamation was rebuffed by the opposition. At 3 p.m. the next day, the leaders of SPA met in the capital, and staked out three demands, namely: reinstitution of the old parliament; formation of an all-party government; and elections to a Constituent Assembly that will draft a new constitution.

Reinstitution of Parliament

In a nationally televised address, King Gyanendra reinstated the old Nepal House of Representatives on April 24, 2006. The King called upon the Seven Party Alliance to bear the responsibility of taking the nation on the path to national unity and prosperity, while ensuring permanent peace and safeguarding multiparty democracy. The reinstitution of Parliament was accepted by the SPA. It declared that Girija Prasad Koirala would lead the new government. The SPA stated that the new parliament will hold elections for a body that would write a new constitution.

The move was rejected by the maoists. Baburam Bhattarai stated that merely restoring the parliament was not going to resolve the problems and that the rebels planned to continue fighting against government forces. They still demand the formation of a Constituent Assembly and abolition of the monarchy.

On April 27, however, the Maoist insurgents responded to demands by Girija Prasad Koirala and announced a unilateral three-month truce in the Nepal Civil War. In addition to this, on May 1, Bhattarai announced that if "the elections [to a Constituent Assembly] are free and fair, one has to respect the result of the elections. Then of course we will abide by the verdict of the people." This was seen as a large step forward as it shows the first signs of Maoist acceptance of the democratic process.

On May 2, Koirala announced the new government cabinet including himself and three other ministers from the Nepali Congress: K.P. Sharma Oli from CPN (UML), Gopal Man Shrestha from Nepali Congress (Democratic) and Prabhu Narayan Chaudhari from the United Left Front. This was followed on May 12 by the arrest of four ministers from the ousted royalist government and an investigation into alleged human rights violations by the army during the General Strike.

May 18 Act

The most dramatic move of the post-Loktantra Andolan government came on May 18, 2006 when the Parliament unanimously voted to strip the King of many of his powers. The bill included:

- Putting 90,000 troops in the hands of the parliament
- Placing a tax on the royal family and its assets
- Ending the Raj Parishad, a royal advisory council
- Eliminating royal references from army and government titles
- Declaring Nepal a secular country, not a Hindu Kingdom
- Scrapping the national anthem until a new one is made
- Scrapping the king's position as the Supreme Commander of the Army

The act overrides the 1990 Constitution, written up following the Jana Andolan and has been described as a Nepalese Magna Carta. According to Prime Minister Koirala, "This proclamation represents the feelings of all the people."

May 18 has already been named *Loktantrik Day* (Democracy Day) by some. Although the constitution was accepted, it was always intended to be temporary and on May 29, 2008 a new constitution was voted on by the Nepalese Parliament, which declared that the monarchy would be deposed and a new parliamentary republic would become the Nepalese political framework.

8

Kingdom of Nepal

GORKHA RULE

After decades of rivalry between the medieval kingdoms, modern Nepal was reunified in the latter half of the 18th century, whenPrithvi Narayan Shah, the ruler of the small principality of Gorkha, formed a unified country from a number of independent hill states.Prithvi Narayan Shah dedicated himself at an early age to the conquest of the Kathmandu Valley and the creation of a single state, which he achieved in 1768.

The country was frequently called the Gorkha Kingdom. It is a misconception that the Gorkhali took their name from the Gorkha region of Nepal; actually, the region was given its name after the Gorkhali had established their control of these areas. The Gorkhali take their name from the legendary 8th-century Hindu warrior-saint Guru Gorakhnath. The Gorkhali claimed descent from the HinduRajputs and Brahmins, who entered Nepal from the west.

After Shah's death, the Shah dynasty began to expand their kingdom into much of South Asia. Between 1788 and 1791, during theSino-Nepalese War, Nepal invaded Tibet and robbed Tashilhunpo Monastery in Shigatse. Alarmed the Qianlong Emperor of the Chinese Qing Dynasty appointed Fuk'anggan commander-in-chief of the Tibetan campaign; Fuk'anggan defeated the Gorkhali army and halted their northward expansion.

After 1800, the heirs of Prithvi Narayan Shah proved unable to maintain firm political control over Nepal. A period of internal turmoil followed.

Rivalry between Nepal and the British East India Company over the princely states bordering Nepal and British-India eventually led to the Anglo-Nepalese War (1814–16), in which Nepal suffered a heavy defeat. The Treaty of Sugauli was signed in 1816, ceding large parts of the Nepali territories of Terai, (nearly one third of the country), to the British.

JUNG BAHADUR RANA

Maharaja Jung Bahadur Rana (June 18, 1816, Kathmandu, Nepal -February 25, 1877, Borlang, Gorkha) was a ruler of Nepal and founder of the Rana dynasty of Nepal. His real name was Bir Narsingh Kunwar but he became famous by the name Jung Bahadur, given to him by Mathebar Thapa, his maternal uncle.

During his lifetime, he eliminated the factional fighting at the court, introduced innovations into the bureaucracy and the judiciary, and made efforts to "modernize" Nepal.

He remains one of the most important figures in Nepalese history, though modern historians have also blamed Jung Bahadur for setting up the dictatorship that repressed the nation for more than 100 years and left it in a primitive economic condition.

Others exclusively blame his nephews, the Shumsher Ranas, for Nepal's dark period of history. Rana rule was marked by tyranny, debauchery, economic exploitation and religious persecution.

Immediate Ancestors

His father, Bal Narsingh Kunwar (aka Bala Narsingh Kunwar), was in court the day Rana Bahadur Shah was murdered by his own half-brother Sher Bahadur Shah; as a retaliation Bal Narsingh killed him on the spot. For this action, he was rewarded with the position of *Kaji*, which was made hereditary in his family, also he was the only person allowed to carry weapons inside the court.

Early Life

Jung Bahadur Kunwar joined the military service (1832–33) at the age of sixteen. As maternal grandson of Bhimsen Thapa, he lost his job and his property when the latter fell. After wandering in north India for several years, he returned to Nepal as a captain in the artillery in 1840. In November 1841, he was asked by the king to join his bodyguard, and in January 1842 he began work as Kaji in the palace. When his maternal uncle Mathbar Singh Thapa returned to power, Jung Bahadur rose with him. However Mathbar Singh disliked Jung Bahadur's ambition and had him removed to a lesser position on the staff of the heir apparent. When Fateh Jung Chautaria came to power, Jung Bahadur became fourth in the hierarchy of the coalition government and took pains to flatter the queen while showing no signs of ambition to general Gagan Singh Bhandari. A career opportunist, he was ready and waiting when the time came to act at the Kot massacre.

Queen Lakshmidevi, the favorite wife of King Rajendra Bikram was not pleased by the new prime minister. She conspired to eliminate Jung Bahadur Kunwar and elevate her son to the throne. The Basnyat Conspiracy—so called because many of its participants belonged to one of the last leading noble families, the Basnyat—was betrayed and its ringleaders were rounded up and executed in 1846 at Bhandarkhal Parva. A meeting of leading notables packed with Rana supporters found the queen guilty of complicity in the plot, stripped her of her powers, and sent her into exile in Banaras along with King Rajendra. The king still had delusions of grandeur and began plotting his return from India. In 1847 Jung Bahadur informed the troops of the exiled king's treasonous activities, announced his dethronement, and elevated Rajendra's son to the throne as Surendra Bikram Shah (1847–81). King Rajendra Bikram was captured later that year in the Tarai and brought back as a prisoner to Bhadgaon, where he spent the rest of his life under house arrest.

By 1850 Jung Bahadur had eliminated all of his major rivals, installed his own candidate on the throne, appointed his brothers and cronies to all the important posts, and ensured that major administrative decisions were made by himself as prime minister. At this point, he took the unprecedented step of travelling to Britain and France, leaving fromCalcutta in April 1850 and returning to Kathmandu in February 1851. Although he unsuccessfully tried to deal directly with the British government while he was there, the main result of the tour was a great increase in goodwill between the British and Nepal. Recognizing the power of industrialized Europe, he became convinced that close cooperation with the British was the best way to guarantee Nepal's independence. From then on, European architecture, fashion, and furnishings became more prevalent in Kathmandu and among the Nepalese aristocracy in general.

Muluki Ain

As part of his modernization plans, Jung Bahadur commissioned leading administrators and interpreters of texts on dharma to revise and codify the legal system of the nation into a single body of laws, a process that had not been carried out since the seventeenth century under Ram Shah of Gorkha. The result was the 1,400-page Muluki Ain of 1854, a collection of administrative procedures and legal frameworks for interpreting civil and criminal matters, revenue collection, landlord and peasant relations, intercaste disputes, and marriage and family law. In contrast to the older system, which had allowed execution or bodily mutilation for a wide range of offences, the Muluki Ain severely limited—without abolishing—corporal punishment. For example, the old system gave wide scope for blood vengeance by aggrieved parties, such as cuckolded husbands, but the Muluki Ain restricted such opportunities. Substitutions included confiscation of property or prison terms. Torture to obtain confessions was abolished. Strict penalties were set down for the abusers of judicial positions and also for persons maliciously accusing judges of corruption. There were statutes of limitations for judicial actions. Caste-based differences in the degree of punishments remained throughout, with higher castes (for example, Brahmans) exempt from the corporal punishments and heavy fines that lower-caste members incurred for the same crimes. This distinction was in keeping with the traditional approach of the dharma shastras, or ancient legal treatises.

Control of Nepal

After Jung Bahadur's visit to Europe, he took steps to increase his hold over the country. He reduced the King of Nepal to a prisoner in his own palace, surrounded by agents of the Prime Minister being restricted and supervised at all times. No one outside the King's immediate family could see the King without permission from the Prime Minister. All communications in the name of the king were censored, and he was allowed to read only approved literature. In 1856 the king issued a royal decree (sanad) that formalized the dominance of the Kunwar family. There were three main provisions in this crucial document.

First, the prime minister had complete authority over all internal administration, including civil, military, and judicial affairs, and all foreign relations, including the powers to make war and peace.

Second, Jung Bahadur was made great king (maharajah) of Kaski and Lamjung districts, in effect serving as their independent ruler. The Shah king retained the title of *Maharajadhiraja* (Supreme King) and the right to use the honorific term *Shri* five times with his name. The prime minister could use shri three times with his name. In this way, Jung Bahadur stopped short of taking the throne outright but elevated his family to a level second only to the royal house, which remained as a symbol of the nation. Finally, provisions were established for hereditary succession to the post of prime minister. Brothers and then sons would inherit the position in order of seniority. These provisions meant that the dictatorship of the Kunwar family, a virtual monarchy within the monarchy, would be passed down in the family for generations, with no legal mechanism for changing the government. Later, Jung Bahadur established official Rolls of Succession that ranked all his descendants in relation to their hereditary rights to the office of prime minister.

Jung Bahadur sealed the arrangement with the Shah Dynasty by arranging marriages between his heirs and the royal house. In 1854, his eldest son Jagat Jung (aged eight) married the eldest daughter (aged six) of king Surendra. In 1855 his second son married the second daughter of the king. The ultimate test was passed in 1857, when heir apparent Trilokya Bir Bikram married two daughters of Jung Bahadur. A son of this union, Prithvi Bir Bikram Shah, ascended to the throne in 1881.

Foreign Relations

Nepal began to experience some successes in international affairs during the tenure of Jung Bahadur. To the north, relations with Tibethad been mediated through China since Nepal's defeat in 1792, and during the early nineteenth century embassies had to make the arduous journey to Beijing every five years with local products as tribute to the Qing emperor. By 1854, however, China was in decline and had fallen into a protracted period of disturbances, including the Taiping Rebellion (1851–64), revolts by Muslim ethnic groups north of Tibet, and war with European powers. The Nepalese mission to Beijing in 1852, just after the death of the sixth Panchen Lama, was allegedly mistreated in Tibet. Because of this slight, the Nepalese government sent a protest letter to Beijing and Lhasa outlining several grievances, including excessive customs duties on Nepalese trade. In 1855 Nepalese troops overran the Kuti and Kairang areas. TheNepalese-Tibetan War lasted for about a year, with successes and failures on both sides, until a treaty negotiated by the Chinese resident and ratified in March 1856 gave Nepalese merchants duty-free trade privileges, forced Tibet to pay an annual tribute of 10,000 rupees to Nepal, and allowed a Nepalese resident in Lhasa. In return, Nepal gave up territorial gains and agreed that it, as well as Tibet, would remain a tributary state subject to China. As the Qing Empire disintegrated later in the century, this tributary status was allowed to lapse, and even Tibet began to shake off its subordination.

Prime-Minister of Nepal and Maharaja of Kaski & Lamjung, Jung Bahadur Rana was the first Rajah and Prime-Minister to get state honors in the court of Queen Victoria in 1850. Nepal and Britain became strong allies after Jung Bahadur's return from England visit.

The outbreak of disorder to the south also allowed the Nepalese army to take a more active role in international affairs. The Indian Rebellion of 1857, beginning in May 1857, was a series of related uprisings throughout north India that threatened to topple the power of the British East India Company. The uprisings began with widespread mutinies in the company's army and spread to include peasant revolts and alliances of the old Mughal aristocracy against the foreigner.

Most of the major cities west of Bengal fell into rebel hands, and the aged Mughal emperor, Bahadur Shah II, was proclaimed the leader of a national revolution. Initially there was some fear in British circles that Nepal would side with the rebels and turn the tide irrevocably against the British East India Company, but Jung Bahadur proved to be a loyal and reliable ally.

At that point, immediately following hostilities in Tibet, the army of Nepal had grown to around 25,000 troops. Jung Bahadur sent several columns ahead and then marched with 9,000 troops into northern India in December 1857. Heading an army of 15,000 troops, he fought several hard battles and aided the British in their campaigns around Gorakhpur and Lucknow. The prime minister returned to Nepal triumphantly in March 1858 and continued to aid the British in rooting out "rebels" who had been dislocated during the chaos and sought refuge in the Tarai.

After the Sepoy Rebellion had been crushed and Britain had abolished the British East India Company and taken direct control of India in 1858, Nepal received a reward for its loyalty. Western sections of the Tarai that had been ceded through the Sugauli Treaty in 1816 were returned. Henceforth, the British were firm supporters of Jung Bahadur's government, and Nepal later became an important source of military recruits for the British army.

In 1858 King Surendra bestowed upon Jung Bahadur Kunwar the honorific title of Rana, an old title denoting martial glory used by Rajput princes in northern India. He then became Jung Bahadur Rana, and the later prime ministers descended from his family added his name to their own in honor of his accomplishments. Their line became known as the house of the Ranas. Jung Bahadur remained prime minister until 1877, suppressing conspiracies and local revolts and enjoying the fruits of his early successes. He exercised almost unlimited power over internal affairs, taking for his own use whatever funds were available in the treasury. He lived in the high style of an Anglicised native prince in the British Raj, although unlike the Indian princes he was the ruler of a truly independent nation, an ally rather than a subordinate of the British.

Lineage

Maharaja Sir Jung Bahadur Rana's eldest son was Gen. Jagat Jung, known as "Mukhiya Jarnel". His eldest grandson and Gen. Jagat Jung's eldest son was Gen. Yuddha Pratap Jung, known as "Naati Jarnel". Their descendants currently live in Manohara, Kathmandu.

Most of the people's lineage, who carry the middle and last name 'Jung Thapa', can be traced to Colonel Gajraj Singh Thapa. Colonel Thapa was Jung Bahadur's eldest son-in-law. He was married to Jung Bahadur's eldest daughter Maharajkumari Badan Kumari Rana.

It is said that Jung Bahadur personally insisted his son-in-law to replace the middle name of Thapa's children to Jung from Singh in an attempt to signify his own name. Henceforth, Colonel Thapa's only son was named Harka 'Jung' Thapa; the ancestor of all modern Jung Thapas. However, in the present context it is important to understand that even normal Thapas have started giving the middle name Jung to their children and this does not mean they hold Jung Bahadur's lineage.

Presently if someone carries the name Shumsher Jung Bahadur Rana, then they come from Dhir Shumsher's lineage (Jung Bahadur's younger brother) whose son Bir Shumsher committed thecoup d'etat of 1885 murdering most of Jung Bahadur's sons and forcing the remaining sons, as well as, Prince General Dhoj Narsingh Rana (adopted son of the childless Prime Minister Ranodip Singh) to seek refuge in India. The descendants of Jung and Ranodip live today in North India (mainly Dehra Dun, Allahabad and Udaipur) and Toronto, Ontario, Canada, some did return to Nepal and live in Kathmandu, Nepalgunj and Pokhara. Presently if someone carries the name Bikram Rana they are the descendants from Junga Bahadur's older brother Maharaja Gen.Bhakta Bikram Rana who is widely known as Buda General (old General). His grand son Gen.Rishi Bikram Rana represented Nepalese army in World War II. Another branch of descendants of Jung Bahadur are from two of his sons Gen. Ranabir Jung and Commander-in-Chief Gen. Padma Jung Bahadur Rana KIH Gold Medal 1877 who were escorted to Allahabad. Gen. Ranabir Jung later attempted to reclaim his position, after having raised an army, but was thwarted and finally killed in battle. Ranabir Jungs descendants with the title Bir Jung Bahadur are very widespread, and live in Kathmandu, Dehra Dun, Delhi, Kolkata, Australia and The UK.

Descendants of Commander-in-Chief Gen Padma Jung Bahadur Rana today live in Allahabad, Nepalgunj, Dehradun, Kathmandu, New York, Australia and United Kingdom. Gen. Padma Jung Bahadur Rana later wrote the book called "Life of Sir Jung Bahadur" which was published in early 1900 in India.

His sons and grandsons fought and commanded forces in places like France, Italy, Afghanistan, Burma, Flanders, Egypt, Mesopotamia and Wazirstan during World War I andWorld War II and won long list of medals.

Maharaja and SIR Jung Bahadur's Grandson (Maharajkumar Gen. Padma Jung's son) was first Indian of Nepali-origin to be trained as commanding officer at RMAS Royal Military Academy Sandhurst. He was commissioned as one of the First KCIO King's Commissioned Indian Officer. He later became Commander-in-Chief of Tripura Forces and retired as full Col. of British Raj. He fought gallantly in World War I. At the Battle of Loos he fought bravely and received five bullet wounds in his neck and upper shoulder. He was awarded many medals and honors during his long military career. His name was Rana Jodha Jung Bahadur.

During World War I at the Battle of Loos, in the MID of British Military London News, following was mentioned:

"Rana Jodha Jang Bahadur, who, in spite of being wounded, continued to lead his men against the Germans, and did not desist until a second wound in the neck rendered him unconscious. The Rana displayed great tenacity, leadership and conspicuous gallantry by leading his company right up to the German defenses in the face of heavy fire"

His titles read: Commander-in-Chief Tripura State Forces, Col. Rana Jodha Jung Bahadur, MBE; MIC, MID, GSM, Victory, Jubilee, War and Coronation Medals; KCIO 1st King Commissioned Officer.

Maharajkumar General Padma Jung's daughters, grand daughters and great-granddaughters were/are married to various Maharajas of Indian Principality States. His own sister was Queen of Nepal (married to Sree-Panch Maharajdhiraj Trilokya). Similarly many of his sons, grandsons and great-grandsons were/are married to various Pricesses of Indian Royal Houses.

Maharaja Sir Jung Bahadur Rana of Kaski & Lamjung himself started the process of marrying Rana Gentlemen and Ladies to the Indian Royal Households in the mid-19th century. Commander-in-Chief Gen. Padma Jung continued the process of marrying his sons and daughters to the Indian Royal Households in the late 19th century.

One of his great-granddaughters, Sita Rani Devi, is Rajmata of former Indian Princely State of Makrai. Another great-granddaughter is Geeta Rani Rana, who is married to Late Thakuri Prachanda Singh of former principality/state Royal House of Tulsipur.

Present titular rulers of former kingdoms and states such as Kingdom of Nepal, Jajorkot, Bajhang and Indian Princely States such asJhalai, Jubbal, Bagribari, Tripura, Oel Kaimara, Khairagarh, Rajgarh, Tehri-Garhwal, Khajurgaon Thalrai, Benaras, Ramnagar, Mayurbanj, Poonch,Sikar and many other states share a direct bloodline with Commander-in-Chief Gen. Padma Jung Bahadur Rana and Maharaja of Kaski & Lamjung Sir Jung Bahadur Rana.

RANA RULE

Jung Bahadur was the first ruler from this dynasty. Rana rulers were titled "Shri Teen" and "Maharaja", whereas Shah kings were "Shri Panch" and "Maharajdiraj". Both the Rana dynasty and Shah dynasty are Rajput caste in the Hindu tradition in contrast with the native Himalayan culture which is largely Buddhist and Bön. Jung Bahadur codified laws and modernized the state's bureaucracy. In 1855 he attempted to impose his influence in Tibet but was sliftment of the untouchable class, public access to education, etc. but these dreams were short-lived when in the coup d'état of 1885 the nephews of Jung Bahadur and Ranodip Singh (the Shumshers J.B., S.J.B. or Satra (17) Family) murdered Ranodip Singh and the sons of Jung Bahadur, stole the name of Jung Bahadur and took control of Nepal. Nine Rana rulers took the hereditary office of Prime Minister. All were styled (self proclaimed) Maharaja of Lambjang and Kaski.

20th century

In December 1923 Britain and Nepal formally signed a "treaty of perpetual peace and friendship" superseding the Sugauli Treaty of 1816 and upgrading the British resident in Kathmandu to an envoy.

Slavery was abolished in Nepal in 1924.

Revolution of 1951

Revolution of 1951 started when dissatisfaction against the family rule of the Ranas had started emerging from among the few educated people, who had studied in various South Asian schools and colleges, and also from within the Ranas, many of whom were marginalized within the ruling Rana hierarchy. Many of these Nepalese in exile had actively taken part in the Indian Independence struggle and wanted to liberate Nepal as well from the autocratic Rana occupation.

The political parties such as *The Prajaparishad* and *Nepali Congress* were already formed in exile by leaders such as B. P. Koirala, Ganesh Man Singh, Subarna Sumsher Rana, Krishna Prasad Bhattarai, Girija Prasad Koirala, and many other patriotic-minded Nepalis who urged the military and popular political movement in Nepal to overthrow the autocratic Rana Regime.

Thus Nepali congress formed a military wing Nepali Congress's Liberation Army Among the prominent martyrs to die for the cause, executed at the hands of the Ranas, were Dharma Bhakta Mathema, Shukraraj Shastri, Gangalal Shrestha, and Dasharath Chand. This turmoil culminated in King Tribhuvan, a direct descendant of Prithvi Narayan Shah, fleeing from his "palace prison" in 1950, to newly created country called India, touching off an armed revolt against the Rana administration. This eventually ended in the return of the Shah family to power and the appointment of a non-Rana as prime minister. A period of quasi-constitutional rule followed, during which the monarch, assisted by the leaders of fledgling political parties, governed the country. During the 1950s, efforts were made to frame a constitution for Nepal that would establish a representative form of government, based on a British model.

ROYAL COUP BY KING MAHENDRA

Declaring parliamentary democracy a failure, King Mahendra carried out a royal coup 18 months later, in 1960. He dismissed the elected Koirala government, declared that a 'party less' Panchayat system would govern Nepal, and promulgated another new constitution on December 16, 1960.

Subsequently, the elected Prime Minister, Members of Parliament and hundreds of democratic activists were arrested. (In fact, this trend of arrest of political activists and democratic supporters continued for the entire 30 year period of partyless Panchayati System under King Mahendra and then his son, King Birendra).

The new constitution established a "partyless" system of panchayats (councils) which King Mahendra considered to be a democratic form of government, closer to Nepalese traditions. As a pyramidal structure, progressing from village assemblies to a Rastriya Panchayat (National Parliament), the Panchayat system constitutionalized the absolute power of the monarchy and kept the King as head of state with sole authority over all governmental institutions, including the Cabinet (Council of Ministers) and the Parliament. One-state-one-language became the national policy in an effort to carry out state unification, uniting various ethnic and regional groups into a singular Nepali nationalist bond. The Back to the Village National Campaign, launched in 1967, was one of the main rural development programs of the Panchayat system.

King Mahendra was succeeded by his 27-year-old son, King Birendra, in 1972. Amid student demonstrations and anti-regime activities in 1979, King Birendra called for a national referendum to decide on the nature of Nepal's government: either the continuation of the panchayat system with democratic reforms or the establishment of a multiparty system. The referendum was held in May 1980, and the panchayat system won a narrow victory. The king carried out the promised reforms, including selection of the prime minister by the Rastriya Panchayat.

People in rural areas had expected that their interests would be better represented after the adoption of parliamentary democracy in 1990. The Nepali Congress with support of "Alliance of leftist parties" decided to launch a decisive agitational movement, Jana Andolan, which forced the monarchy to accept constitutional reforms and to establish amultiparty parliament. In May 1991, Nepal held its first parliamentary elections in nearly 50 years. The Nepali Congress won 110 of the 205 seats and formed the first elected government in 32 years.

Civil Strife

In 1992, in a situation of economic crisis and chaos, with spiraling prices as a result of implementation of changes in policy of the new Congress government, the radical left stepped up their political agitation. A Joint People's Agitation Committee was set up by the various groups. A general strike was called for April 6. Violent incidents began to occur on the evening before the strike. The Joint People's Agitation Committee had called for a 30-minute 'lights out' in the capital, and violence erupted outside Bir Hospital when activists tried to enforce the 'lights out'. At dawn on April 6, clashes between strike activists and police, outside a police station in Pulchok (Patan), left two activists dead.

Later in the day, a mass rally of the Agitation Committee at Tundikhel in the capital Kathmandu was attacked by police forces. As a result, riots broke out and the Nepal Telecommunications building was set on fire; police opened fire at the crowd, killing several persons. The Human Rights Organisation of Nepal estimated that 14 persons, including several onlockers, had been killed in police firing.

When promised land reforms failed to appear, people in some districts started to organize to enact their own land reform and to gain some power over their lives in the face of usurious landlords. However, this movement was repressed by the Nepali government, in "Operation Romeo" and "Operation Kilo Sera II", which took the lives of many of the leading activists of the struggle. As a result, many witnesses to this repression became radicalized.

THE ADMINISTRATIVE SYSTEM

The *panchayat* system represented "democracy at the grassroots," and until April 1990 it included four integrated levels:

local or village, district, zonal, and national—the Rashtriya Panchayat. Only the village *panchayat* was directly elected by the people. Championing *panchayat* rule as a political system, king Mahendra was able to tap into nascent Nepalese nationalism and also to outmaneuver the evolving political parties which had posed a challenge to the monarchy's vested power.

The country was divided into fourteen zones and seventy-five districts in support of the complex hierarchy of the *panchayat* system. The lowest unit of government was the *gaun panchayat* (village committee or council), of which there were 3,524. A locality with a population of more than 10,000 persons was organized as a *nagar panchayat* (town committee or council). The number of *nagar panchayat* varied from zone to zone. Above the *gaun panchayat* and *nagar panchayat* was the district *panchayat*, of which there were seventyfive. At the apex of the *panchayat* system was the Rashtriya Panchayat, which served as the unicameral national legislature from 1962 until 1990.

The district *panchayat* had broad powers for supervising and coordinating the development programs of the village and carried out development projects through the district development boards and centres. Each of the seventy-five districts was headed by a chief district officer, who was an elected official, responsible for maintaining law and order, and for coordinating the work of the field agencies of the various ministries.

The zonal *panchayat* was responsible for implementing development plans forwarded by the central government, formulating and executing programs of its own, and planning, supervising, and coordinating district development programs within its jurisdiction. Zonal commissioners exercised full administrative and quasijudicial powers. Each zone was administered by a zonal commissioner and one or two assistant zonal commissioners, all directly appointed by the king. Zones and districts were further regrouped into five development zones in 1971-72, an administrative division that remained in effect in 1991.

A drive for political liberalization, which had begun shortly after the 1959 constitution was abrogated and all political activities were banned in 1960, did not climax until the prodemocracy movement of 1990. At that point, ongoing debilitating interparty conflicts and halting demands for reforms of the political system ended, and national energy focused on a movement to achieve democratic rights. During the prodemocracy movement, some of the *pancha* (*panchayat* members) loyalists even were openly friendly with their former adversaries.

The interim government that was installed in April 1990 consisted of strange bedfellows, who, however, succeeded in steering the nation to its first free and fair elections in thirtytwo years. In April 1990, the *nagar panchayat* was renamed *nagar polika* (municipal development committee), and the *gaun panchayat* became *gaun bikas samiti*, or village development committee. The Ministry of Local Development posted an officer to each district to help with the various programs of the development committees. In mid-1991, a Nepali Congress Party government was in power, and a conglomerate of communist parties was playing the role of constitutional opposition. At that time, there were 4,015 village development committees and thirty-three municipal development committees. Elections for the heads of the development committees were scheduled for June 1992.

The Panchayat System

For centuries the government had been run by a number of interrelated aristocratic families. Despite the limitations of a royal ban on political parties and other impediments, political parties did exist and operated clandestinely. To escape harassment or imprisonment, many political leaders went to India, where they also received logistical and other support.

Under the *panchayat* system, there were six government-sponsored class and professional organizations for peasants, laborers, students, women, former military personnel, and college graduates. These organizations were substitutes for the prohibited political parties and provided alternate channels for the articulation of group or class—rather than national—interests The professional and class organizations were warned repeatedly against engaging in political activity; nevertheless, they offered the only political forum open to many Nepalese, and even some Nepali Congress

Party and communist partisans considered them worthy of infiltration.

The king also launched an independent national student association, the National Independent Student Council (Rashtriya Swatantra Vidyarthi Parishad), to control the political activities of the students. The association failed to gain support, and successful student agitation in 1979 forced the king not only to abolish it but also to initiate constitutional reforms leading to the national referendum of 1980. Also in 1980, a group of dissident *pancha* brought a no-confidence motion against Prime Minister Surya Bahadur Thapa on charges of bureaucratic corruption, food shortages, and lack of economic discipline. Surya Bahadur, however, was a perennial political survivor and was returned to office in 1981.

King Birendra devised the Back-to-the-Village National Campaign (BVNC) in 1975. The BVNC was intended to circumvent the possibility of opposition within the *panchayat* and to create a loyal core of elites to select and endorse candidates for political office, thereby neutralizing the influence of underground political party organizers in the rural areas. Although it was envisioned as a means to mobilize the people for the implementation of development plans and projects, the shortlived BVNC—it was suspended in 1979—was in reality an ideological campaign to reinforce the importance of the partyless system. The campaign stressed that the partyless system was appropriate to the ways of the Nepalese people; the party system was a divisive and culturally alien institution.

Each zonal committee had a BVNC structure, with a secretary nominated by the king. The BVNC network was extended to the district and village levels so as to reinforce a national communication system. However inasmuch as the government paid the BVNC central and zonal committee members and restricted chances for popular participation, the committees carried out the same activities as the *panchayat*. In actuality, the BVNC was created by the king to ensure a loyal organization and circumvent active party members from gaining seats in the *panchayat* elections. The BVNC became an organization of centrally controlled loyal *panchayat* elites and an insurance policy for palace initiatives.

The only significant opposition to the monarchy came from the Nepali Congress Party, which operated from exile in India. Other parties either accepted and operated within the *panchayat* system on a supposedly nonpartisan basis or merged with the exiled Nepali Congress Party, polarizing politics over the issue of monarchical rule. Even the Communist Party of Nepal, divided on the tactical question of whether to seek the direct and immediate overthrow of the monarchical system or to work within it, had split into factions—a radical wing operated in India and a moderate wing underground in Nepal. Some party members, to gain tactical advantage over the Nepali Congress Party, entered the *panchayat* system with the tacit approval of the palace. Ethnic plurality, income disparity, linguistic diversity, pervading regional loyalties, underdeveloped communications, and a paucity of written and electronic media also hindered party organization. The dominant high-caste political leaders were more interested in sharing or gaining access to power than in developing lasting foundations for party politics.

Reportedly, before political organizations were banned, there were sixty-nine political parties, most of which were characteristically fluid in their membership and inconsistent in their loyalties. Personalities rather than ideologies brought individuals and groups under the nominal canopy of a party. Fragmentation, recombination, and alliances for convenience were the outstanding aspects of party behavior. In the polarized political climate, the monarchy looked at the *panchayat* system as its only dependable support base. The *panchayat* apparatus provided access for politically motivated individuals to form a new elite.

Although the political leadership and following of the Nepali Congress Party initially stayed away from the *panchayat* system, over time, and in the absence of an outlet for political activities, some defections took place. Nevertheless, the lateral entry of some pro-Nepali Congress Party elements did not substantially change the character of the *panchayat* leadership, which was dominated by rural elites of the Hill Region rather than the urban Kathmandu and Tarai Region elites who had been in the forefront of political activities. The system was designed so that the established parties would gradually shrink and lose their influence and control. Once the new *panchayat* leadership matured, however, some members became restive under the excessive control of the palace. This group of the *panchayat* elite opposed the system from within and overtly joined the prodemocracy movement.

In the last four decades, there was significant progress towards democracy in Nepal's traditionally authoritarian political system. The first national elections in Nepal took place in 1959— some eight years after the overthrow of the Rana system. The Nepali Congress Party-dominated government, victorious in the 1959 parliamentary elections, was overthrown by King Mahendra within two years—resulting in the ban on political parties. The pattern that developed over the following decades was that of a monarchy reinforcing its power through the traditional institution of the *panchayat*. The *panchayat* system, co-opted and easily manipulated by the monarchy to suit its political ends, nevertheless was slowly but steadily subjected to pressures to change. Over time the monarchy was forced by necessity to expand the role of elections in response to the mounting discontent of a citizenry living in an age of heightened political awareness and rising expectations. This trend culminated in May 1991 with the first truly free elections in over thirty years, ushering in a new political era. The Nepali Congress Party obtained a workable majority within the framework of a constitutional monarchy and affirmed the rise of a nascent democratic force.

One of the ramifications of the prodemocracy movement was the beginning of a process of integration in national politics and decision making. With an elected Parliament and demands for an equitable allocation of resources to different regions, it was likely that all regions would compete for equality in national politics and that the monopoly of power by select families would erode, as would the excessive influence of the Kathmandu Valley Brahman, Chhetri, and Newar elites.

At the beginning of 1990, the *panchayat* system still dominated Nepal. Although the institution itself was the object of derision from opponents of the *panchayat* system, it appeared unthreatened. Within a few months, however, its position eroded and then crumbled with bewildering speed. The surge of the successful prodemocracy movement sweeping Eastern Europe, parts of the Soviet Union, and several Asian countries profoundly inspired the Nepalese people. Also contributing to the sudden transformation were the economic woes of Nepal, exacerbated by India's refusal to renew a trade and transit agreement; widespread bureaucratic inefficiency and corruption at all levels of government; the misgivings openly expressed by the international donors over the country's inefficient use of aid; and a deplorable record on human rights.

In January 1990, the Nepali Congress Party held its first national convention in thirty years in Kathmandu. It was well attended by party delegates from all districts and observers from all political parties. Also present was a multiparty delegation from India, headed by Janata Dal (People's Party) leader Chandra Shekhar, who subsequently became Indian's prime minister. The Nepali Congress Party cooperated with the United Left Front parties, a coalition of seven communist factions, in a joint program to replace the *panchayat* system with a multiparty political system and launched the Movement for the Restoration of Democracy, or prodemocracy movement.

Beginning on February 18, 1990—the thirty-ninth anniversary of King Tribhuvan's declaration of a multiparty democracy and the thirtieth anniversary of the antidemocratic usurpation of power by the palace—a series of spontaneous and sometimes turbulent mass demonstrations rocked major cities. People took to the streets to demand the restoration of a multiparty democracy, human rights, and fundamental freedoms. The success of the Kathmandu *bandh* (general strike) by prodemocracy forces on March 2 was repeated in other parts of the country over the course of seven weeks. By the time the movement succeeded in totally uprooting the *panchayat* system, at least fifty people were dead, and thousands were injured as a result of the force used by the authorities in suppressing the agitation. The government also had incarcerated national and district-level leaders of both the Nepali Congress Party and the United Left Front.

Unable to contain the widespread public agitation against the *panchayat* system and the mounting casualties, and fearing for the survival of his own monarchical status, King Birendra lifted the ban on political parties on April 8. The unrest persisted. In the midst of continued violence, a royal proclamation on April 16 dissolved the Rashtriya Panchayat and invalidated provisions of the 1962 constitution inconsistent with multiparty democracy. The next day, the king named Nepali Congress Party President K.P. Bhattarai, a moderate who had spent fourteen years as a political prisoner, as prime minister and head of the interim government. The government also freed all political prisoners, lifted control of all domestic and foreign publications, and established a commission, known as the Mullick Commission, to investigate the recent loss of life and property.

The eleven-member Bhattarai cabinet, composed of four members of the Nepali Congress Party, three members of the United Left Front, two human rights activists, and two royal nominees, was immediately entrusted with the task of preparing a new constitution and holding a general election. Pending the adoption of a new constitution, the interim government agreed that Nepal should remain under the 1962 constitution. In the interest of continuity and orderly management of public business, the interim government resisted demands from the left for a mass purge of the bureaucracy and die-hard *panchayat* elements. Bhattarai's goal was national reconciliation in a multiparty democracy.

After nine months of politicking, the constitution was proclaimed on November 9, 1990. Elections to the House of Representatives were held on May 12, 1991. The new government faced the immediate problems of restoring law and order, providing economic relief to the populace, and establishing its claim to sound administration, a somewhat difficult task because the parties of the interim government had been in the opposition for a long period of time. Furthermore, pro-*panchayat* thugs who had tried to foment chaos and law and order problems to discredit the new government had to be brought under control. The situation improved as many former *panchayat* leaders who had previously supported moves for a multiparty democracy openly supported the political changes and offered to cooperate with the new government--taking advantage of political opportunism.

POLITICAL PARTIES SYSTEM

The Nepali Congress Party

The Nepali Congress Party, a reform-oriented centrist party, has been in continuous operation since it was founded under a slightly different name in 1947. Elected to office in 1959 in a landslide victory, the Nepali Congress Party government sought to liberalize society through a democratic process. The palace coup of 1960 led to the imprisonment of the powerful Nepali Congress Party leader, B.P. Koirala, and other party stalwarts; many other members sought sanctuary in exile in India.

Although political parties were prohibited from 1960 to 1963 and continued to be outlawed during the *panchayat* system under the aegis of the Associations and Organizations (Control) Act of 1963, the Nepali Congress Party persisted. The party placed great emphasis on eliminating the feudal economy and building a basis for socioeconomic development. It proposed nationalizing basic industries and instituting progressive taxes on land, urban housing, salaries, profits, and foreign investments. While in exile, the Nepali Congress Party served as the nucleus around which other opposition groups clustered and even instigated popular uprisings in the Hill and Tarai regions. During this time, the Nepali Congress Party refused the overtures of a radical faction of the Communist Party of Nepal for a tactical alliance.

Although the Nepali Congress Party demonstrated its ability to endure, it was weakened over time by defection, factionalism, and external pressures. Nevertheless, it continued to be the only organized party to press for democratization. In the 1980 referendum, it supported the multiparty option in opposition to the *panchayat* system. In 1981 the party boycotted the Rashtriya Panchayat elections and rejected the new government. The death in 1982 of B.P. Koirala, who had consistently advocated constitutional reforms and a broad-based policy of national reconciliation, further weakened the party.

In the 1980s, the Nepali Congress Party abandoned its socialistic economic program in favor of a mixed economy, privatization, and a market economy in certain sectors. Its foreign policy orientation was to nonalignment and good relations with India. Although the party also boycotted the 1986 elections to the Rashtriya Panchayat, its members were allowed to run in the 1987 local elections. In defiance of the ban on demonstrations, the Nepali Congress Party organized mass rallies in January 1990 that ultimately triggered the prodemocracy movement.

Following the humiliating defeat of party leader K.P. Bhattarai by the communist factions in the 1991 parliamentary elections, Girija Prasad (G.P.) Koirala was chosen by the Nepali Congress Party as leader of its Parliamentary Board. As prime minister, he formed the first elected democratic government in Nepal in thirtytwo years. G.P. Koirala was the third of the Koirala brothers to become prime minister. Along with his elder brother, B.P. Koirala, he was arrested in 1960 and was not released until 1967. After a period of exile that began in 1971, he returned to Nepal in 1979 under a general amnesty. He was elected general secretary of the party in 1976 in a convention at Patna and played a key role in the prodemocracy movement. G.P. Koirala was known for favoring reconciliation with the left, but he also wanted to pursue national unity and Western-style democracy.

The Communist Parties

Like the Nepali Congress Party, the fractured communist movement was deeply indebted to its Indian counterpart, whose initiative had helped to found the Communist Party of Nepal (Marxist) in 1949 in Calcutta. Nepalese communists looked askance at the Nepali Congress Party leadership as willing collaborators of Indian expansionism and called for broad-based alliances of all progressive forces for the establishment of a people's democracy.

As many as seventeen factions, ranging from the quasiestablishment royal communists to extremely radical fringe groups, vied for leadership and control, preventing the movement from making significant gains. The proscription of political parties in 1960 affected the communists less severely than other parties because communist factions proved better at organizing and operating underground and at making the transition to covert activity. Little effort was exerted to detain communist leaders, and in the months following the palace coup d'état in 1960, the

Communist Party of Nepal (Marxist) was allowed to operate with a perceptibly greater amount of freedom than any other party. The Communist Party of Nepal (Marxist-Leninist) was established in 1978, one of many splinter groups under the name Communist Party of Nepal. In spite of many vicissitudes encountered since the movement's inception, the communists maintained national attention because of continued support from the peasant and worker organizations and the fact that the country's poverty and deprivation offered a fertile ground for Marxist ideals. Support was maintained through the All Peasants Union and the Nepal Trade Union Congress.

Communist groups wielded significant influence in the universities and professional groups. The movement had a dedicated cadre of motivated youth who followed party discipline strictly. Whereas the Nepali Congress Party seemed to accommodate the old guard at the expense of the younger generation, communists more ardently sought younger members. Most of the mainstream communist groups in the 1980s believed in democracy and a multiparty system, recognized no international communist headquarters or leaders, and abjured the Maoism many had embraced earlier.

The United Left Front coalition, organized in late 1989, supported multiparty democracy. During the prodemocracy movement, it played a crucial role by joining the interim government led by the Nepali Congress Party and by submerging serious differences of opinion. Although differences in the communist camp were endemic when the movement was underground, the internal conflicts lessened as communists operated openly and began to look toward future electoral gains.

The success of the communist parties in the May 12, 1991, election, came as a shock to the Nepali Congress Party, which had failed to repeat its 1959 landslide victory. Although there was some unity among the communist factions of the United Left Front, there was no agreement to share seats with the other factions or groups. The Communist Party of Nepal (United Marxist-Leninist) faction—formed as a result of a merger between the Communist Party of Nepal (Marxist) and the Communist Party of Nepal (MarxistLeninist)—came in second to the Nepali Congress Party. The head of the communist leadership echelon was Madan Bhandari, son of a Brahman priest, who was working to turn his Communist Party of Nepal (United Marxist-Leninist) into a formidable political power. He stunned the Nepali Congress Party in the 1991 elections by narrowly defeating its leader, K.P. Bhattarai, for a parliamentary seat in Kathmandu.

As a partner in the interim coalition government, the Communist Party of Nepal (United Marxist-Leninist) had endorsed, although reluctantly, the new constitution, which retained the monarchy. The communists received popular support for their allegations that the Nepali Congress Party was too close to India and was a threat to Nepal's sovereignty. Other mainstream communist leaders were Man Mohan Adhikari and Sahana Pradhan, both originally of the Communist Party of Nepal (Marxist); and Bishnu Bahadur Manandhar of the Communist Party of Nepal (Manandhar), another communist faction.

Other Political Parties

There was a phenomenal rise in the number of political parties--particularly between May and September 1990—as strategic maneuvers to participate in parliamentary elections and find a niche in postelection Nepal occurred. The Nepal Sadbhavana Party (Good Will Party), one of several regional and ethnic parties, was founded in April 1990. It aimed at promoting the interests of the Tarai Region, including the expulsion of the Hill people from Tarai and the establishment of a special relationship with India in the framework of nonalignment. A forum for people of Indian descent, the party also favored the introduction of Hindi as the second national language. Its ideology supported a democratic socialist society. Other Tarai Region parties included the Nepal Tarai Unity Forum, the Nepal Tarai Association, and the Nepal Tarai Muslim Congress Party.

Among the several ethnic parties were the National People's Liberation Front (Nepal Rashtriya Jana Mukti Morcha), the National Mongol Organization (Rashtriya Mongol Sanghatan), SETAMAGURALI (an acronym of names of different ethnic groups of eastern Nepal including the Tamang, Magar, and Gurung), the

Front of the Kirat Aborigines (Nepal Kirat Adhibasi Janajiti Morch), the Freedom Front of the Limbu People (Limbuwan Mukli Morcha), and the Nepal Nationalist Gorkha Parishad, or Parishad (Nepal Rashtrabadi Gorkha Parishad). The Parishad, revived in September 1990, was founded in 1951 as part of Rana revivalist politics and had placed second in the 1959 general elections. Some of its senior leaders later joined the Nepali Congress or *pancha* camps.

Of those groups favoring the monarchy, two conservative parties received considerable attention. Hastily founded by two former prime ministers, both parties were called the National Democratic Party—suffixed with the names Thapa or Chand enclosed within brackets. Other parties of this political bent included the National Democratic Unity Panchayat Party (Rashtriya Prajatantrik Ekata Panchayat Party), Nepal Welfare Party (Nepal Janahit Party), United Democratic Party (Samyukti Prajatantra Party), and Nepal Panchayat Council (Nepal Panchayat Parishad). Besides the Nepali Congress Party, fifteen centrist parties also had emerged. Most of these parties were founded by former members of the Nepali Congress Party and defecting *pancha* who had shifted allegiance to the multiparty system. The Women's Democratic Party aimed at promoting the rights, interests, and freedoms of Nepalese women.

ELECTIONS

The 1981 Elections

Growing political unrest, accompanied by massive demonstrations, forced King Birendra, as a palliative tactic, to call for a nationwide referendum to choose the form of government. Following the May 2, 1980, referendum—the subject of charges of rigging—the *panchayat* system was reaffirmed. However, members of the Rashtriya Panchayat would henceforth be elected directly by the people on the basis of universal adult suffrage. In May 1981, the king promulgated the third amendment to the 1962 constitution incorporating the results of the referendum. There was no change in the fundamental principle of partylessness; all candidates for the Rashtriya Panchayat competed as individuals.

The first direct election to the Rashtriya Panchayat was held in May 1981. In the midst of an election boycott by the Nepali Congress Party and other banned political parties, the exercise only legitimized the administration of Prime Minister Thapa as a democratically elected popular government. Indirectly, however, the election was counterproductive because it intensified further the increasingly sharp divisions within the various *panchayat* and the continued opposition of the Nepali Congress Party, various communist factions, and peasants' and workers' organizations. There were 1,096 candidates contesting 112 seats in the 1981 elections. Campaign appeals were made on regional, ethnic, and caste lines rather than on broad national issues. Among the contestants were forty-five candidates from pro-Moscow communist factions, thirty-six candidates from the Nepali Congress Party, and several multiparty *pancha*. Voter turnout was 63 percent. Despite Thapa's reelection, more than 70 percent of the official candidates were defeated. Candidates who supported the multiparty system also fared poorly. The election of fifty-nine new members in the Rashtriya Panchayat indicated the voters' rejection of the old guard. The indirect participation of the political parties was a symbolic gesture toward national consensus and reconciliation; the chief protagonist was the moderate Nepali Congress Party leader, B.P. Koirala.

In the tradition of *panchayat* political patterns of instability, the quick fix of a referendum and new elections failed to restore political equilibrium to the system. Corruption and general administrative inertia further vitiated the political climate. Even senior *panchayat* leaders, who were openly critical of the system, became willing participants in intrigues, which only precipitated counterplots by paranoid palace advisers. Clashes between students, which were at times supported by faculty members, created disturbances throughout the country.

The 1986 Elections

Between the 1981 and 1986 elections, there was a growing rift among the *pancha*. Without a viable economic and political program, disillusionment with the *panchayat* system increased. In the face of a deteriorating economy, faltering development plans, and the failure of the *panchayati raj* to inspire motivation and confidence in an already demoralized bureaucracy, the credibility of the government waned. The banned political parties, especially the Nepali Congress Party, after initial efforts at reconciliation, concentrated on organizational work and the demand for political pluralism. Most political activities, however, were noticeable only within the *panchayat* system itself. Appointed in 1983, the new prime minister, Lokendra Bahadur Chand, had a no-confidence motion filed against him immediately after taking office. The motion was declared inadmissible on the grounds of errors in drafting, but this power struggle among different groups of *pancha* further undermined the *panchayat* system.

The uneasy political stalemate was upset when in late May 1985, the Nepali Congress Party, in preparation for the 1986 election, decided to launch a *satyagraha* (civil disobedience) campaign—in which many communists also participated—to demand reforms in the political system. A large number of Nepali Congress Party activists were quickly arrested. Although the campaign generally lacked popular support, it received considerable attention and interest among intellectuals and students, caused tension within the government, and further divided the already fractured *panchayat*. Kathmandu also was subjected to violence, including explosions that rocked the royal palace and other key buildings. There was further discontent when, at the *panchayat* workers' annual congress, the moot issue of government accountability to the legislature was disallowed from discussion.

In a politically charged atmosphere, the second quinquennial nationwide election to the Rashtriya Panchayat was held in May 1986. Slightly more than 9 million voters cast their ballots for 1,584 candidates for 112 seats. According to official sources, 60 percent of all eligible voters participated in the election.

The election was marked by a lack of enthusiasm, which partly reflected the Nepali Congress Party's boycott. A few communist factions contested the election. About 20 percent of the candidates were elected either on the basis of their roles as champions of the opposition or for their stand against the elite. Allegations of electoral malpractice also were widely voiced. The electoral success of forty-five Chettris and Thakuris, sixteen Hill Brahmans, and seven Newars indicated that the traditional power structure remained largely unaffected. Marich Man Singh Shrestha, a Newar, was appointed prime minister. Three women were elected to the Rashtriya Panchayat from the Tarai Region, but no Muslims were elected.

Local Elections in 1987

In contrast to the procedure followed in the 1986 elections, the Nepali Congress Party and a number of communist factions allowed their members to participate as individuals in the 1987 local elections. The Nepali Congress Party also made it clear that its local election strategy did not mean an end to its opposition or resistance to the *panchayat* system. In urban areas, especially in the Tarai Region, certain party members, as well as some communists, did very well and were returned to office in substantial numbers.

The 1991 Elections

For many Nepalese, participation in the democratic process meant either walking for hours along mountain paths or riding a yak to cast a ballot. Since most voters were illiterate, they had to choose a candidate according to the party's symbol as authorized by the election commission; for example, a tree signified the Nepali Congress Party and a sun represented the Communist Party of Nepal (United Marxist-Leninist).

Although forty-four parties were recognized by the Election Commission, only twenty parties actually contested the elections. The twenty parties ranged across the political spectrum from radical right to loyalist leftist and all except a leftwing radical faction, Masal (Torch), eagerly participated in the elections. Twelve parties did not win a single seat and obtained a total of only about 82,500 votes, slightly more than 1 percent of the total valid votes. Many voters seemed to have fallen back on their ageold identification with caste or ethnic community. Younger voters favored the progressive leftist parties, as did voters in the urban areas.

The Nepali Congress Party won the first multiparty election in thirty-two years, taking 110 seats in the 205-member House of

Representatives. The results of the elections, however, demonstrated that a coalition of various communist parties was a major political force in Nepalese politics, defying the international trend of dismantling communist parties and regimes. The Communist Party of Nepal (United Marxist-Leninist), a constituent of the United Left Front, won sixty-nine seats. The three other communist parties of the United Left Front coalition won a total of thirteen seats. Besides the Nepali Congress Party and the Communist Party of Nepal (United Marxist-Leninist) alliance, four other parties qualified for national party status, which meant they polled more than 3 percent of the total votes cast.

The election was marked by heavy voter turnout. Of a total of more than 11 million voters, about 7 million, or 65 percent, cast ballots, of which slightly more than 4 percent were declared invalid on technical grounds. The election results made it very clear that the promonarchists and those in favor of the panchayat system lacked national support. Communist parties won in the Kathmandu Valley and some parts of the eastern Tarai Region. The Nepali Congress Party won in other parts of the Tarai Region and in western Nepal. The National Democratic Party (Chand) won three seats and the National Democratic Party (Thapa) won only one seat. The four members of those parties, six Nepal Sadbhavana Party members, and independents were expected to join the moderate Nepali Congress Party. All leftist elements under the Communist Party of Nepal (United Marxist-Leninist) umbrella were likely to form a solid opposition in Parliament to the Nepali Congress Party government.

The new House of Representatives included thirteen members of the dissolved Rashtriya Panchayat, five Muslims, seven women, and six members of the Parliament that had been dissolved in 1960. Although the number of women representatives was much lower than was hoped for, Muslim representation was comparable to their proportion of the population. Also notable was the performance of the ethnic or regional parties, in particular the Tarai-based Nepal Sadbhavana Party, which polled 4 percent of the valid votes, allowing it to claim the status of a national party. Out of the five seats in Kathmandu, the Nepali Congress Party won one seat; the rest were swept by the Communist Party of Nepal (United Marxist-Leninist). The average age of the newly elected members of the House of Representatives was forty-three.

Kathmandu citizens made it clear that they had enough of political dynasties. The son and wife of Nepali Congress Party figurehead Ganesh Man Singh ran for two of the high-profile seats; both were defeated by communist candidates. In the prestigious contest for a seat in Kathmandu, the Communist Party of Nepal (United Marxist-Leninist) general secretary, Madan Bhandari, defeated interim Prime Minister K.P. Bhattarai. The poor showing of the Nepali Congress Party in the urban areas may also be attributed to the fact that, given that the communists had been banned for thirty years, the party did not see them as potential opposition and was overconfident.

The continuing transition from a partyless *panchayat* system to a multiparty democracy was relatively peaceful, although there were some incidents of sporadic violence. Six deaths in preelection violence were reported, but no election-related deaths were confirmed on polling day. Police enforced a curfew during the long wait for election results. Because of election irregularities and violence, the Election Commission—which enjoyed the confidence of all the parties—ordered repolling at 44 of 8,225 polling centres, affecting 31 constituencies.

In response to the interim government's invitation to international observers, a host of Asians, Europeans, and North Americans journeyed to Kathmandu. Among the observers was a sixtyfour member international observation delegation, representing twenty-two countries, which was organized by Nepal's National Election Observation Committee. The committee was an offshoot of Nepal's Forum for the Protection of Human Rights. The international delegation concluded that the elections generally were conducted in a fair, free, and open manner and that the parties were able to campaign unimpaired. Complaints were received that equal and adequate access to radio and television was denied, however, and that the code of conduct and campaign spending limitations were violated. The delegation also recognized that, as confirmed by the Election Commission, from 5 to 10 percent of eligible voters were not registered and that there were some inaccuracies in voter lists.

On May 29, 1991, a Nepali Congress Party government was installed with G.P. Koirala as prime minister. The first session of Parliament was held on June 20. The new government faced two enormous tasks, both of which concerned India: the negotiation of a new trade and transit treaty, and the exploitation of Nepal's only major natural resource, water, for hydroelectric power for purchase by India. Further, although the Communist Party of Nepal (United Marxist-Leninist) faction wanted to end recruitment of the Gurkhas into the British and Indian armies, the Nepali Congress Party wanted neither to outrage the Gurkhas nor to deprive the country of the foreign remittances sent by the soldiers.

THE CONSTITUTION OF THE KINGDOM OF NEPAL, 1990

The Constitution of the Kingdom of Nepal promulgated in 1990 has been modelled after the West-Minister style of parliamentary form of government, which is highly centralized and exclusionary. Indeed, winner takes all in such a system. Given socio-cultural diversity of the Nepalese society and culture, the Constitution discriminates and excludes minorities in many ways. The Consultative workshop organized by Nepal Federation of Nationalities (NEFEN) with support from Minority Rights Group International (MRG), has identified 26 provisions in the Constitution and 49 legal Acts that discriminates against indigenous nationalities. There are many such provisions that discriminate against other minorities. Also, caste-based untouchability has been made illegal but lack of laws has made it meaningless in practices.

There has been a strong demand for secularism not only by the non-Hindus but also by the Hindu Dalits who have been forced to face caste-based untouchability by their "upper caste" Hindu counterparts. In spite of a fact that Nepal is a multi-religious country and a historical fact that about 150,000 people demonstrated in the streets of Kathmandu, which was the largest gathering ever in the history of Nepal, demanding for secularism, the Constitution of the Kingdom of Nepal, 1990 declared Nepal as a Hindu State, prohibited to form any political parties on the basis of religion. According to the Article (4) of the Constitution, 'Nepal is a multiethnic, multilingual, democratic, independent, indivisible, sovereign, Hindu and Constitutional Monarchical Kingdom.'

Another most discriminatory provision is the distinction between "nation's language" and "national languages." The Constitution declared Nepali language as the only official language. Article 6 of the Constitution states, '(1) The Nepali language in the Devnagari script is the language of the nation of Nepal. The Nepali language shall be the official language. (2) All the languages spoken as the mother tongue in the various parts of Nepal are the national languages of Nepal.'

Article 18 (2) in the Fundamental Rights, the Constitution has restricted the right to education in one's own mother tongue with such restriction, 'Each community shall have the right to operate schools up to the primary level in its own mother tongue for imparting education to its children.' Such a provision restricts the right of education in mother tongues beyond grade five.

Many indigenous nationalities of Nepal have a culture of eating beef ("cow meat"). The National Code of Nepal (Muluki Ain) prohibits killing of cow and the offender gets life sentence. Instead of declaring national animal with full cultural sensitivity, Article 7 (2) of the Constitution declared cow, which is sacred for the Hindus only, as the national animal. Therefore, indigenous nationalities are prohibited to slaughter cow and eat its meat.

A study conducted by the Forum for Women, Law and development (FWLD) in 2000 stated, 'there are 118 Clauses/Section/ Rules, two Rules in their entirety, and 67 Schedules/Annexes/ Forms in 54 different laws including the Constitution which have discriminatory provisions'. The Constitution and laws discriminate women in every field including citizenship, property, education, employment, health, marriage & family, legal & court proceedings. For example, Article 9 of the Constitution discriminates women thus, '(1) A person who is born after the commencement of this Constitution and whose father is a citizen of Nepal at the birth of the child shall be a citizen of Nepal by descent. (2) Every child who is found in within the Kingdom of Nepal and the whereabouts of whose parents are not known shall, until the father of the child is traced, be deemed to be a citizen of Nepal by descent.'

Forms and Origins of Discrimination

There are several historical markers of domination and discrimination against indigenous nationalities and other minorities in Nepal. These are as follows:

The main historical marker of Hindu domination begins with caste restructuring by King Jayasthiti Malla in the Kathmandu Valley in the fourteenth century. The King invited five Brahmin priests from India to Kathmandu. Based on their advice, the King restructured the Newars, the indigenous nationalities of the Kathmandu Valley, into 64 castes based on occupational division of labour. These caste divisions were neither based on hierarchic Hindu varna model, that is, Brahmin at the top followed by Kshyatriya, Vaisya and Sudra at the bottom, nor on inscription. It indeed paved a way for intensification of the processes of Hinduization or Sanskritization of indigenous nationalities of Nepal.

The second historical marker of Hindu Bahun-Chhetri domination is the conspiratorial attack against the Magar King of Lig-Lig Kot by King Drabya Shah, who later won a war against the Khadka King of Gorkha in 1559 A.D.. This was the beginning of the downfall of independence of indigenous nationalities in Nepal.

The third historical marker of continuing Hindu Bahun-Chhetri domination is the territorial "unification" of Nepal in 1769 by King Prithvinaryan Shah. Prior to 1769, indigenous nationalities had their own rule in their respective traditional homelands. King Prithvinarayn Shah annexed small but independent kingdoms, "22 and 24 principalities," of different indigenous nationalities either through defeat in war or through mutual agreement of autonomy within the centralized state. After the defeat of Kirtipur in the Kathmandu Valley, King Prithvinaryan Shah ordered to chop off nose tips and ear of the peoples of Kirtipur that weighed 18 dharnis, i.e. about 8 kilos. Thus, one can imagine the extent of brutal physical violence and humiliation to minorities and indigenous nationalities under the sword of Prithvinarayan Shah. The King accepted that Nepal is a country 'a garden of four castes and thirty-six varna' but his mission was to make Nepal a "real India" ("*Asali Hindustan*"). The main consequence of the "territorial unification" was that all indigenous nationalities lost their independence and gradually lost their rights to land, water, forests, mines, rivers and pastures. Thus, indigenous nationalities began to loose their language, religion, culture and indigenous knowledge system.

The fourth historical marker is the Muluki Ain (National Code of Nepal) of 1854 implemented by Junga Bahadur Rana, the founder Prime Minister of 104-years of autocratic Rana rule. The National Code, the first ever codified law applicable in all parts of Nepal, restructured caste and ethnic groups and divided them into fourfold social hierarchy. The Tagadhari (sacred thread wearing or twice-born) caste was the top, followed by the Matawali ("alcohol drinking castes"). They were sub-divided into namasine (enslavable) and masine (slavable) groups. Although, indigenous nationalities never belonged to Hindu social hierarchy but the Rana ruler legally included them in the second in the hierarchy as "alcohol drinking caste." Pani nachalne chhoee chhito halnu naparne (impure but touchable castes) were third and pani nachalne chhoee chhito halnu parne (impure and untouchable castes) belonged to the bottom of the social hierarchy. The whole National Code, including the punishments was based on caste discrimination. Thus during the 104-years of Rana rule, indigenous nationalities of Nepal were Hinduized and Sanskritized. As its consequences, many indigenous nationalities began to loose their language, religion and culture. The most devastating events in this period was confiscation of traditional Kipat land tenure and re-distribution of land to state elites, i.e. Bahun, Chhetri, Rana and Thakuri, through Birta and Jagir land tenures and exploitation of Indigenous Nationalities and Dalits through forced free labour such as jahra, rakam, beth and beggar. The Rana rulers prevented Tamangs, one of the Indigenous Nationalities of Nepal, from joining British-India Army and any government jobs in Nepal, except as Pipa (porter) in Pipa Goswara office in Singha Durbar.

During the Partyless Panchayat rule from 1960-90 under the direct and active rule of King Mahendra and King Birendra, the rulers launched a campaign of "One King, One Country; One Language, One Dress." The project of "melting pot" was intensified in a country characterized by "salad bowl" of caste, ethnicity, language, religion, culture and region. Any organized effort to preserve and promote indigenous nationalities' language, religion and culture was charged as "anti-King," "anti-constitution," "anti-national," and "communal." Also, caste-based untouchability was abolished in the revised National Code of 1963 but due to lack of necessary laws, its practice continues unabated The People's Movement of 1990, following the pro-democracy wave in the Soviet Union, eastern-European countries, and other parts of the world, jointly organized by the Nepali Congress Party and the United Left Front, including the Nepal Communist Party (Marxist-Leninist), demolished the autocratic partyless Panchayat political system and restored democracy in Nepal. It raised a lot of hope and expectation to reduce socio-cultural and political inequalities. The hope remained unfulfilled.

Finally, the Maoist "People's War" that started in February 1996 has brought the issues of indigenous nationalities, Dalits, women and other minority groups to the forefront. The government security forces tend to treat them with hostility as potential "terrorist."

Indigenous Nationalities & Minorities

Although there is commonality among different minority groups in Nepal, that is, all of them are discriminated due to the dominance of Brahmanistic ideology, policy and practices. This is, however, manifested in somewhat different forms with similar and/or different consequences among different minority groups. Common contested prime issues of all minorities are elimination of all forms of domination and discrimination, secularism, affirmative action, representation in decision-making positions, and factual census data. Nevertheless, there are some issues very specific to each of the minority groups. This section will analyse the contested prime issues of indigenous nationalities, Dalits, linguistic groups, religious groups, Madhesi and women. They all have raised their respective issues in a peaceful way through interaction programs, seminars, workshops, conferences, press release, memorandum, street demonstration, publications and so on. These all groups are never tired of making demands with His Majesty's Government of Nepal but the latter hardly hear these voices and raise frustration of these right-based activists. If HMG-N and donors do not hear these voices, Nepal will be entangled in disastrous civil war sooner or later.

Indigenous nationalities: Indigenous nationalities and other minorities are against domination, subjugation, suppression, oppression, depression, compression, exploitation, monopoly etc. by dominant castes (Bahun-Chhetri), religion (Hindu), language (Nepali) and culture (Hindu), sex (male), region (the Kathmandu Valley). They all are against all forms of discrimination. They are indeed for inclusive democracy through elimination of Bahunism (Brahminism); land rights; right-to-self determination; federalism; proportional representation; secularism; caste/ethnic; linguistic, religious, gender, regional and cultural equality; mainstreaming caste/ethnicity, language, religion, gender, and region; empowerment of caste/ethnic, linguistic, religious, gender, regional and cultural groups; and effective implementation of international instruments of human rights, including indigenous nationalities right, minority rights and women's rights.

Before 1990, demands of organized indigenous nationalities were branded as "anti-national," "anti-King," "anti-political system," "anti-constitution," "divisive," and "secessionist" by the dominant group. Although, the Tharu had formed the Tharu Kalyankari Sabha in 1950 and the Tamang and the Thakali also formed their own organizations, these organizations were confined to purely cultural activities only. It was the Newar of the Kathmandu Valley who raised their voice for language rights since the time of the autocratic Rana rule and they intensified their demand during the autocratic partyless Panchayat rule. Some indigenous nationalities made efforts during late 1970s to form a federation of different indigenous nationalities, such as the SETAMAGURALI, but the rulers suppressed any such effort. After the people's movement and the restoration of democracy in 1990, those indigenous nationalities who were already organized intensified their efforts and unorganized ones also began to organize.

Such a hopeless situation changed after the people's movement of 1990 that overthrew the autocratic partyless Panchayat political system, which was based on the active leadership of the King. The Constitution of the Kingdom of Nepal, 1990 declared, in its preamble, that human rights, freedom and equality will be guaranteed through the parliamentary form of government, constitutional monarchy and multi-party democracy. Although the Constitution accepted Nepal as a multi-caste/ethnic country but also it declared Nepal as a Hindu kingdom and Nepali language as the only official language of the country. Unfortunately, during the first half of the last twelve years, any organized efforts or their demands were labelled as "communal," "secessionist," "disintegrative" etc. by the dominant group. Despite of negative perception of the dominant group, indigenous nationalities expanded and intensified their movement for equal rights since 1990, the dominant group was forced to accept, since mid-nineties, that indigenous nationalities have been indeed discriminated by the State in the last two and a quarter centuries. Till now indigenous nationalities are against the domination of Bahun-Chhteris. They are against them in many issues. They, therefore, have been demanding for equity and equality.

Dalits: Although the term "Dalit" is still controversial, however, the Dalit leaders and their organizations have now accepted to identify their community by this term not to loose its historical, ideological, social, cultural and political contexts. In the past, Dalits were referred by several terms including "untouchables," "Sudra," "pariganit," "water unacceptable caste," and "Harijan" ("god's people"). The New National Code of 1963 abolished caste-based untouchability, but due to lack of laws, its practices continue unabated. A recent study conducted by Bhattachan *et al.* (2001) revealed at least 205 different forms of caste-based untouchability are practiced in different parts of Nepal. Another study conducted by Dahal *et al.* (2002) revealed that Dalits are marginalized in every field due to caste-based discrimination.

In spite of Dalits being Hindus and Nepal being the only Hindu kingdom in the world, Hindu "high caste" peoples continue to treat Dalits very inhumanly as untouchable peoples. Practices of untouchability exist not only between the Dalit and non-Dalit but also within the Dalits, between "high caste" and "low caste" Dalits. For example, Kami is at the top of the social hierarchy, followed by Sarki, Damai and at the bottom are the Dom. Such practices were legally enforced by the National Code of 1854. Therefore, it is not a creation of the Dalit community as such. Similarly, some Hinduized or Sanskritized indigenous nationalities also practice caste-based untouchabilty because of the same Code.

The National Code of 1854 placed Dalits in the third and last in the four-fold social hierarchy as untouchables and the whole legal system discriminated on the bases of castes, Dalits were oppressed and suppressed in every sphere. They were not able to get organized and raise their voice until mid-1940s. It was, the Kapalis of Kathmandu Valley initiated Dalit movement with a demand for entry in Hindu temples, including the temple of Pashupatinath in Kathmandu. Since then other Hill Dalits, particularly, Blacksmith and Tailor (Damai or Pariyar) intensified the Dalit movement with demands for elimination of all forms of caste-based unotuchability. By now, the Hill Dalits, particularly, Kami, Sarki and Damai are better organized and other Hill Dalits and Madhesi Dalits are yet to get organized and intensify the Dalit movement. As an exception, recent Chamar movement in Siraha was very powerful and successful in their struggle against caste-based untouchability.

Linguistic Minorities: Among the linguistic minorities, the Nepal Bhasa speaking Newars have been in the front line of equal language right movements since the time of autocratic Rana rule. The Madhesis, who have their own mother tongues, also intensified the movement for equal language rights since the dawn of democracy in 1950. HMG-N's following language policy adopted in 1956 was nothing but a predatory for mother tongues ,

'Nepali should be the medium of instruction, exclusively from the third grade on, and as much as possible in the first two grades.

No other languages should be taught, even optionally, in the primary school because: few children will have need for them, they would hinder the teaching of Nepali. ...'

This policy was pursued vigorously during the partyless Panchayat rule from 1960 to 1990. The Newars, with support of other indigenous nationalities continued to intensify the language movement but the dominant group branded such efforts as "anti-national," "communal," "anti-constitutional" and "secessionist".

The movement received legitimacy after the promulgation of the Constitution of the Kingdom of Nepal, 1990, which accepted Nepal as a multi-lingual country but unfortunately, differentiated between nation's language and national languages and declared Nepali as the only official language of Nepal. Thus, the new Constitution worked as catalysis of struggle for equal language rights. Due to mounting pressure from the equal language rights, HMG-N set up the National Languages Policy Recommendation Commission in 1993. The government did not implement the recommendations made by the Commission but as a window dressing, the government set-up a committee to identify the languages in which news could be broadcasted from the government owned Radio Nepal. Initially, five-minutes news was broadcasted in nine languages and now it is broadcasted in 16 languages, including Sanskrit. Equal language rights activists have been denouncing that the government's negative attitude towards mother tongues is exhibited by giving priority to Sanskrit, a dead language, against other live languages.

The Local Self-Government Act of 1998 gave rights to local bodies, DDCs, VDCs and Municipalities to preserve and promote national languages. In the course of its implementation, Kathmandu Municipality, Rajbiraj Municipality and Dhanusha DDC decided that Nepal Bhasa (Newari language) will be used as an additional official language and Rajbiraj Municipality and Dhanusha DDC decided that Maithil language will be used as an additional official language in their respective local bodies. Later, in a writ petition against the use of national languages as official languages, the Supreme Court of Nepal made a ruling on June 1, 1999 that none of the government bodies, including local government bodies, must use Khasa/Nepali language as the only official language. Protesting against such court decision, equal language right activists closed down the Kathmandu Valley for one day and since then

Language discrimination has deprived mother tongue speakers from education, including under Basic and Primary Education Project (BPEP) and being literate, right to information, and right to development. As a consequence, they are deprived from getting scholarship for higher education abroad and passing examination taken by Public service Commission for various gazetted and non-gazetted civil service posts.

Religious Minorities: Given the out of proportion representation of Hindus in executive, legislature and judiciary and also in media, minority religious groups, including Kirants, Buddhists, Islams and Christians, have been systematically marginalized by the dominant Hindu religious group. All these minority religious groups are against Hindu domination but some religious groups, particularly Kirants and Buddhists are vocal critics whereas other groups such as Islams and Christians are in defensive posture due to fear of backlash from the Hindus.

Although, political leaders, policy makers, planners, development practitioners etc. never get tired of saying that Nepal is characterized by religious harmony, the reality is entirely different. It is true that in the past, different religious groups have not resorted to violence and insurgency but it does not mean that there were no incidences of communal clashes at different places in different times. For example, there were several cases of Hindu-Muslim clashes in some Terai districts, including Banke, Rautahat and Kapilvastu. In such clashes, often referred as "communal clashes," the local administrators, security personnel and political leaders, who mostly belong to dominant Hindus, organize meetings involving all groups and find out solutions, which invariably favours the Hindus.

Another example of Hindu-Buddhist conflict was the so-called "Hindu-Buddhist unity conference" organized by the Hindus in Lumbini in the year 2000.

Madhesi: Madhesis have been treated as second-class citizens after the territorial integration of Nepal by King Prithvinaryan Shah in 1769. During the autocratic Rana rule, Madhesis were required to obtain visa to visit the Kathmandu Valley. Madhesi representation in Army, civil service, judiciary is negligible but their representation in cabinet, Parliament, and political parties is low. Due to marginalization of Madhesi by the dominant caste, they formed the Nepal Sadavabana Party, a region-based political party and formed coalition government time and again. In the last twelve years of democracy, all political parties, including the Sadvabana Party failed to address the fundamental problems facing the Madhesi community. Many Madhesis, therefore, formed the Madhesi Liberation Front as a wing of the Nepal Communist Party (Maoist), who is waging an insurgency for the lat seven years. Madhesi movement as a social movement is between the political party and liberation front. They are mainly against Khasa-Brahmanism. They are for regional autonomy.

Often Madhesi are wrongly stereotyped as "Indians" by the Hill people. They are as Nepalese as any other Nepalese people. Due to centuries of suppression and oppression against Madhesis, they generally shy away from speaking out loudly against such practices. However, the communal tension between the Hill peoples and Madhesis that broke out for few days in December of 2001 indicated that the bond that ties between the Hill people and Madhesi are very fragile and that Madhesi have courage to speak out against suppression and oppression against them.

Women

Women comprise a little more than a half of the total 22.3 million population of Nepal. The Nepalese women are not a homogenous group. Instead, it is characterized by diversity in terms of race, caste, ethnicity, language, religion, culture, and region. All Nepalese women are victims of gender discrimination but the nature, forms, degree and intensity differs among different caste/ethnic, religious and cultural groups. Therefore, some Nepalese women are victimized more than other women. The so-called high caste women of the Hills are single victim of gender discrimination but of the Madhes (Terai region) are victims of gender and regional discrimination. Similarly, women belonging to indigenous nationalities are multiple victims, one from gender discrimination and other from ethnic, linguistic, cultural and religious discrimination. Hill Dalit women are victims of gender and caste-based discrimination but Madhesi Dalit women are additional victims of regional, cultural and linguistic discrimination.

The extreme forms of gender discrimination are found among the Hindus whose society is characterized by patriarchy. Hindu women have no access to and control over property and have restricted mobility. They are dependent to men throughout their life, that is, daughters are dependent to fathers, wives to husbands and mothers to sons. In contrast, women belonging to indigenous nationalities have relatively more freedom, social mobility, access to and control over resources than their Hindu counterpart, but they are underrepresented not only in women's rights movement but also in public positions as the latter dominate them.

Women's rights movement has a history of about five decades. The movement has been dominated mainly by women belonging to the dominant Bahun-Chhetri castes and the Hinduized Newar women. To assert their due place in both the women's rights movement and the national development, indigenous women have formed their organizations and federated in National Indigenous Women's federation (NIWF) and Dalit women have formed Feminist Dalit Organization (FEDO). Among the minorities, international donors have been giving support, both technical and financial, to women's movement and women's empowerment since the seventies in the names of Women in Development (WID), Women and Development (WAD) and Gender and Development (GAD). In the seventies and eighties, women's movement was more focused on income generation but since the nineties its focus is on rights-based movement. The Nepalese women are against all forms of discrimination against women. They are indeed for gender equity and equality.

Violence on Indigenous Nationalities & Minorities

Till now there has been no caste or ethnic, linguistic and religious insurgency in Nepal in the past but now there is such possibility. The Nepal Communist Party (Maoist) has been waging a Maoist insurgency in the form of "People's War" since February 13, 1996 with support of different minorities—women, Dalits, indigenous nationalities and Madhesi. It has been primarily a class based internal (civil) war but interestingly class has been blended with caste/ethnic, regional and gender components. The rationale for the "People's War" given by the Maoist are twofold: one, stop imperialism and expansionism of the external forces and two, eliminate internal social and spatial contradictions of a semi-feudal political-economic system.

The immediate reason for the birth of insurgency appeared to be the failure of HMG-N led by Prime Minister Sher Bahadur Deuba of Nepali Congress Party to address 40-points demands submitted to be as a memorandum. However, the main reasons for the rise of insurgency include lack of decentralization of power and authority, rising corruption, nepotism and favouritism, lack of democratic culture in political parties, poverty, failure of foreign aid to address the burning issues of the peoples at the grassroots level, and soicocultural discrimination against Indigenous Nationalities, Dalits, Madhesi, and linguistic, religious and regional groups.

9

Political Condition in Nepal

The mass movement of April 2006 in Nepal sought to restore parliament for the democratic process to continue and to initiate a peace process for the end of a ten-year long armed conflict. This required the Communist Party of Nepal (Maoist) to join democratic competition which in turn necessitated the devising of a constitution to manage root causes of conflicts afflicting the nation.

Hence, a Constituent Assembly (CA) election, that would pave the way for an inclusive state responsive of social diversity and sustainable peace, was seen as the compromise solution among all the political forces. A train of processes and events was thus set off resulting in the advent of current Nepalese politics. A Comprehensive Peace Agreement (CPA) was signed between an alliance of the seven political parties (six after the merger of Nepali Congress and Nepali Congress-Democratic) and the CPN (Maoist) on November 21, 2006. An Interim Constitution drafted and the restored parliament dissolved to pave the way for an interim legislature and interim government that included the CPN (Maoist) in 2007. The ruling seven-party alliance (SPA) announced substantive structural reforms, such as declaration of the country secular, federal and republican. Civilian control of Nepal Army (NA), nationalization of royal property, empowerment of the Premier as head of state, abolition of the national unification day and substitution of the national anthem were announced as time went by. There were also reform measures such as greater inclusiveness regarding marginalized people in the CA, the bureaucracy and police. However, all these measures have allowed a neo-patrimonial regime to incubate, sapping the political will necessary to alter the policy and strategic development vital to transform the "structural causes of conflicts". This has hindered efforts for cultural, social, economic and political transformation needed to establish a well-organized virtuous state capable of instituting sound democratic governance. The political transition has remained highly turbulent due to the open-ended nature of the conflict system. It is, therefore, hard to say whether Nepal has actually entered a post-conflict phase.

The continuation of high political dynamics in the country now indicates a steady erosion of the writ of state and the low level of constitutional and government's stability. This has resulted in a new bargaining environment for armed non-state actors and movement-oriented ethno-regional forces thus further limiting the scope for complex reforms, both involving long-term institutional restructuring and short-term policy interventions. The weakness of state institutions has further spoiled efforts to promote relief to vulnerable sections of the population and address conflict residues. Social movements of marginalized groups—women, Dalits (untouchable underclass), Janajatis (ethnic groups), Aadibasis (indigenous groups) and Madhesis (people living in the southern plains) — for identity, proportional representation, federalism and self-determination and insurrectionary activities of two-dozen non-state armed actors have upset the coherence of state-society relations in an unprecedented manner. While the mainstream parties have interest in restructuring the state, the social forces favour restructuring political parties to expand the social base of politics.

As a result, the SPA has missed three deadlines (June 14 and 20 and November 22) for the CA elections to draft a new constitution. It was forced to amend the Interim Constitution three times in eight months-(May 9, June 14 and December 18) to give in to rising demands that the political process was exacting and to give in to the voice of various agitating groups. Among the provisions included in the amendments the more significant ones empower the parliament to abolish the monarchy, if found plotting against the CA elections, and declare the country a federal democratic republic, subject to ratification by the elected CA, or even before that by a two-thirds legislators if the King poses a threat to the elections. Despite voices emerging for a space for monarchy and efforts of CPN (Maoist), NC and CPN-UML to woo its supporters, King Gynendra remains aloof from the power struggle. All this has not changed the political dynamics for the better. The Madhesi People's Rights Forum (MPRF), a group which organized violent protests in the Tarai where scores of people were killed last year, is demanding a fourth revision of the constitution to address the grievances of the Madhesis.

HISTORICAL CIRCUMSTANCE TO THE PRESENT POLITICAL POSITION

Nepal has been an independent kingdom since 1768. Never colonized, the country was almost totally isolated from outside influence until the early 1950s. A transition from strict rule by the king to constitutional monarchy began in 1959, when then-King Mahendra issued a new constitution and held the country's first democratic elections. In 1960, however, the king declared the parliamentary system a failure, dismissed the fledgling government, suspended the constitution, and established a partyless system of rule under the monarchy. Although officially banned, political parties continued to exist and to agitate for a return to constitutional democracy. In February 1990, student groups and the major political parties launched the Movement for the Restoration of Democracy.

The centrist Nepali Congress (NC) party joined with the leftist parties to hold peaceful demonstrations in Nepal's urban centres. In April 1990, after more than 50 people were killed when police fired on a crowd of demonstrators, then-King Birendra turned power over to an interim government. This government drafted a constitution in November 1990 establishing Nepal as a parliamentary democracy with a constitutional monarch as head of state. The king at that time retained limited powers, including the right to declare a state of emergency with the approval of a two-thirds majority of parliament. In February 1996, the leaders of the underground CPN-M launched a "People's War" in the mid-western region of Nepal, with the aim of replacing the constitutional monarchy with a one-party Communist regime. The uprising appears to have been fuelled by widespread perceptions of government corruption and failure to improve the quality of life of citizens, including providing access to cultivable land. The Maoists ran a parallel government, established their own tax system, burned land records, and redistributed seized property and food to the poor, in 45 districts. The insurgency was waged, in part, through torture, killings, and bombings targeting police, the military, and public officials. A number of bank robberies, combined with "revolutionary tax" revenue, made the Nepali Maoists one of the wealthiest rebel groups in Asia. The Kathmandu government faced additional turmoil in June 2001, when Crown Prince Dipendra shot and killed his parents, King Birendra and Queen Aishwarya, seven other members of the royal family, and himself reportedly after a disagreement over whom he should marry.

This incident did much to undermine the legitimacy of the monarchy. King Gyanendra, the former king's brother, was crowned on June 4, 2001, and he appointed a commission to investigate the assassinations. By mid-June, the country began returning to normal following rioting and widespread refusal to believe official accounts of the massacre. In July 2001, Prime Minister Girija Prasad Koirala stepped down amid fears of continuing instability and his government's failure to deal with the growing Maoist insurgency. He was replaced by NC leader Sher Bahadur Deuba, who then became the head of Nepal's eleventh government in as many years.

Constitutional Crisis

During the summer of 2002, the government of Nepal was thrown into a constitutional crisis that interfered with its ability to effectively combat the Maoist insurgency. The crisis began in late May, when King Gyanendra, at the request of the prime minister, dissolved parliament and unilaterally declared a three-month extension of emergency rule, which had expired on May 24, 2002. The prime minister, who also scheduled early elections for November 2002, reportedly took such action after his centrist

Nepali Congress party refused to support his plan to extend emergency rule. Following the prime minister's actions, 56 former members of parliament filed a lawsuit against him, claiming there was no constitutional precedent for the dissolution of parliament during emergency rule. In August 2002, the Supreme Court rejected this lawsuit. Although opponents of the prime minister agreed to accept the verdict, they emphasized the difficulty of holding free and fair elections two years ahead of schedule when much of the country was under either rebel or army control. Although the prime minister pledged that there would be no emergency rule during the scheduled November 2002 elections, Maoist attacks and threatened strikes prompted the government to consider various measures to prevent a Maoist disruption of the polls.

The government discussed imposing a partial state of emergency in areas most affected by the insurgency. However, opposition parties, which urged the government to open a dialogue with the Maoists, argued that by curbing civil liberties, emergency rule would inhibit free and fair elections. As an alternative, the government announced in September 2002 that it would hold the elections in six stages over two months, starting in mid-November, so that government troops could be transferred around the country to protect voters and candidates. After further deliberation, however, Nepal's cabinet concluded that the security situation was too risky to hold elections. On October 3, 2002, the cabinet asked King Gyanendra to postpone the national elections for one year. The next day, the king dismissed the prime minister, disbanded his cabinet, and assumed executive powers.

The King's Takeover

The security situation in Nepal deteriorated after the collapse of the ceasefire between the Maoists and the government on August 27, 2003. The Maoists favoured drafting a new constitution that would abolish the monarchy. The king opposed such a move and wanted the Maoists to relinquish their weapons. Accommodation between the king and opposition democratic elements had been thought to be key to creating the unified front necessary to defeat the Maoists. With his direct assumption of powers, and arrest of opposition democratic elements, the king decided to try to defeat the Maoists on his own. This move proved to be the beginning of the end of the power of the monarchy in Nepal. After seizing direct power in February 2005, King Gyanendra exerted control over democratic elements, but made little progress in the struggle against the Maoists. The king reportedly thought he could take advantage of a split in the Maoist leadership and disarray amongst democrats to seize control and use the Royal Nepal Army (RNA) to defeat the Maoists. The seizure of power by the king appears to have been aimed as much, if not more so, at asserting the king's control over democratic forces.

Many observers felt that a military solution to the conflict with the Maoists was not achievable and that a concerted effort by the king and the democrats was needed to establish a unified front to defeat the Maoists. When the king assumed power he stated that he would take steps to reinstate a constitutional democracy within 100 days, which he then failed to do. Although some political prisoners were released by the king, hundreds of others remained under arrest and restrictions on civil liberties, such as public assembly and freedom of the press, remained in place. A U.N. Office of the High Commissioner of Human Rights team was established in Nepal in April 2005 to monitor the observance of human rights and international humanitarian law.

By moving against the democrats, who under different circumstances could have worked with the king against the Maoists, the king strengthened the position of the Maoists. By some estimates almost half of the RNA was occupied with palace security, civil administration, and efforts to restrict communications and civil rights. The king's legitimacy with the people was weakened due to the circumstances under which he assumed the throne, the way he seized direct rule, and due to poor popular perceptions of his son, Prince Paras Shah. The former Crown prince was unpopular with Nepalis "for his drunken antics and playboy lifestyle." Maoist Reaction. From February 13 to 27, 2005, the Maoists reacted to the king's actions by blockading major highways linking the country's 75 districts, as well as international road links to India and China. This led to clashes between Maoists and the RNA and brought trade by road to a standstill. The army organized armed convoys which allowed limited trade to continue. The Maoists had earlier cut off land routes to Kathmandu in August 2004. During the week-long blockade in 2004, prices of some basic foods more than doubled and fuel was rationed. This increase in food prices reportedly recurred in the 2005 blockade. By blockading Kathmandu, the Maoists successfully increased pressure on the king's government and demonstrated their power.

Democratic Rebellion

On April 24, 2006, mounting popular resistance in support of the political parties led King Gyanendra to hand over power to the Seven Party Alliance. This followed weeks of violent protests and demonstrations against direct royal rule in Nepal. The Seven Party Alliance that opposed the king in April included the parties. The Maoists were not part of the Seven Party Alliance, though they worked with the alliance to oppose the monarchy. This was made possible by the king's political crackdown on the democrats.

- The Nepali Congress (NC)
- Communist Party of Nepal Unified Marxist Leninist CPN (UML)
- Nepali Congress (Democratic) or NC (D)
- Nepal Sadbhavana Party (Anandi Devi) or NSP (A)
- Jana Morcha Nepal
- Samyukta Baam Morcha (United Left Front) or ULF
- Nepal Workers and Peasants Party (NWPP).

The seven parties worked together through their alliance to promote a more democratic Nepal in the face of direct rule by the king. In May 2006, six of the seven political parties formed a coalition government. On November 8, 2006, the Seven Party Alliance and the Maoists reached a peace agreement ending a decade-old insurgency that claimed over 13,000 lives. In it, the Maoists agreed to put down their arms and postpone a decision on the future disposition of the monarchy until after the election of a Constituent Assembly. Under the peace agreement, Constituent Assembly elections were to be held by the end of June 2007. The June election date slipped but Constituent Assembly elections were eventually held in April 2008.

COMMUNIST PARTY OF NEPAL

The Communist Party of Nepal (Maoist) adheres to the ideals, aspirations and course of action based on Mao's style of dictatorship of the proletariat. As one of the extreme left organisation, its main objective is to 'establish a 'people's government' through a 'people's war.' The executive head of the CPN (Maoist) is its general secretary Pushpa Kamal Dahal (Prachanda). Baburam Bhattarai, considered a moderate, is the political face of the Maoists. The political party structure consists of a politburo central committee, regional bureaus, sub-regional bureaus, district committees and cell committees. The party has emphasised its course of action on political and military strategies. For administrative convenience it has divided the country into three zones and twenty-seven districts. On the military front it has a central military commission, regional military commissions and the district military commissions. The Maoists have maintained fraternal and ideological linkages with the People's War Group and Maoist Communist Centre in India who also provide them with arms and ammunition.'

The Communist Party of Nepal (Maoist) is a member of the Revolutionary Internationalist Movement (RIM). It has links especially with the Maoists in Peru, India, Turkey, Philippines, Bangladesh, Sri Lanka, Iran, Italy, New Zealand and the United States. The CPN (Maoist) has support groups and solidarity forums outside the country in India, Hong Kong, Germany and in Belgium.

In 1990, the two major communist factions united into the United Marxist-Leninist party 'UML'. The Communist Party (UML) emerged as the second main party in the parliament during the first general elections, held in 1991. The Nepali Congress, led by G. P. Koirala, emerged as the major party and formed the government. However, G. P. Koirala resigned in 1994, and during the ensuing mid-term elections the Communist Party (UML) won and formed the government under the leadership of Manmohan Adhikari. However, the communist government was not able to perform well and fell after nine months. According to Bertil Lintner, 'the CPN (UML) was not radical enough; it resembled a European social democrat party rather than a militant organisation that was going to introduce any radical political or economic changes.' It was because of these reasons that differences arose within the party and the main factions, Samyukta Jana Morcha (United People's Front), under the leadership of Dr. Baburam Bhattarai, left the Communist Party (UML). This faction had won nine seats during the 1991 elections. Dr. Baburam Bhattarai was dissatisfied with the working of the left parties who according to him, had digressed from the Marxist goal of creating a classless society. The Samyukta Jana Morcha united with the Communist Party (Maoist) and launched the 'People's War' in 1996.

CPN (MAOIST)'S PEOPLE'S WAR

The Communist Party of Nepal (Maoist) launched the 'People's War' on February 13, 1996, with the aim 'to smash the existing semi-feudal and semi-colonial state and build a people's New Democratic State.' According to Dr. Baburam Bhattarai, Chairman United People's Front, 'An armed People's War has been initiated in Nepal from February 13, 1996 under the leadership of the Communist Party of Nepal (Maoist) with the proclaimed aim of establishing a New Democratic socio-economic system and state by overthrowing the present socio-economic structure and state. This should be understood under the background that Nepal has slided to the status of the second poorest country in the world in terms of physical and cultural developments.'

Explaining the rationale behind the 'People's War', Dr. Baburam Bhattarai emphasised that 'the Nepalese Maoists' attempt to create a new democratic system through People's War began only after all attempts to carry out reforms within the old semi-feudal and semi-colonial system had failed. The ruling classes want to continuously exploit the people through the present socio-economic system, and international forces also exploit the people through internal means.

From this point of view the People's War in Nepal is part of the world anti-imperialist national liberation movement.' Ms. Li Onesto, a commentator for the Pacific News Service, in 1999 visited the Maoist-controlled areas in western, central and eastern Nepal. In her reports, she stated that the rural areas were underdeveloped, without electricity, running water and basic sanitation. The statistics of deprivation according to Shom Prasad Luitel, that make Nepal the second poorest country in the world are: '71% of the population is below absolute poverty level; 46.5% of national income is in the hands of 10% of the richest people; more than 60% of its total population are illiterate, more than 90% of its total population live in rural areas and 81% of the labour force is engaged in backward agricultural occupations; 10% are totally unemployed and 60% are under-employed or in disguised employment.'

As commented by Ms. Onesto, the rural population, including farmers and women, supported the Maoists as they were advocating land ownership rights, development and equality for women. According to other reports, the Maoists in these regions, 'burned property-ownership records and redistributed land among farmers. Women, in these areas, were also given various rights.' Thus, the Maoists gained support at the grass roots level by appealing to their sense of deprivation and grievances.

The CPN (Maoist) has two organisational structures, the political front, and the military front. The political front's responsibility is to organize, create awareness and spread Maoist ideas. The military front organises attacks on police and other targets. It has around 5000-armed personnel; including the militia. Various other organisations affiliated with the Maoist party are the All-Nepal National Free Students Union (Revolutionary), All Nepal Women's Association (Revolutionary), All Nepal Trade Union Federation and National People's Movement Coordination Committee.

When in 1994 the Samyukta Jana Morcha, led by Baburam Bhattarai disassociated itself from the Communist party (UML) and continued its armed rebellion in the rural areas, the State authorities intensified their campaign to crush the movement. The Nepali government launched 'Operation Romeo' in November 1995 against the extreme communists.

It was in this backdrop that Samyukta Jana Morcha united with the Communist Party (Maoist) and launched the People's War. According to Bertil Lintner this campaign is based on the Peru's Shining Path model. 'It has established strongholds in remote mountain regions, where police outposts are few and far between, enabling the guerrillas to move about freely.' Their arms are primitive and generally collected in the villages from farmers or snatched from the police in encounters. However, some small arms, as pointed by Lintner, were bought in the black arms market in the Indian State of Bihar. During this period there was anti-India feeling among the Nepalese because of the water and hydroelectric power issue (the Mahakali Treaty). The Maoists also exploited these nationalist feelings and won support in the rural community. Dr. Bhattarai in his article 'Politico-economic Rationale of People's War' states: 'the biggest direct manifestation of world imperialist oppression and exploitation in Nepal is Indian expansionist exploitation and oppression.' The CPN (Maoist)'s political front, as part of it People's War in 1996, put forward forty demands to the government headed by Nepali Congress Party. These were within the following categories:

Demands Related to Nationalism

1) Regarding the 1950 Treaty between India and Nepal, all unequal stipulations and agreements should be removed.
2) The Government (HMG) should admit that the anti-nationalist Tanakpur agreement was wrong, and the Mahakali Treaty, incorporating the same, should be nullified.
3) The entire Nepal-Indian border should be controlled and systematized. Cars with Indian number plates, which are plying the roads of Nepal, should not be allowed.
4) Gorkha recruiting centres should be closed and decent jobs should be arranged for the recruits.
5) In several areas of Nepal, where foreign technicians are given precedence over Nepali technicians for certain local jobs, a system of work permits should be instituted for the foreigners.
6) The monopoly of foreign capital in Nepal's industry, trade and economic sector should be stopped.
7) Sufficient income should be generated from customs duties for the country's economic development.

8) The cultural pollution of imperialists and expansionists should be stopped. Hindi video, cinema, and all kinds of such newspapers and magazines should be completely stopped. Inside Nepal, import and distribution of vulgar Hindi films, video cassettes and magazines should be stopped.
9) Regarding NGOs and INGOs: bribing by imperialists and expansionists in the name of NGOs and INGOs should be stopped.

Demands Related to the Public and its Well-being

10) A new Constitution has to be drafted by the people's elected representatives.
11) All the special rights and privileges of the King and his family should be ended.
12) Army, police and administration should be under the peoples' control.
13) The Security Act and all other repressive acts should be abolished.
14) All the false charges against the people of Rukum, Rolpa, Jajarkot, Gorkha, Kavre, Sindhuphalchowk, Sindhuli, Dhanusha and Ramechap should be withdrawn and all the people falsely charged should be released.
15) Armed police operations in the different districts should immediately be stopped.
16) Regarding Dilip Chaudhary, Bhuvan Thapa Magar, Prabhakar Subedi and other people who disappeared from police custody at different times, the government should constitute a special investigating committee to look into these crimes and the culprits should be punished and appropriate compensation given to their families.
17) People who died during the movement should be declared as martyrs and their families, and those who have been wounded and disabled should be given proper compensation. Strong action should be taken against the killers.
18) Nepal should be declared a secular state.

19) Girls should be given equal property rights to those of their brothers.
20) All kinds of exploitation and prejudice based on caste should be ended. In areas having a majority of one ethnic group, that group should have autonomy over that area.
21) The status of dalits as untouchables should be ended and the system of untouchability should be ended once and for all.
22) All languages should be given equal status. Up to the middle-high school level (uccha-madyamic) arrangements should be made for education to be given in the children's mother tongue.
23) There should be guarantee of free speech and free press. The communications media should be completely autonomous.
24) Intellectuals, historians, artists and academicians engaged in other cultural activities should be guaranteed intellectual freedom.
25) In both the terai and hilly regions there is prejudice and misunderstanding in backward areas. This should be ended and the backward areas should be assisted. Good relations should be established between the villages and the city.
26) Decentralization in real terms should be applied to local areas, which should have local rights, autonomy and control over their own resources.

Demands Related to the People's Living

27) Those who cultivate the land should own it. (The tiller should have right to the soil he/she tills.) The land of rich landlords should be confiscated and distributed to the homeless and others who have no land.
28) Brokers and commission agents should have their property confiscated and that money should be invested in industry.
29) All should be guaranteed work and should be given a stipend until jobs are found for them.
30) The government (HMG) should pass strong laws ensuring

that people involved in industry and agriculture should receive minimum wages.

31) The homeless should be given suitable accommodation. Until the government (HMG) can provide such accommodation they should not be removed from where they are squatting.

32) Poor farmers should be completely freed from debt. Loans from the Agricultural Development Bank by poor farmers should be completely written off. Small industries should be given loans.

33) Fertilizer and seeds should be easily and cheaply available, and the farmers should be given a proper market price for their production.

34) Flood and drought victims should be given all necessary help.

35) All should be given free and scientific medical service and education and education for profit should be completely stopped.

36) Inflation should be controlled and salaries of labourers should be raised in direct ratio with the rise in prices. Daily essential goods should be made cheap and easily available.

37) Arrangements should be made for drinking water, good roads, and electricity in the villages.

38) Cottage and other small industries should be granted special facilities and protection.

39) Corruption, black marketing, smuggling, bribing, the taking of commissions, etc. should all be stopped.

40) Orphans, the disabled, the elderly and children should be given help and protection.

The government of Nepali Congress Party rejected these demands and adopted repressive measures to suppress the Maoist activities. In reaction, the Maoists increased their guerrilla activity. According to official reports, since 1996 about 1800 people have died, whereas unofficial reports claim about 4,000 deaths, mostly of Maoists, police and villagers. The Maoists have influence in sixty-eight of Nepal's seventy-five districts. According to Government sources thirty-two are regarded as 'hardest hit' areas. In five western districts the Maoists have organised a parallel government. Theses are Rolpa, Rukum, Jararkot, Salyam and Kalikot.

In the Maoist related issues, human rights groups in Nepal have been active in two respects. First, they have supported an end to human rights violations. Second, they have stressed upon and mediated peace talks between the Maoists and the government. The Maoists have also shown a more accommodating attitude towards the human rights institutions and activists.

International organisations have called for respect of human rights by the Government of Nepal and by the Maoists. For example, Amnesty International in one of its reports says: 'Amnesty International joins human rights defenders in Nepal in demanding accountability from the authorities in upholding the fundamental human rights guaranteed in Nepal's Constitution. We also urge the leadership of the CPN (Maoist) to put an end to abuses and issue strict orders to its cadres not to attack civilians, take hostages, kill or torture prisoners or recruit children into their ranks.'

COMPOSITION OF POLITICS AND ADMINISTRATION OF NEPAL

The most crucial area of domination against minorities by the dominant group is indeed politics and administration. According to the *Nepal Human Development Report* 1998 ,

'There is an astonishing continuity in the predominance of the high caste and specific ethnic groups in state administration since the formation of the Nepali state more than two centuries and a quarter ago, which appear to have occupied 98 percent of the top civil service posts in 1854. More than one century later, in 1969, this percentage came down to only marginally, to 93 percent. At present, of the 454 top-level civil (Special Class and First Class) positions, 417 (92 percent) are still occupied by the same groups.'

Although, the Newar, one of the 59 indigenous nationalities, has high representation in the top level civil service positions but they are not the decision-makers. Thus, it took 144 years to get down from 98 per cent to 92 per cent or 24 years for 1 per cent. If it should descend with this rate in future and about 30 per cent of Bahun-Chhetri population should hold 30 per cent of the total top civil service posts, it would take 1,488 years to strike a balance in which the dominant caste Bahun-Chhetri has to loose nothing. About three-fourth of the administrative posts at different levels are held by Bahun-Chhetris.

Justices in the Courts at all levels are mostly male Bahun-Chhetris and remaining ones are male Hinduized Newar. In a multi-lingual country, Khasa-Nepali language is the only official language used in the Court. Therefore, overwhelming majority of population who speak different mother tongues and who belong to minorities are denied of access to justice. Also, lack of gender sensitivity has denied access to justice to women and girl child.

In the Parliament, about 60 per cent of the total 60 members of National Assembly (Upper House) and 205 members of House of Representative (Lower House) are Bahun-Chhetris. Most of the remaining members who come from minorities, mostly Hinduized and "dominant" groups within the minorities, speak the language of the dominant caste. It was amazing that there was not even a single representation from the Dalit community, who comprise about one-fifth of the total population of Nepal, in the House of Representative. Although women comprise a half of the total population of Nepal, there were only 12 women representatives in the House of Representative.

In the Constitutional bodies such as the Public Service Commission and powerful non-constitutional body such as the National Planning Commission most of the key positions are controlled by the dominant Bahun-Chhetris. The National Planning Commission is crucial as it is the central authority to prepare perspective and five year plans. The members are comprised invariably of Bahun-Chhetri and Newar.

In the local bodies such as the District Development Committees (DDC), Municipalities and Village Development Committees (VDC), it appears to be fifty-fifty between the dominant and minorities. However, one the one hand Bahun-Chhetris hold positions 100 per cent more than their population size and on the other, local bodies are powerless bodies due to highly centralized power and authority due to failure to devolve power and authority.

Almost all main political parties are controlled by Bahun-Chhetri and most of the workers and followers are the minorities. The central committee members in the two largest political parties are mostly Bahun-Chhetri and in other main political parties although there are representations of different minorities but the former dominate.

Women's participation in local elections, professional jobs and administrative jobs, cabinet, Parliament, judiciary etc. is very low. Most of these women belong to Bahun-Chhetri and the Newar groups. The results of such an out of proportion representation of the dominant caste—Bahun-Chhetri—in various decision-making bodies is that the minorities can neither find their due place in such bodies nor can they stop any legislation, policy, plans and programs that have adverse impact on their identity, language, religion and culture. As long as there is no structural mechanism for fair representation of minorities and affirmative action, both remedial and preferential, the continuing domination of the dominant group could hardly change.

The Politics of Foreign Aid

Nepal's economic policies continue to hinge, directly or indirectly, on poverty reduction and poverty reduction policies are influenced substantially by foreign aid (Gsanger and Viopio 2000). Both, economic policies of HMG-N and foreign aid has affected natural environment, which is the lifeline of indigenous nationalities.

Foreign aid began to trickle from India and the United States of America from early fifties and from China and the Soviet Union in the later fifties. In 1950/51, out of the total budget US $ 3.2, foreign aid comprised 4.1 per cent. it was highest in 1958/1959 with 76.8 per cent, and in 2000/2001, out of the total budget of US $ 1,118.61, it is 30.8 per cent only. Currently one of the largest donors are Japan, EU countries, the World Bank and the Asian Development Bank. Over the years multi-lateral aid supersede bi-lateral aid, loans and technical support supersede grant and commodity aid. Nepal's development programs are fully donor dependent. Bhattachan reported, "There is no disagreement among all the respondents that poverty has never been alleviated or reduced or controlled, let alone eradicated, but on the contrary, it has been definitely accentuated or escalated." In a similar vein, Acharya (2002:1) writes,

'Lately, foreign aid in Nepal has begun to be watched with critical reservation. It is publicly held that it has not brought about the economic and social development that it had promised. On the contrary, aid is held to have widened gaps in economic opportunities between the rich and poor. Foreign aid has also been charged of propelling the pace and magnitude of corruption in the country. It is said to have disempowered the Nepali state, its people and government.'

Donors, multi-lateral, bi-lateral and INGOs work primarily with HMG-N. Due to high level of corruption and red tapism in the Nepalese bureaucracy, donors supported NGOs in both advocacy and service delivery in different parts of Nepal. They have supported mostly to women's rights since the eighties and to some extent to the Dalits since the mid-nineties. All donors have ignored indigenous nationalities. According to Bhattachan (2001:76), the main reason for such a situation is,

'The Bahunbadi policy makers, bureaucrats, development experts, decision makers and politicians scare the donors—bilateral, multilateral and INGOs—away by telling them not to "play politics" by directly helping the disadvantaged groups on caste or ethnic, religious and linguistic bases. They feel the heat even in contemplating to help them. Even if some of them are bold enough to take one step forward, once their Bahunbadi colleagues scare them away, they do not hesitate to go four step backward.'

However, due to escalation of violence and counter violence between the Maoist insurgents and the security forces of HMG-N, donor's community has lately realized a need for mainstreaming caste, ethnic and regional groups. What is unfortunate is that those who are involved in peace building, conflict management and mainstreaming of caste, ethnicity and region are mostly from the dominant groups. Such efforts may further escalate ensuing conflict and explode in the form of caste, ethnic, linguistic, religious and regional violence, counter violence and insurgencies.

Foreign aid and economic policies have, by and large, adverse impact on minorities. For example, forest is one of the areas where donors have helped optimally and they are proud of improving forest resources, which depleted very rapidly until the eighties. The forest policy has displaced many indigenous nationalities from forest to those who lived in forest and alienated from ownership to those who owned forests. According to Bajracharya and Thapa ,

'...early conservation efforts resembled the western system wherein national parks were demarcated, the people forfeited their traditional rights to use the resources within the boundaries, neither were they provided with other alternatives. In other words, the concerns of people living in the park periphery were ignored. This raised an intense park-people conflict, thereby negating the achievements in terms of conservation. The strict conservation policy, incorporating only flora and fauna conservation, added further pressure and increased conflict between the park and the people.'

HMG-N enacted many forest laws. The minorities, specially indigenous nationalities did not even know while making and implementing these laws. The government has categorized forests into protected forest (it comprise about 14 per cent of the total forest), religious forest, community forest (it comprise about 11 per cent of the total forest), leasehold forest, and government-managed forest, that is, residual forest managed by the Department of Forestry of HMG-N. Similarly some private forest is registered with the government and some are not. The Royal Chitwan National Park (RCNP), the first national park in Nepal, was established in 1973. By now 8 national parks, 5 wildlife reserve and 3 conservation areas cover about 20 percent of the total land of the country. All these different types of forest have indeed displaced many peoples belonging to different indigenous nationalities from their own forestland. For example, Tharus have been affected by the Shukla Phant Wildlife Reserve, the Royal Bardiya National Park, the Royal Chitwan National Park and Parsa Wildlife Reserve. Magars are affected by the Shey-Phoksundo National Park. Gurungs, Magars, Thakalis, Pacnhgaunles and Baragaunles are affected by the Annapuran Conservation Area Project (ACAP) Tamangs are affected by the Langtang National Park. Sherpas and Rais are affected by Sagarmatha National Park. Rais and Limbus are affected by Makalu-Barun National Park and Kanchanjunga Conservation Area. Some indigenous nationalities who are allowed to live in wild life parks under the park and people program, they wonder whether animals or human beings have right to life because if animals are killed suspected individuals are arrested and punished but if human beings die no one really cares. Similarly, the life of the Rautes, the last nomads, have been threatened from living their traditional life due to restriction on mobility imposed by different forest authorities, including the community forest groups. Also, many Chepangs who live in the forest and stone caves did not know that they had already lost their forests with the enforcement of government laws and as about 85 per cent of the total 52,237 Chepang population do not have neither land registration certificate nor citizenship certificate.

Indigenous nationalities are expert of natural environment but in the last 230 years but they have been made homeless in their own traditional homeland. Non-indigenous nationalities have never lived in forests but they have either cleared forest or some have earned degrees on forest but indigenous nationalities have been deprived from using forest and other natural resources.

Till now HMG-N requests donors to go to remote or poor areas yet do not allow implementing any programs or projects that directly deals with caste/ethnic, language and religion. Also, the state-led, market-led, NGO-led and "community" or "people" based development strategies has failed to reach and benefit minorities. Most of the foreign aid evaporates at the top and hardly trickles down to the bottom. Among different minority groups, donors have provided financial and technical support mostly to gender issues and to some extent to Dalits. Indigenous nationalities, Madhesis, Muslims, linguistic and religious minorities have not yet been reached out. The dominant group does not want donors support these issues. Donors also find it difficult to go against the dominant groups' interest. Most of the donor funded development programs have adverse impact on minority groups. The World Bank has now initiated to conduct social assessment with special focus on adverse impact on indigenous nationalities and other minority groups.

Dor Bahadur Bista (1991:151-2) has analyzed in detail about the relationship between Hindu fatalism manifested in the form of Brahmanism and continuing underdevelopment of Nepal. He has criticized both economic and cultural policies of both HMG-N and donors. He aptly writes,

'The Nepali population that has remained untouched by Hindu caste principles is Nepal's greatest treasure. This is a very sizable proportion of the population. But presently they live in remote areas, at a little above subsistence level, with little or no education, and no opportunities to develop and actualize their aspirations. Their values are not the values of hierarchic Bahunism. They do know the importance of hard work, of endurance, and the role of individual effort in the improvement of ones' circumstances. And they have the positive qualities of strong cooperative behaviour and an appreciation of the general well being and importance of the group or community as a whole. The Jyapu of Kathmandu Valley, and the others who are even less affected by Hindu caste hierarchy, such as the Sherpa, Tamang, Magar and Limbus are untapped resources of the nation. Only when foreign aid can reach these people, in sufficient quantity and of the right kind, will Nepal genuinely be able to establish the basis of her future prosperity.'

INTERNATIONAL MIGRATION IN NEPAL

History and trend: One of the big problems of research particularly in the developing countries like Nepal is the lack of availability, reliability and systematic publication of data and migration sector cannot be excluded from this situation. Hence, a detail analysis of migration phenomenon from the perspective of poverty, gender and development at various levels of spatial aggregation is difficult. Even though the Government of Nepal started collecting data on migration since 1920 it was not accessible as published material. Kansakar (2003) reports that the population data published for the first time in Nepal was in the Appendix of the speech made by Prime Minister Chandra Shumsher Jung Bahadur Rana in the booklet Maharaja Chandra Shamsher Jung Bahadur Rana's Appeal to the People of Nepal for the Emancipation of Slave and Abolition of Slavery in the Country in 1925. Another classic source of migration data was the Population Census of 1952/54. The report contains an analysis of different characteristics of the population of Nepal. Though Nepal has a census history of almost a century, more detailed account of migration data were made available only after the census 1991. The census of 2001 has a bit more detailed information, including a comprehensive account of the respective areas of destination, the purpose of migration (type of work the migrants engaged in), and gender specific data including the population structure and so on.

Nepalese labour out-migration is not a new phenomenon. Nepali migrant workers have been sending their earnings to their families for around 200 years. The first evidence of out-migration found in literature is that in early nineteenth century, the first Nepalese men migrated to Lahore (in present day's Pakistan) to join the army of Sikh ruler Ranjit Singh. Afterwards, both they and later migrants are termed as "Lahure". Literally, the nickname lahure is given to the people who join the armed force of India, Hong Kong, Singapore, United Kingdom, and so on; but it also designates people living abroad particularly having the working class jobs.

The distinction here is essential because people living abroad for study or working in the universities and 'big' organizations like UN, FAO, and ADB are not necessarily called lahures. The labourers working in the working class jobs are recently termed as 'New Lahures'. This is an indication of socioeconomic position of migrant households in Nepal, who goes where and who does what.

Another metaphor used for Nepalese migrants working abroad is the Gurkhas: particularly known as the Nepalese who work in Gurkha Regiment for British or Indian forces. After a war in the Gorkha area with the British East India Company (1814/1816), an increasing number of Gurkhas (mostly, but not exclusively from present-day Nepal) also joined the British Army in India, starting a tradition that continues today.

During the World War I and II, Gurkhas were sent as courtesy from Nepalese government to support allied force where they fought courageously and established an image of "Gurkhas". Even to date Gurkhas as Nepal Armies and Police are popularly recognized as good peace keeping force worldwide, some examples are their involvement in UN peace keeping force in Kosovo, Lebanon, Congo etc. In other words, Nepalese out-migration started from the history of Nepali soldiers who joined forces of other countries though it was not well accounted. With respect to the census 1942, Kansakar (2003: 107) reports, "The census seems to have not recorded the Nepali troops sent from Nepal in different fronts to assist the allied forces and might have been included only those who went abroad for livelihood".

Nepal's international border with India and China remained almost open for the movement of people from both of her neighbours. With China, it became closed one after 1950, while it has remained open with India to date with no restriction on the movement of people of both countries. Hence, because of open border, cultural similarities, and no need of documentary evidence to show migration to and from India is pre-historic and even unaccounted. Throughout the 19th century and well into the 20th, Nepalese men served in India, often accompanied by their wives and other family members. As the Gurkha settlements increased in number and size, they also attracted Nepali workers seeking civilian employment in India. The brothels developed in these new centres may well have included women from Nepal and from the surrounding areas (Seddon 2005). He further illustrates that the development of tea estates in Assam and Darjeeling in India also increased the demand for labour, which resulted in a substantial increase in the number of both men and women workers from Nepal, ultimately increased the expatriate Nepali community in those areas.

Data show that Nepal is witnessing an increasing trend of out-migration since 1942, the first year from which we have the information. In this period of six decades, the migrated population reaches from 88 thousands in 1942 to more than a million in 2008, over 12-fold growth in an increasing rate.

Not all persons represented by the figure mean the labour migration rather they are the people absent at households during census period, which also include labour migrants. Because of data problem, we have to take the whole group of out-migrants into a single category but they can be disaggregated into labour migrants, trafficked people, students, emigrants (under diversity visa [DV] program in USA, skilled manpower immigration program in UK, Canada, New Zealand, and Australia), Gurkhas, and the people working in diplomatic missions and NGOs, and so on.

The growth was not so high until 1981 but it took a bigger leap between the years 1981 and 1991. This can be related to first popular movement in 1990 that restored democracy in Nepal. This actuated labour out-migration in two ways: a) democracy provided an increased access to information and opportunity, and also to freedom and autonomy in decision-making; b) the restored democracy could not solve the problem of unemployment and people's expectation, which made them explore a better opportunity and go abroad. As a means of pull factor could be the increased labour demand from Gulf countries and other Asian countries where the economy was (and still is) booming because of their industrial development. Another leap observed in the figure is from 2001 to 2005. This corresponds with a period of political instability (the period of Maoist insurgency) and surprisingly increased development of information technology that made it easy for the people to access to information.

This trend is ever increasing. A very recent figure of DLEP shows that the size of Nepalese labour force in the year 2007/08 totalled 215,639 persons, an increase of 22.44 percent compared to the previous year (Kantipur 2008).

Patterns of migration: The Government of Nepal officially opened its door for citizens to go abroad for work in late 1980s. Before that people used to work only in India because of open border and people did not have access to other countries. After having labour agreements with a number of Gulf States the number of migrant workers has increased substantially since 1996 with the increasing demand every year. According to the population census 2001, India remains to be the main recipient of Nepalese migrant workers with about 600,000 migrants living there. India is followed by the Gulf countries in aggregate (111,000) such as Saudi Arabia, Qatar, United Arab Emirates, Bahrain, and so on. Other countries account for about 62,000 Nepalese migrants. Europe is still not visible in terms of Nepalese migrant population size and the proportion in other developed countries is also negligible with respect to size.

A study carried out by Seddon et al. (2002) gives a good account of Nepalese workers living abroad especially in the West. They illustrate that there are few Nepalese living and working in 'the West' and they send remittances back home. Many, particularly in North America, are professionals who live with their families. These are predominantly of urban origin. According to their estimate for 1997, a total of 12,500 Nepali migrants were working in Europe and might be 2,500 in North America—making a total of around 15,000 in the West as a whole. The largest number of Nepalese in any one country is in Britain, with 3,600 (mainly Gurkhas) officially registered and 8,000 unofficial workers. Likewise, in Japan, most of the estimated 10,000-plus Nepali migrant workers are illegal.

If we take out India from the picture, Gulf becomes the prime destination of Nepalese migrant workers. According to DLEP, Malaysia (36%) remains to be the largest recipient as per the country-wise calculation till now (2008), which is followed by Qatar (29%), Kingdom of Saudi Arabia (19%), and United Arab Emirates (12%) and so on. European and American countries are still out of access for the Nepalese migrant workers. Clearly, one should note that the data are entirely work-related migration, which does not include students, refugees, permanent emigrants, and the expatriates.

It is also interesting to observe that probably because of open access to information and impact of globalization the out-migration towards countries other than India is being increased. Previously. people only had access to India because of a number of reasons such as transportation, information. demands from other countries, and other policies and governing rules but gradually people are moving to other countries in the world. In 1981 about 93 percent of out-migrants went to India while only 7 percent found their destination to other countries. The tendency of migrating to outside India kept on increasing and reached 23 percent in 2001 while going to India has been reduced to 77 percent in the same year.

On contrary to above calculation based on the cumulative country-wise calculation, the trend of migration to Malaysia has been reduced since 2005/06 while this trend of the Gulf countries has increased. This is because of a relatively low wage rate in Malaysia as compared to the Gulf countries. My short newspaper survey during June-July 2008 showed that the demand from Malaysia seems to be only working class labourers with the name "Production Workers" or "Production Operators" while in the Gulf countries the demand is more disaggregated. Furthermore, the demand of skilled and semi-skilled labourers like mason, mechanic, salesman/girls, security guards, and engineers is increasing from Gulf States. It is also important to note that many workers returned from Malaysia because of the work they had to engage in are found different form the work they were told they would get during the process. Another important de-motivating factor to Malaysia is the levy charged by the Government of Malaysia from workers. A foreign employment agent (broker) in Jhapa said that if levy was removed the tendency would increase again. In Malaysia, one has to pay up to 150 Ringgit per month to the government, which Nepali workers consider as a financial burden against a relatively low salary.

Gender dimension of migration: Even though, at a global level, almost half of world migrant population is female, Nepal has predominantly male out-migration, with 89 percent of the total migrant population. It is partly attributed by the patrilineal social structure where men have greater access to productive resources, public sphere activities, and a breadwinning role that men are supposed to take such steps and earn to make a living. Ideally, a general social expectation from men in Nepal is to manage resources and make available a livelihood while women are expected to maintain the family and households by allocating resources for the benefit of members. In terms of productive activities, Seddon et al. (2002) analyzed 77 percent women's involvement in agriculture whereas men involved mainly (57 percent) in outside agriculture. This suggests why male out-migration is predominantly high in Nepal. The country-wise gender composition of out-migrants from Nepal. Hong Kong has the largest proportion of female migrants. Hong Kong is one of the main destinations for Gurkhas, who are also accompanied by their wives and children. The Hong Kong born children of British armies received their citizenship from Hong Kong government that made them attracted to reside there and hence increased the number. Another reason could be that there has been increasing demand of domestic help which preferably women like to do.

The data show that in the western countries the proportion of women migrants is higher as compared to that of in Moslim countries like Malaysia and the Gulf countries. On contrary to the situation in Southeast Asian countries like Indonesia and the Philippines, the female out-migration from Nepal to the Gulf countries is not so motivating because of the cultural factor and the nature of jobs available. Neither it can be of target for women to apply for as a factory labourer or farm worker nor can they accompany their spouses during migration (due to possibly low wage rate to run their family there). Higher proportion of women migration in the cluster of USA, Canada and Mexico reveals the diversity visa (DV) program in the USA, increasing target of students to US education and immigration program in Canada. These are relatively gender neutral interventions as compared to the labour migration to the Gulf countries and Malaysia.

Apart from the spouses of Indian armies and other civilian workers in India, a huge proportion of women migrants are working in the Indian brothels. Since 1989, when a number of Nepali women from the red light districts of Mumbai were deported, it showed that large numbers of Nepali women are employed in the Indian commercial sex industry. Maiti Nepal, a non-governmental organization working in the field of women trafficking in Nepal, estimates that about 150,000 to 300,000 girls are exploited in different brothels in India. However, a scientific investigation is needed to prove whether they are exploited and trafficked. Same situation is prevailed in Hong Kong and Middle Eastern Countries. Due to open border with India the actual number of migrants may surpass the government estimations. Similarly, people trafficked (as a form of human trafficking) through illegal channels are not counted on official figures.

Remittance as a product of migration: Literally, remittance is the transfer of money by foreign workers, but literature also includes other forms of transfers such as social remittances (diffusion of various types of social practices, ideas and values), knowledge or technology remittances (knowledge, skills and technology brought back by returning migrants), and political remittances as changing identities and political awareness after return. Labour migration and remittance is becoming the important mainstay of Nepalese economy. The official statistics does not reflect the actual situation. Seddon et al. (2002) estimate the actual remittance in Nepal is about 10 to 20 times greater than the amount shown by the official statistics, which is equivalent to almost 25 percent of national gross domestic product (GDP). This shows an importance of remittance especially to the rural households. It means rural livelihoods have never been wholly reliant on agriculture, and labour migration has long been an important feature of rural existence in Nepal.

Like pattern of migration (number of migrants) the scale of remittances differs depending upon the countries of destination but in different ways. We have observed that India is the largest recipient of Nepalese migrant workers. However, the remittances from India are not as high as the number of migrants working there. Out of total number of remittances (one remittance means the remittance sent at a time) sent back home, about 40 percent is from India and the corresponding value of remittance is about one third of total remittances entered into the country. On contrary, a negligible number of remittances (3 percent) from outside India produce almost a quarter of the total amount of remittances. It gives a critical importance of remittances from abroad (outside India) to policy and research arena. Similarly, remittances from urban areas and rural areas of the country are also significant, though they are out of the scope of this chapter. Remittances from abroad constituted 76 percent of the total amount of remittances received in Nepal in 2004. As migration to India is decreasing the remittance thereof is also decreasing. Using the data from Nepal Living Standard Survey 2003/04 show the largest share of international remittances came from Saudi Arabia, Qatar, and the United Arab Emirates (35 percent), followed by 30 percent from India, 17 percent from other Asian countries, and the remainder from United Kingdom, United States, and other countries. In sum, it is revealed that the scale and pattern of migration and remittances have different consequences. One country (as the country of destination) may have relatively fewer number of migrants but would have high amount of remittances and in some cases a large number of migrants may produce a relatively smaller amount of remittances, for example, number of migrants and their remittances from India. The influence in aggregate may be different from the influence at household or individual level, so they have to be treated accordingly.

MEDIA AND DEMOCRACY IN NEPAL

If innovation and novelty are things to be cherished, then Nepal, a developing nation in South Asia, does not seem to despise experimentation of new ideas. An article in the *New York Times* recognized this fact when it declared: Nepal's capital Kathmandu, "long a symbol of spiritualism, is now also a centre for research and innovation". *The Times* may be right in its observation, but the question remains if innovations and researches have brought any substantial change in the democratic landscape of this great city.

Commentators agree that in the past decade, Nepali journalism, too, has seen innovations. The few positive instances in rural journalism and community radio projects, however, remain overshadowed by a number of problems that confront the local press as well as the public. Although, as one veteran journalist put it, like "a beacon atop the Himalayas," the efforts of Nepalese journalists might have "shone into the lives of people there and in surrounding countries as well," the Nepali press has not done as much as it could have in covering issues of public concerns in the local level. Kathmandu's adoration for all things "South Asian," especially following the establishment in 1984 of the permanent secretariat of the South Asian Association for Regional Cooperation (SAARC), the Subcontinent's equivalent of European Union, has made this city preoccupied with hoards of regional and international agendas. Since 1996, much of that regional attention has been diverted to a bloody internal Maoist insurgency which continues to weaken democracy and threaten press freedom.

Whatever the shift, national issues continue to top the media agenda. Nationalism, national unity in ethnic and cultural diversity, and nation-building have always remained major issues in Nepal. More than anything else, *desh nirman* (nation-building), *desh vikash* (national development), and *rastriya rajniti* (national politics), or *prajatantra* (democracy) are all time favorite journalistic jargons. Hence, politics and development remain the two important facets of the Nepali press. The political model of the press assumes that the press as the fourth estate has the obligation to act as a check to the power of the other branches of the state. The watchdog role of the press, however, is concerned to this day more with party politics than with the politics for and by the people. However, in recent years, the idea of "good governance" is being disseminated by the press, the indication of an attempt to make politics more relevant to the lives of the general public.

In contrast, development model, embraced in the mid-80s by some journalists disgusted with the press obsessed with *real politik,* attempts to bring the public, the communities, and the social and economic life of the local people into the media spotlight. Naturally, in an impoverished country like Nepal, *vikash* remains on top of the national agenda. Nevertheless, one can argue if it should be *desh viskash* or *jana vikash* (citizens' development). This is an important point given the failure of the so-called grass-roots Panchayat democracy (1960-1990) in delivering its promises to the people. King Mahendra, the ideologue of that system, could not realize a thriving civil society and an informed, responsible and pro-active citizenry largely because he could not make people's empowerment as central to his indigenous form of democracy. The king's attempt at populist politics, seemingly the first-ever organized attempt at participatory democracy in the history of the country, failed to produce the desired results, and finally, it was replaced by the western style parliamentary democracy in 1990. Yet, king Mahedra's unique experiment helped to single out some of the most important factors that contribute to the grim picture of the Nepali problem. For one thing, the party-less grass-roots Panchayat system was more of a response to Nepal's need to maintain its identity amid diversity.

Scholars like Joshi and Rose (1966, p.397), tracing the roots of Panchayat, describe it as an instrument of caste administration and a body in the implementation of Brahmanic social regulations. King Mahendra developed it to a full-fledged political system that granted some autonomy to the villages. However, the emphasis was on nation-building, national identity and national security, rather than human security or the security or prosperity of the general people. Hence, King Mahendra was essentially concerned with the national order— the international image and security of Nepal— than with civic empowerment. The King fell prey to the historical circumstances— the height of the Cold War and Nepal's geopolitical reality. Indeed, there could not have been citizens without a nation. Mahendra's guided democracy had no place for the civil society, special interest organizations and ethnic groupism were outlawed. His *gaon farka andolan* (Back to the Village Movement) was more of a royal decree than a democratic art. And the media, as always, did care little to look beyond the king, and national politics.

For instance, when Nepal Press Institute (established in 1984) did a survey of newspaper content in the mid-1980s, it was found that about 95 per cent of news and views was on national politics, directly or indirectly related to the King, politicians and the government (Koirala, 2003). The establishment of specialized media organizations during the 1990s marked the beginning of concentrated focus on areas of press performance. While Nepal Forum of Environmental Journalists. (NEFEJ, established 1986) helped raise consciousness about deforestation, pollution, environmental degradation and its impact on people, Sancharika Samuha (est.1995) monitored gender issues in the media. The formation and growth of Centre for Investigative Journalism (1996) and a dozen of organizations concerned with media freedom and performance paralleled with the government's institutional initiatives to nurture the hard-won democracy in 1990. But despite the efforts of these organizations and despite the establishment of democracy; the lives of the general public largely remained unaffected. Media experts, such as Bharat Koirala, bemoaned (Koirala, 2003) that most of the newspapers, a majority of them political weeklies, thrived on sensationalism and overtly political events and paid little attention to social and economic development.

Political leadership, however, seemed confident about the virtues and future of democracy in the country. For instance, the former Prime Minister K.P. Bhattarai, who was himself a crusading journalist at one time and who wrote against the autocratic Rana Regime (1846-1951), believed that "democracy has a solid future in Nepal". Such strong faith in the procedural democracy—emphasizing elections, party system, independent judiciary and a free press, etc.—received a heavy jolt in February 2005 when the king took over full power and declared a state of emergency amid an intensifying and bloody Maoist rebellion. The evolution of a substantive, participatory democracy in Nepal has been constrained visibly by the violent conflict and more insidiously by the continued presence of ethnic backwardness, social inequities, casteism, untouchability and discrimination against women and minorities. Despite having set up institutions for good governance, these institutions were not capable of ensuring the same even before the pre-February 2005 environment. The government media, which still holds a greater chunk of the market, could not be free from its subservient role to the ruling political party. The role of judiciary in timely and impartial delivery of justice often remained questionable. The country also saw little transparency in public appointments. The bureaucracy is yet to emerge as a professional and efficient organ of the government.

Corruption, perceived as one of the country's major maladies, was exacerbated by, among others, discretionary power vested upon decision-makers with little sense of accountability, lack of transparency, no provision for public hearings and low salary structure in the civil services. The Royal Commission for Corruption

Control, formed by the King after the February coup, charged several high-level ministers and government officials of corruption and embezzlement, including former Prime Minister Sher Bahadur Deuba. Throughout the 1990s, the electoral process, another of democracy's important attributes, saw some of the most undemocratic practices, especially with the increase in the influence of money, muscle and public media in elections. Political parties and candidates were often reported to be taking graft and donation from businessmen for election funding.

Where does the media figure in this democratic equation? Issues of accountability and the question of corruption continued to be highlighted by the media, but the factual reportage or the investigative reporting of such issues is aimed more at boosting sales rather than at citizen participation, public mobilization and bureaucratic reforms.

The crisis of credibility of both public and private sector media worries many a professional who aspires for reforms. Despite some progress in the field, Koirala (1995) wrote that Nepali journalists were yet to be conversant with the norms of fair journalistic practice. They had not given up character assassination and confining to individualistic or partisan interest. Women were very few and their voices and problem least covered in the media. Regarding the content of Nepali media, he observed that the most important spaces of newspapers were covered with boring speech, government communiqué, details of *shilanyas* (laying foundations) and inaugurations, politics and election reports. Thus, newspaper could not be taken as reliant means for social change. Although there must have been some progress in press performance over the last few years, Koirala's critique is still relevant here in that it sheds light on the foundational behaviour of the Nepali press vis-à-vis issues of importance to the general public.

Naturally, the question is how Nepali citizens could come together to discuss their problems when the very society they live in is so diverse and divided along the lines of languages, castes, gender, wealth, education, influence and power. This problem is not typical of hierarchical and class society; even the classless and supposedly the most democratic nation like the U.S. has, in recent years, seen dialogue gaps in the public arena, especially concerning race relations, neighborhood crime, drugs and so on. Citizens' participation in public affairs, including the elections, is dwindling to the extent that newspapers have devised new ways, such as civic journalism, in an attempt to tackle the problem. Civic journalism, also called public journalism, is defined in a number of ways. There is no one common agreement on its definition. Edmund B. Lambeth, who is at times sympathetic to the civic journalism movement, attempts an all-inclusive definition in terms of the goals of this new form of journalism. According to him, civic journalism seeks to 1) listen systematically to the stories and ideas of citizens even while protecting its freedom to choose what to cover; 2) examine alternative ways to frame stories on important community issues; 3) choose frames that stand the best chance to stimulate citizen deliberation and build public understanding of issues; 4) take the initiative to report on major public problems in a way that advances a public knowledge of possible solution and the values served by alternative courses of action; and 5) pay continuing and systematic attention to how well and how credibly it is communicating with the public.

Critics will be quick to note that importing a western tool to fix a local problem should precede some forethought. Following Lambeth's definition, my argument is that public journalism—in terms of its focus on citizens—is not absolutely new to newspapers in Nepal. During the party-less system, government mouthpieces often spoke authoritatively to the "citizens" on behalf of the government. However, the citizens were passive consumers of the governmental propaganda. The news media's emphasis on unity, consensus, and compromise; rather than on division or disagreement; portrayed the public as passive actors. Theoretically, the post February 2005 Nepal may not be a democratic state. But the King continues to insist on a multiparty democracy and constitutional monarchy and has categorically termed his takeover as only a temporary move in his fight against the Maoists and the corrupt politicians. In other words, if a democratic system recognizing the vital role of citizenship as well as the press in the polity of the country is to be sustained, the problems associated with democracy and governance also deserve a more democratic news media. With some local adjustment, public-oriented journalism, if not fully public journalism, could be useful in this regard.

POLITICAL DIMENSION OF NEPAL'S ECONOMIC POLICY

Diplomacy is the power game. It is a game to control others, neutralize them or use them to one's advantage. It is a new form of war. Although economic diplomacy is being understood as the mobilization of foreign policy for creating opportunities of economic growth and prosperity, the birth of nations, wars, imperialism, colonialism, international organizations, treaties and conventions are basically reflection of the same interest. Agreements and treaties are also influenced by balance of power. According to Adam Smith: *"Exportation was encouraged by drawback, sometimes by bounties, sometimes by advantageous treaties of commerce with foreign states, and sometimes by the establishment of colonies in distant countries"*

The first and second points referred to by Smith relate to enhancing competitiveness of goods while the last two points help develop friendly market. Taking advantage of external markets without the need for indentifying areas of comparative advantage is a far more pragmatic course.

According to Khanal (2059 BS), developed countries tend to mobilize unlimited resources for the promotion of their global interests which are preserved through technical, strategic, military, political and economic organizations at the national, regional and international levels.

This shows that no assistance, loan and grant provided by multi-lateral, regional or international NGOs are free from strategic and political interests of major powers. This perspective has been formulated even more forcefully by Fukuyama, who argues for the use of American soft power for promoting the emergence of middle class attuned to the American value system and its global interest and the establishment of democratic regimes He also describes the sponsored propaganda of vote rigging in Ukraine, Serbia arid Georgia, mobilization of the, popular revolt and the establishment of regimes suited to the American interests, and named several persons who led the civil society at the time. Fukuyama also refers to several world organizations like the United Nations, which are either incapable of taking quick decisions favoring American national interest or are dominated by countries whose interests clash with those of the United States and recommends creation of global organizations that endorses the American decisions or give legitimacy to American interventions.

According to Khanal, there is a general tendency in Nepal to link a particular policy to an individual. For example, China's domestic modernization and the liberalization of her foreign policy is linked to the policy of Deng Xioping. This could be true to a certain extent....However, we must understand that serious strategic and economic interests (rather than individuals) have governed the policy changes in China and the United States. What are involved are national interests of each countries involved, and the individuals are superfluous. The perspectives of someone recognized as the architect of Nepal's modern diplomacy indicates that national interests are at the core of foreign policy of a country.. The government has been providing a grant of Rs.1 million to each of the village development committees. However, the Indian Embassy can provide lump sum Rs.50 million to any VDC without even asking any agency of the Nepal government.

A former member of the National Planning Commission told an interaction that once the Indian Embassy wrote a letter to the Nepal government, asking to raise the ceiling of amount it could provide to any one in Nepal from Rs.30 million to Rs.50 million. As required, the approval of the NPC was sought. The NPC formally discussed the proposal but rejected on the grounds that the loyalty of the party leaders or workers negotiating such assistance between the recipient and the Indian government would be towards the Indian government. However, the very next day the news by the official media said the Indian proposal has been accepted and approved. The major beneficiaries of such assistance have been the leaders and workers of all political parties.

It is true that Nepali bureaucrats, security officials, traders, businessmen and leaders and workers of the political parties thus favoured by India have invested their income in India. Even today, the sons and other relatives of most Nepalis including the Prime Minister and political leaders are studying in India under Indian scholarships. Most scholarships are provided at the recommendation of the political leaders. This is the spider web of Indian diplomacy, which is one of the several reasons why the growing trade deficit between Nepal and India has not been able to be narrowed down.

On the other hand, the legitimacy of any state power or government is measured in terms of the country's economic prosperity and the opportunities available to the people. Most of the third world countries had survived on the goodwill of superpowers in the post-colonial period when the world was bipolar led respectively by the United States and the Soviet Union. The demand for rights and prosperity of the people were suppressed with the help of the masters. This situation changed dramatically following the end of the Cold War in 1990s. The legitimacy of the regimes now depends on the popular support, thus the emphasis on economic development.

Economic policy of any country is no more a matter of independent choice. Global integration of the economies is the reality. Countries such as North Korea and to some extent Myanmar that have failed to march with global economy are sick and fragile. Independent policies without adjusting to the policies of the World Trade Organization, World Bank and International Monetary Fund are next to impossible. Those with power and money dominate such multilateral organizations. It is for this reason also that the representation of developing countries has shrunk in the structures of these organizations.

The world economy is being managed on the basis of Washington consensus. However, the consensus has weakened gradually. As a consequence, efforts are. being' made for creating the Beijing Consensus as an alternative and make structural changes in the World Bank on the basis of the changing balance of power in order to enhance the roles of emerging powers such as China, Russia, India, South Africa and Brazil.

The Beijing Consensus has two important aspects. The first aspect is to end the dominance of dollar in the world market and create an alternative world currency. This is primarily aimed at reflecting the reduced economic influence of the United States and its developed capitalist allies. It takes into account a number of factors including the origin of the global economic meltdown in 2008 and the Chinese investment of US$150 billion in US bonds (Stiglitz 2010). The second aspect is the kind of challenge it poses to the US political value sc,,stem on which its foreign policy is based (Subedi 2010).

Only recently, China has overtaken Japan as the world's second largest economy. China is the emerging world power. Emerging powers like China and others exert pressures on the US dominated institutions to open up for democratic reforms. Until 10 years ago, the trade between China and India was to the tune of $1 billion. That was the time when it was said that Chinese goods had swamped India. Today the total volume of trade between the two countries has swelled to $50 billion, and the balance of trade is favourable to India. The growing trade would have impact on their relations. Nepal should take the advantage out of this flourishing trade at least as a transit country as the travel distance between India's Siliguri and Delhi via Nepal is much shorter by hundreds of kilometers.

CIVIL SOCIETY IN NEPAL

Civil society in Nepal is so variegated and disparate in terms of size, nature, function, character and identity that it is difficult to develop a precise definition. Historians trace its genealogy with the birth of civility, public spiritedness, community building and norm-governed associational life which liberated the Nepalese citizens from the state of nature. Associational life in Nepal had flourished with the *vedic* age (2000 BC) when *dharma* (institutional duties), *shastras* (moral and legal treatises) and *shastrartha* (philosophical discourses) shaped the knowledge and habits of the subjects and monarchs, rationalized the governing norms of the polity according to *barnashram dharma* (social division of labour), *rajdharma* (statecraft) and *sanatan dharma* (cosmological ordering) and oriented them towards living together and act collectively for peace, public welfare and social harmony. The ties of the scholarship of *rishis* and *munies* (sages and ascetics) and public life were indissoluble and independent of state discipline and punishment.

The Hindu treatise *Bhagawad Gita* states that those who are actively engaged in the welfare of all beings, attain *mokchha,* emancipation. Kautilya's *Arthashastra* argues for the mutual obligations of states and people. In the West knowledge is power while in Vedic-Buddhist culture it is a means for the self-realization of all. In the West duty is the derivative of individual rights while in the Vedic tradition the *dharma*-mediated ethical system embedded individual identity in a web of moral and social duties and relationships. Philosophical discourse framed enlightenment for all, built human connections and helped to resolve various conflicts. A duty-based society naturally lays down rules governing the discourse, challenge status quo and seeks what Gandhi called *ashimsa,* non-violent resolution of social conflict. This essence of *dharma* was followed in all the ancient *nitishastra* (public policy treatises) that were written as a as a guide to public policy. Codes of social, political and economic behaviour were laid down with the central *dharma* theme in mind, rather than political or economic expeditiousness. Legal systems were based on the treatises and their remnants are still found in today's laws and public policy.

The Buddha's teaching of *Panch Sheela* that evolved around 2,500 years ago laid down five rules of life— refrain from killing, stealing, adultery, alcohol drinking and lies—which corresponds to the great five sins of Hindus. The Hindu-Buddhist religions emphasized the need to dissolve personal ego for emancipation, Buddhist by *nirvana* and Hindu by attaining *mokchha* and set the vicious cycle into reverse. Nepalese civic life also draws legacy from scholarly king Janak of Mithila who freed power from its repressive role and fostered a culture of enlightened discourse and coexistence. Discourse performed in his palace was a rational process of deflating dogmas and reaching mutual understanding and consensus among all the concerned participants, mediation of radical disagreements and application of reason and various perspectives for conflict resolution.

Discourse made self-righteousness difficult and self-criticism quite easy. This had facilitated the non-violent resolution of conflict and enabled citizens to become peaceful members of the community. In the economic and social modernization of Tarai, the charity works of private sector have played a great role in minimizing the rationality of conflict.

Lumbini in the southern part and Gandak region and Kathmandu valley in the north are often regarded as the pinnacle of Nepalese civilization where Buddhist *bihars* (monasteries) and *sangha* (mass organization), Hindu temples, *gurukuls* (voluntary schools run by community) and *panchali pratha* (local arbitration system) were the springs of public sphere for education and rational contestation of ideas. Buddha also founded *sangha* for women. As these factors were embedded in the sociology of knowledge, the political acculturation process was natural.

The *guthis* (trust) of today demonstrates the resiliency of *gosthis* of the Lichchhvi state and resonates the continuity of cultural consciousness and associational life. By definition, *guthi* is a group of people founded as a community based on extended families, clans and lineage groups for the promotion of their social, cultural and economic interests. It is also an endowment of land for philanthropic purposes to thicken individual's connections with the society and the state. The Buddhist *suttas* situates individuals into historical and social context and links their fate to the fate of community. Accordingly, "peace has to be understood in nature space, human space, social space and world space". Over ritualization, however, diluted the rational potential of Hinduism and Buddhism and they began to impose their own taboos on the public domain, conflict avoidance strategies and lack of contestation of ideas for enlightenment. Still, as faith both will outlast contemporary ideologies.

Jayasthiti Malla (1380 AD) codified, strengthened and enforced a stable social life based on the caste system. The Malla kings reared literary societies, constructed roads, arts and aesthetics, temples, *pati pauwas,* (resting places), irrigation works, public *dharas* (water sprouts), temples, preservation of *gampa* land, etc. to enrich spiritual, social and culture life and cherish the connection between knowledge and human solidarity. They evolved *panch kachhahari* (council of five elders) for the peaceful resolution of conflicts on local matters (Shrestha and Bhattarai, 2004:81-82). After Prithvi Narayan Shaha unified the country into a modern nation-state Nepal, in 1769, he articulated the pluralist social space of the nation. Land grants to different sets of citizens, economic mercantilism and Hindu caste universe then underlined the state's strength to integrate society and organize social capital to acquire state-society synergy. The dawn of the Rana regime in September 1846 too did not roll over the autonomy of local social and cultural spaces constituted by the people themselves. Tribal heads having their own claim to local resources and their own system of rights ran village units. Ranas, however, made the state captive of the aristocracy, crushed dissension and fostered a political culture of clientilism as they treated the citizens as *raitis*— the subjects, not the public.

They enacted the *Muluki Ain* (the Civil Code) in 1854 and amended in 1910, to dispense justice on the basis of caste ordering. Ranas also commenced social engineering—*Sanskritization* of non-*Sanskritic* communities, introduced reforms in the governing institutions, encouraged the process of *Nepalization* of language and culture, applied modernity, executed social reforms such as abolition of the slavery system, custom of *sati pratha* (self-immolation by widow), etc. and secured the sovereignty of the nation. Like the Greeks, they inherited a system of governance based on the exclusion of Dalits, Women and tribes from the public realm. In the 1940s, the then civil society formed in Nepal and by the Nepalese in India set up an associational arena for participatory politics.

The pluralistic Hindu-Buddhist society provided a rich ground for a liberal regime. During the anti-Rana movement, *Arya Samaj* (civic society or a society of noble citizens) was set up in 1909 to free the Nepalese and to abolish discrimination against women, child labour, child marriage, legitimize widow marriage, initiate social reforms and direct the society on a rational course. Subsequently, a *Malami Guthi* (trust) was established. In 1926, a public trust called *Kamadhenu Charkha Pracharak Mahaguthi* emerged as a modern form of social organization. In 1937, *Nepal Nagrik Adhikar Samiti* (Committee on Citizens' Rights) began to inspire the public through the narration of *Geeta* and liberate the oppressed. Prem Bahadur Kansakar and his friends established *Prajatantra Sangh* (Democratic Association), Daya Bir Singh Kansakar set up the *Paropakar Sansthan* (Charity Association) and several literary societies had been formed for the renewal of the commoners' interest in public life. The Sanskrit school of Kathmandu in the name of *Jayatu Sanskritam* waved anti-Rana flags in 1947. They wanted to modernize the syllabus of Sanskrit teaching by including social science and animate the spirit of ethical life, political modernization, nationalism and public welfare. Likewise, in 1947, a workers' strike broke out in Biratnagar with professional demands. These organizations and activities were seeking emancipation of people from feudalism and dynasticism through the establishment of a political state. Greater social energy for political freedom brought the collapse of more than a century old rule of Rana oligarchy in 1950 and the establishment of multiparty polity. This opened Nepal into international political discourse.

In the 1950s, there was a faint vision of modernity derived from European Enlightenment to pull the public to a new realm of promise based not only on self-interest but also compassion. An Interim Constitution was promulgated in 1951 reflecting power sharing among the King, the Ranas and the political parties. Yet, personalized form of leadership and erosion of civic institutions, including the inability of political parties to reach out to remote areas, owing to their fierce power struggle, undermined the legitimacy of the system. The leadership failed to create democratic citizenship and civic culture as they dissociated themselves from the populace and began to tie up with the aristocratic classes leaving the people on the edge of despair. In February 1959 a new Constitution was introduced. Yet, a constitutional culture did not evolve which could hold the loyalty of the public to democratic institutions and see the fiery dawn of human freedom.

This factor provoked the King to invoke tradition, order and nationalism and invent a partyless Panchayat system under the Constitution of 1962. The Panchayat polity banned political parties, but allowed the opening of class-based organizations, enlarged the elite base of the system and initiated the process of social mobilization of citizens at the grassroots level through local government institutions and Back to Village National Campaign. After the referendum of 1980, it opened the space for several demand-articulating civil society organizations, a representative parliament and professional groupings. The global wave of democratization and the growth of a critical mass in the civil society of urban areas weakened the levers of feudal power in rural areas and helped the revival of political parties. After the success of the People's Movement in 1990 multiparty democracy, constitutional monarchy, sovereignty of people and human rights of citizens became the sources for defining state-civil society ties on the basis of universally sharable democratic values and resolution of social conflicts "without the need to resort to mutual violence (head are counted, not severed)".

INTERNATIONAL RELATIONS

Relations with the United States

The United States seeks to promote democracy and civil society in Nepal and provide developmental assistance to its people. The United States became Nepal's first bilateral aid donor in January 1951 and has since contributed more than $1 billion in bilateral development assistance to the country. The United States has viewed the Maoists' past plans to institute a one-party republic, collectivize agriculture, re-educate "class enemies" and export revolution as undermining regional stability as well as the promotion of democracy and development for Nepal. The United States is now presented with the situation of having to develop a relationship with a democratically elected group that it recently opposed. The United States has been described as taking "quiet steps to reorient its policy" towards Nepal. Prime Minister Dahal travelled to the United States in September 2008 to attend the United Nations General Assembly. During his eightday visit in the United States he met with a number of foreign leaders, including President Bush, whom he reportedly met only briefly. Dahal reportedly asked President Bush for support and assistance. Dahal also met with U.S. Assistant Secretary of State Richard Boucher and expressed his concern that his Maoist organization remained on the U.S. list of terrorist groups. Deputy Assistant Secretary of State for South and Central Asian Affairs Evan Feigenbaum explained in May 2008 that while the Maoists were included on the Terrorist Exclusion List and the Specially Designated List, they were not on the Foreign Terrorist Organization (FTO) list. The FTO has a more stringent set of requirements than the other two lists. Feigenbaum added that "... the degree to which we can work with parties in Nepal will depend very directly on the degree to which they continue to embrace the political process and abandon violence."

In October 2008 it was reported that while the United States would support the elected government of Nepal it would not change its policy towards the CPN-M. That said, travel bans on Maoist leaders were relaxed and a dialogue had been established with Maoists by the Fall of 2008. U.S. Foreign Assistance. In recent years, U.S. attention to Nepal has focused on issues related to the past Maoist insurgency, though non-military assistance has been far greater. The United States provided former Nepali governments with light weaponry and other military assistance to help the previous government of Nepal in its former fight against the Maoists. U.S. assistance to Nepal has also focused on strengthening Nepal's democratic institutions. Economic Support Funds (ESF), Development Assistance (DA), and Child Survival and Health (CSH) programs have sought to enhance stability and security while seeking to strengthen governance and protect human rights. International Military Education and Training (IMET) programs have sought to develop Nepal's military's ability to conduct operations while "following the rules of engagement that respect the rule of law, international human rights standards, and democratic values."

Nepal is heavily dependent on India as the primary source of imports, the main market for exports, and for access to the sea through the major port of Calcutta. A significant percentage of all foreign investment in Nepal is thought to come from India. Moreover, the Himalayan mountain range along Nepal's northern border limits access to China, whereas the 500-mile southern border with India is relatively open. India has considered Nepal a strategic link in its northern border defences. New Delhi has viewed Nepali instability as a potential catalyst for the destabilization of India's own troubled northeastern states. Maoist success in Nepal may also have a negative impact on India's own Maoist problem, which has increased in recent years. It has been reported that India will support a Maoist-led government in Nepal and that the Maoists may demand a review of Nepal's treaties with India including the 1950 Treaty of Peace and Friendship.

While leftists in India welcomed the electoral outcome of the April 2008 CA election, the opposition Hindu right was reportedly "seething" over the result and viewed the Indian government as "derelict of its duties [and] violative of its oath of office to safeguard the country's interests...." It is thought by some observers that much of this concern stems from a fear by some in India that China's power in the region would grow as a result of the outcome of the CA election.

China

The Nepali leadership has long resented Indian economic influence and has sought to establish a more independent foreign policy. Kathmandu has at times "played the China card" in seeking to counterbalance what it considers undue pressure from India. Beijing has contributed economic aid to Nepal.

Observers have noted that Nepal's stability is important to China, given that it serves as a buffer between China and India. Nepal also borders Tibet, whose spiritual leader the Dalai Lama has sought a degree of autonomy from Beijing for the Tibetan regions within China. Unrest in Tibet manifested itself most recently in March 2008 through a series of demonstrations marking the 1959 failed Tibetan uprising against Chinese rule. It was reported in September 2008 that China had approved RS 100 million in military assistance to Nepal during a visit to China by Nepal's Minister for Defense Ram Bahadur Thapa. It appears that Nepal will continue with a one China policy and continue to take a hard line on Tibetan refugees as the CPN-M and other major parties will likely be reluctant to offend China.

The United Nations

Formal assistance from the United Nations was requested by the Nepalese government in July 2006. Following this, the U.N. dispatched a pre-assessment mission that helped the seven-party alliance coalition and the Maoists to resolve differences on the issue of arms management. The U.N. monitored the cantonment of combatants and the caching of arms as specified under the peace agreement. The Security Council established the U.N. Political Mission in Nepal (UNMIN) through Resolution 1740 in January 2007. Under Resolution 1740, UNMIN was tasked to monitor the management of arms and armed personnel of both sides; to assist the parties through the Joint Monitoring Coordinating Committee in implementing their agreement; to assist in the monitoring of the cease fire; provide technical support for the planning, preparation and conduct of the election of a Constituent Assembly; and to provide a small team of election monitors. UNMIN's mission has been extended until January 23, 2009, to allow for continued monitoring of former Maoist rebels and their arms. The NC has voiced its criticism of UNMIN, claiming that it has refrained from criticizing violence perpetrated by the Young Communist League and the lack of movement by the Maoists in returning private property confiscated during the Maoist insurrection.

Bhutan

Nepal's relationship with Bhutan is largely defined by tensions over ethnic Nepalis who are in Bhutan or who have fled Bhutan. The Government of Bhutan has been experiencing problems with an estimated 100,000 Bhutanese of Nepali background, many of whom it views as having settled in Bhutan illegally. This Nepali minority group are known as the Lhotshampa. They are a Nepali speaking Hindu people that inhabit Bhutan's southwest. Many Lhotshampa left Bhutan as a result of attempts over recent decades to integrate them into mainstream Bhutanese culture. Such attempts at assimilation have been viewed as a threat to the ethnic Nepalis' own culture. The program was aimed at assimilating the Lhotshampa by having them adopt the Bhutanese language Dzongkha, as well as the Bhutan's Buddhist religion and its cultural dress. This tension led to unrest in the south of Bhutan in the early 1990s. There are some 107,000 Lhotshampa in seven refugee camps in Nepal. The United States agreed to take some 60,000 of the Nepali Bhutanese refugees beginning in 2008.60 Only about 25,000 of the Lhotshampa refugees in Nepal have thus far registered for resettlement in third countries and only 10,000 are expected to be resettled by the end of 2008.61 Some of the Lhotshampa have reportedly been denied citizenship by Bhutan.

CONSTITUENT ASSEMBLY ELECTIONS

The Election Commission (EC) has already published the CA election schedule and enforced the election code of conduct from January 16. The parties contesting it will have to submit their closed list of candidates for proportional representation system by February 22, registration of candidature for direct voting will be opened from February 22 to 25 and the candidates will be given election symbols on March 2. The Interim Constitution recognizes the SPA but says that anyone else willing to register a new political party must submit 10,000 signatures to EC.

Many opposition parties-MPRF (Yadav), MPRF (Bishwas), Rastriy Prajatantra Party (RPP)-Nepal, Rastriya Janashakti Party (RJP), RPP, Nepal Sadbhava Party and Tarai-Madhesh Loktantrik Party (TMLP) have depicted the SPA as undemocratic in spirit and attitude and argued that setting the date for elections without creating a proper security and political environment is meaningless. The MPRF and TMLP blaming the deployment of Special Task Force "for creating terror in Tarai and helping the Maoist-affiliated Young Communist League (YCL), have threatened to stage a decisive agitation if their demands are not addressed by January 18. Nepal Federation of Indigenous Nationalities (NEFIN), a coalition of 54 ethnic groups, has put its dilemma this way: if it wages its movement, the SPA will be demolished; if not, the SPA refuses to implement the 20-pint accord it signed with the government.

The meeting of the high level seven-party coordinating committee, a SPA coordination mechanism, is currently discussing the possibility of conducting elections in two phases, keeping in mind the security situation in the Tarai. It decided to request the EC to postpone the implementation of the code of conduct for 15 days so that local bodies can be constituted. Finance Minister R. S. Mahat has requested Nepal's international development partners to extend an additional assistance of $4.76 million to implement the 23-point accord among the SPA and to hold the elections. At the same time, an influential section of NC has warned of "Tarai disintegration" if election takes place in two phases. The decision of the government to distribute $15,870 to each legislator for the development of their constituency also stoked the fire of protest in the civil society. The pre-election perk out of the government coffer does not make the election competitive process. It is such controversies that overturned the election apple-cart in the past. A badly designed election can easily foment social divisions, fragment the political sphere, institutionalize sub-national conflicts and embroil the nation into the centrifugal pressure of regional geopolitics.

Tarai's Geopolitics

Twenty-two districts in Nepal's southern plains bordering India constitute the Terai or Madhesh. It is fertile area and is linked to Nepal's major supply routes to hills. After the declaration of secular state and talk about redistributive land reforms, the glue that bind hill and Tarai communities got lost The Madhesi movement spearheaded by the MPRF wants the declaration of the Madhesh as an autonomous region, talks with armed Madhesi groups, balanced distribution of state revenue and income to Madhesh, proportional representation in all the governance institutions including the NA, appointment of chief administrators in Madhesh from the Madhesi communities, return weapons captured by Maoists to the concerned people and declaration of those killed during the Madhesh movement as martyrs including compensation for their families. The TMLP has expressed its desire to have its own state organs for the plains. The two radical components of Janatantrik Tarai Mukti Morcha (JTMM) demand international mediators like the UN to resolve their issues and a separate independent state. India's assertion that "Tarai's demands should be addressed," has provoked a prickly reaction from various political forces. Premier Koirala who had earlier assertion that the "Tarai problem can be resolved within a minute with India's cooperation" has led to suspicions about an 'Indian hand' in the unrest.

India's main opposition, Bharatiya Janata Party (BJP), however, criticizes the Indian government for remaining silent on the collusion of Indian and Nepali communists for creating turmoil in both countries and quashing of the symbols of Nepal's stability and unity-Hindu state and monarchy. An open border with India, existence of co-ethnics across the border and affiliation of each group and political party with like-minded ones in India create a context in which resolution of conflict requires confidence-building measures from both sides.

The violent conflict in the Tarai has forced the hill people to migrate to safe places and create their own mechanisms in the area, like the Chure Bhavar Unity Society (CBUS) that positions itself in the foothills bordering the Terai and the mountains, for autonomy and self-defense.

The autonomy movement in the Madhesh has snowballed into ethnic Tharus, Rais, Limbus, Tamangs, Gurungs, Magars, Dalits and Newars also demanding autonomous federal states based on the right to self-determination. But, there is no unity among Madhesi groups due to their multiple caste, language, religious and ethnic identities. For example, TMLP leadership is dominated by high caste groups, MPRF by intermediary caste groups and JTMM by lower caste groups. The government's Special Task Force (STF), deployed in Kathmandu and eight Terai districts, has failed to penetrate, divide and destroy criminal networks and create public security for local governance to operate. Nepal's problems cannot be tackled without taking this regionalism into account and identifying ways to address it. No matter how one looks at this problem, it seems obvious that there is no military solution. The political package must create a situation favorable to all groups where they see they have more to gain through peace than violence. An election in a security and authority vacuum will neither have legitimacy nor ability to institutionalize democratic polity.

Law and Order

The Nepalese army has expressed its commitment to democracy and a nationally-owned security sector reforms. But, Chief of Army Staff, Gen. R. Katawal clearly said "No" to integrate the CPN (Maoist) combatants. The UN has verified 19,602 politically indoctrinated People's Liberation Army (PLA) out of its total force of over 32,000. Premier G. P Koirala agrees with the army's viewpoint and has given options to Maoists-to integrate the PLA into industrial security groups or give them priority in foreign employment. Nepal's total strength of security forces stands at 165,000— NA (92,000), the civilian police (48,000) and Armed Police Force (25,000). The NA is holed up inside barracks as per the peace accord. The existence of these two adversarial structures does not provide any incentive for confidence building and to pursue a viable peace process for the future. Similarly, without disarming all autonomous armed groups and improving civil-military relations, the chances of free and fair elections remain fragile.

Erosion of state monopoly on power, taxation and loyalty of citizens, growth of competitive violence and failure of statehood in governance have confiscated the state's capacity to provide security in the country. As a result the ability of the political system to maintain balance of power between different governance organs is severely undermined which is telling on its capacity to enforce rule of law, provide service delivery and resolve the multi-layered conflict. SPA's control over the legislature the executive control over the judiciary and a lack of legitimate opposition have established monopoly rule. There is an absence of institutions protecting property rights and promotion of collective goods.

Nepal has a very weak middle class and poor mediating agencies to protect the rights and welfare of the poor. Tax contributes 12 percent to GDP and the contribution of public sector output to GDP is only about 7 percent. Foreign aid constitutes 70 percent of development outlays. Domestic revenue raising capacity is very poor. Easy borrowing from international institutions has established the government's autonomy from their tax paying citizens. As a result, the government is less concerned with institutional capacity of the state to deliver governance goals. The substantial contribution of remittance to GDP (17 percent) too has detrimental effect on the accountability of government. GDP growth rate of 2.3 percent hardly balances out the population growth of 2.2 percent. The daily per capita income of $ 1 puts Nepal's human security condition at the bottom of world development statistics. Feudalism, caste hierarchy and patriarchy have suppressed social mobility of the underclass. This lack of social and economic security has made Nepal's politics highly inflammable amidst radical appeals and growing frustration.

Nepal's bureaucracy, police and public institutions are highly politicized along partisan lines, de-motivated, show poor esprit de corps and weak to enforce rule of law and deliver essential public services. "The rulers have no trust in the constitution, leading to its failure," Chairman of the Constitution Drafting Committee, Laxman Aryal said on January 15. To him, the constitution emerged as a compromise among SPA constituents for the transition politics until the CA election is conducted. It, therefore, does not hold the principles of constitutionalism. He added, "We saw nothing during its first year, but chaos and deterioration of law and order." This condition has made national integrity system ineffective in controlling crime, corruption and impunity. Public institutions and enterprises are still monopolized by ruling parties. Sense of public trust in the authority, assuming that the government is trustworthy and acting in the public interest, is sharply declining. Lack of a boundary between leaders' personal and institutional interests has given birth to a political culture of clientalism although new social movements of women, youth, Dalits, indigenous people and ethnic groups are increasingly challenging the position of authority fixed at birth, lineage and patronage. They are seeking to remold the pre-modern political culture of mutual distrust, betrayal and revenge and into post-conflict modern culture of a shared future based on social justice, democracy and peace.

VOICE AND PARTICIPATION OF MARGINALIZED

The struggle for human rights in Nepal for liberation, entitlements and social opportunities still remains unfinished.

Chairman of the National Human Rights Commission of Nepal (NHRC) K. N. Upadhaya stresses the need for joint efforts among the human rights organizations and individuals to mitigate human rights violations in an effective manner. The government's presence is felt to some extent only in Kathmandu and some urban nodes. Killing, kidnapping, extortion, strikes, food shortages, rocketing prices, shrinking job opportunities and growing fear have deteriorated human rights conditions in the periphery. Last year, 130 civilians got killed by various forces.

Seventy-two political parties have applied in the EC for registration. This number represents asymmetry and diversity in Nepalese social life. A number of social groups are struggling for social, gender and inter-generational justice in the party structure of mainstream parties. Internal party democracy is essential to make political power proportional to its representativeness and end the fissiparous tendencies that have sapped their social integration potential.

The country has 102 ethnic groups and more than 82 languages. No single group claims more than 18 percent of the population. This means it is a country of minorities and there is no institutional mechanism to prevent the minority from becoming a majority. Civil society groups are columnized along partisan lines. This condition has marred the possibilities for cooperative action for public service. Despite the legislation of the Right to Information Act, the media is unevenly distributed just like the per capita income and, therefore, people of backward and remote areas have no access to the public sphere in shaping the agenda.

In contrast, the apex body of media persons, Nepal Federation of Journalists, revealed the condition of media freedom this way: Between April 24, 2006 to December 1, 2007 one journalist was killed, one disappeared, 74 detained and 128 threatened. There were 203 attacks on media houses, 129 journalists lost their jobs and 55 media houses were shut down.

Engagement of the International Community

For an international community caught in a fluid political climate, it will be hard to enlarge the development space as agreed in the Basic Operating Guidelines (BOG), other than relief and humanitarian supplies. The presence of the international community in Nepal acts as a deterrence against excessive use of violence and abuse of human rights. Japan has put Nepal in the category of a "fragile state." By definition, a fragile state creates a situation for humanitarian intervention owing to anarchy of free wills, poor governance and failure to enforce rule of law. India has often insisted that elections to the CA must take place on time at any cost, but remained silent when the SPA failed to create a favorable security and law and order situation. The European Union and the US are insisting that the security situation in Nepal must improve for a credible, free and fair election. On January 18, the US Ambassador to Nepal, Nancy J. Powell suggesting the government and political parties to fulfil earlier commitments made in the peace accord said, "The CA polls will not guarantee sustainable peace in Nepal. What is necessary for the sustainable peace is loyalty to the nation."

On January 11, UN Secretary-General Ban Ki-Moon submitted his report to the UN Security Council proposing a six-month extension of UNMIN's mandate to support Nepal's peace process through CA elections. He has advised against downscaling the UN's presence, emphasizing that it could imperil prospects for a successful election, except in the cases of technical assistance which has already been provided. The UN too favors a credible CA election with improved security, government's engagement in a dialogue with disgruntled groups and abolition of the culture of impunity. Unlike the EU, however, India, the US and China have geopolitical priorities. India's role in bringing the SPA together against the 'monarchy' in November 2005 and their joint struggle forced King Gyanendra to hand over power to the political parties. As the SPA established their monopoly over power and resources but failed to maintain security and rule of law, it evoked the security concern of neighbours. China has voiced against "any foreign intervention in Nepal," showed interest to actively involve itself in Nepal's peace process, expressed anxiety about the events taking place in the Tarai and asked the Nepalese leaders to take independent decisions depending less on outside forces.

Bibliography

Adhikari, J. and Gurung, G. 2002. *"Foreign Labour Migration and the Remittance Economy of Nepal."* Critical Asian Studies.

Ajey Lele: *Strategic Technologies for the Military : Breaking New Frontiers*, Sage, Delhi, 2009.

Amitabh Sikdar: *India and China : Strategic Energy Management and Security*, Manas, Delhi, 2009.

Ashok K. : *The Royal Nepal Army : Meeting the Maoist Challenge*, Rupa, Delhi, 2005.

Bandita Sijapati: *A Kingdom Under Siege : Nepal's Maoist Insurgency, 1996 to 2003*, The Printhouse, Delhi, 2003.

Bottomore, Tom: *A Dictionary of Marxist Thought*, New Delhi, Maya Blackwell, 2000.

Cheek, Timothy: *Mao Zedong and China's Revolutions: A Brief History with Documents*. Boston: Bedford/St. Martin's, 2002.

Dasgupta, B.: *The Naxalite Movement*, Bombay: Allied Publishers, 1974.

Dhanalaxmi, Ravuri. *British Attitude to Nepal's Relations with Tibet and China, 1814-1914*. Chandigarh, India: Bahri, 1981.

Digumarti Bhaskara Rao: *Military Conversion : Impact on Science and Technology*, Discovery, Delhi, 2003.

Ellis, F. *Rural Livelihoods and Diversity in Developing Countries*. New York: Oxford University Press, 2000.

Frederick H. *Regionalism and National Unity in Nepal*. Berkeley: University of California Press, 1975.

Geremie R. *Shades of Mao: The Posthumous Cult of the Great Leader*. Armonk, N.Y.: M. E. Sharpe, 1996.

Ghosh, Suniti : *The Historic Turning-Point: A Liberation Anthology*, Calcutta, 1992.

Kansakar, V. B. S.: *"International Migration and Citizenship in Nepal"*. Kathmandu: Central Bureau of Statistics/UNFPA, 2003.

Kant, Adhikari, Krishna. *Nepal under Jang Bahadur, 1846-1877*. Kathmandu: Buku, 1984.

Kumar, Satish. *Rana Polity in Nepal: Origin and Growth*. New York: Asia, 1967.

Leo E. *Nepal: Strategy for Survival*. Berkeley:University of California Press, 1971.

Marie Lecomte : *Hindu Kingship, Ethnic Revival, and Maoist Rebellion in Nepal*, Oxford University Press, Delhi, 2009.

Muni, S.D. : *Maoist Insurgency in Nepal : The Challenge and the Response*, Rupa, Delhi, 2004.

Parmanand. *The Nepali Congress since Its Inception: A Critical Assessment*. Delhi: B.R. Publishing, 1982.

Pemble, John. *The Invasion of Nepal: John Company at War*. Oxford: Oxford University Press, 1971.

Schurmann, Franz: *Ideology and Organization in Communist Nepal*. Berkeley: University of California Press, 1971.

Sharma, P. 1989. *Urbanization in Nepal*. Hawaii: East-West Population Institute.

Sijapati, Li, : *A Kingdom Under Siege : Nepal's Maoist Insurgency, 1996 to 2003*, The Printhouse, Delhi, 2003.

Skeldon, R.: *Migration and Development: a global perspective*. Harlow: Longman, 1997.

Stuart R. Schram: *The Political Thought of Mao Tse-Tung*. New York: Praeger, 1969.

Thapa, Deepak : *Understanding the Maoist Movement of Nepal*, Centre for Social Research and Development, Delhi, 2003.

Tse-tung Mao: *Mao and the Nepali Revolution*. London: Oxford University Press, 1965.

Uddhab P : *Maoist Movement in Nepal: A Sociological Perspective*, Adroit, Delhi, 2007.

Upreti, B C : *Maoists in Nepal : From Insurgency to Political Mainstream*, Kalpaz Pub, Delhi, 2008.

Wapner, Paul : *Environmental Activism and World Civic Politics*, Albany, SUNY Press, 1996.

Wright, Arthur : *Studies in Chinese Buddhism*, New Haven, CT: Yale University Press, 1990.

Index

❑❑❑